EXECUTIVE PRIVILEGE

INTERPRETING AMERICAN POLITICS
Michael Nelson, Series Editor

Gerald S. Strom, *The Logic of Lawmaking: A Spatial Theory Approach*
John P. Burke, *The Institutional Presidency*
Marc Allen Eisner, *Regulatory Politics in Transition*
Mark J. Rozell, *Executive Privilege: The Dilemma of Secrecy and Democratic Accountability*

EXECUTIVE PRIVILEGE

★ ——————————————————————— ★

*The Dilemma of Secrecy and
Democratic Accountability*

MARK J. ROZELL

THE JOHNS HOPKINS UNIVERSITY PRESS

BALTIMORE AND LONDON

© 1994 The Johns Hopkins University Press
All rights reserved. Published 1994
Printed in the United States of America on acid-free paper
03   02   01   00   99   98   97   96   95   94   5   4   3   2   1

The Johns Hopkins University Press
2715 North Charles Street
Baltimore, Maryland 21218-4319
The Johns Hopkins Press Ltd., London

Design and composition by Wilsted & Taylor

ISBN 0-8018-4899-7
ISBN 0-8018-4900-4 (pbk.)

Library of Congress Cataloging-in-Publication Data
will be found at the end of this book.
A catalog record for this book is available from the British Library.

For Lynda

Contents

Series Editor's Foreword

The grandiloquence of legal and constitutional language with which the scope, legitimacy, and proper exercise of executive privilege in the American presidency have typically been debated is matched only by the highly charged, intensely partisan circumstances that have occasioned such debates. Impeachment is another such issue: When is the meaning of the phrase "high crimes and misdemeanors" (the constitutional grounds for impeachment and removal) discussed widely *except* when a particular president is being considered for impeachment? The war powers offer yet another example. The proper allocation between the president and Congress of the authority to conduct war becomes a matter of public concern when hostilities are imminent or ongoing but seldom at other times. Under such circumstances, serious constitutional discussion invariably seems—and often is—little more than a thin patina of respectable verbiage that has been poured on a roiling sea of angry, short-term political conflict between Republicans and Democrats, conservatives and liberals, an assertive president and a hostile Congress.

Executive privilege—the right of the executive to withhold information in the service of his or her understanding of the national interest—provides an especially interesting case study of the unhappy marriage between highblown constitutional discourse and down-and-dirty politics. From the 1930s until the 1960s, an era in which the Democrats usually controlled the White House, executive privilege was championed by lib-

ix

erals and opposed by conservatives. During the 1970s and 1980s, when Republican presidents were the norm, conservatives and liberals changed sides on the issue and, often, exchanged arguments: conservatives who had once emphasized the dangers of executive privilege and found no basis for it in the Constitution now saw what liberals had previously seen (but no longer saw)—namely, that executive privilege is inherent in the executive power. (Liberals, for their part, found the abandoned conservative arguments suddenly persuasive.) President Richard Nixon made things hard for his side by blatantly using executive privilege as a smokescreen to cover up his and his aides' role in the Watergate controversy. But by the late 1980s, supporters of the Reagan administration were once again defending executive privilege unabashedly.

Now comes Mark J. Rozell to shed needed light on the overheated subject of executive privilege. He is the right person (a nonpartisan) writing at the right moment (a no doubt short-lived oasis of time in which no controversy about executive privilege is occurring) and with the right training: Rozell is a political scientist. This last characteristic is especially important because it enables him to see clearly that, for all its constitutional and legal aspects, the issue of executive privilege is by nature an intensely political one and that no progress will be made on it if it is treated otherwise. To be sure, Rozell reviews and critiques the constitutional arguments for and against executive privilege. But he also offers a solid political analysis of the executive privilege controversies that have occurred in the Watergate and post-Watergate eras. This blend of the legal and the political enables Rozell to propose in his final chapter a resolution to what he sees as the great dilemma of executive privilege: How can presidents be allowed to withhold information from others when to do so is appropriate yet still be held properly accountable for their actions by Congress, the courts, and the people?

Michael Nelson

Preface and Acknowledgments

This book is an interpretive analysis of the controversial doctrine of executive privilege. By *executive privilege*, I mean the right of the president and important executive branch officials to withhold information from Congress, the courts, and, ultimately, the public.

For the past two decades, the uncontested leading work on this topic has been historian Raoul Berger's *Executive Privilege: A Constitutional Myth*.[1] As the title of his book makes clear, Berger believes that presidents who have exercised executive privilege have acted outside their constitutional authority. Any form of executive branch secrecy, he maintains, is "an abomination" and cannot be legitimized under democratic government.[2] He argues that the U.S. Congress in particular—the "Grand Inquest" of the nation—has the absolute right to compel the production of all executive branch information.

In part, this book stands as a challenge to Berger's analysis. As Berger himself so eloquently has argued, it is the scholar's responsibility to examine all available evidence on a topic and then to base his or her conclusions on that examination.[3] After having examined comprehensively the academic literature on this topic, the theoretical arguments underlying executive privilege, the history of its exercise, constitutional law, and modern-era executive privilege controversies, I have arrived at a conclusion that differs with Berger's analysis. In brief, I believe that the evidence weighs in favor of the constitutional legitimacy of executive privilege.

As I shall argue, executive privilege clearly is *not* a myth. It also is *not* an unfettered presidential prerogative. Although the president has the right to assert executive privilege, he can do so only for the most compelling reasons. In a liberal democracy, the presumption generally is in favor of openness and freedom of information. Nonetheless, liberal democratic republics, like all governments, have secrecy needs.

In this study, I posit that a dilemma is posed by the doctrine of executive privilege: that a democratically elected president, who ultimately must be held accountable for his actions by the public, and constrained in the exercise of his authority by the coordinate branches of government, can withhold information from the public, Congress, and the courts, and thus effectively deny citizens and members of the coordinate branches the knowledge that they need either to hold the president accountable for his actions or to constrain his exercise of authority. The resolution to this dilemma is not found in proposals for statutory guidelines on the use of executive privilege but, rather, in a proper understanding of the founders' theory of the separation of powers.

It is important not to confuse the concept of executive privilege with that of executive prerogative. That latter concept refers to the right of the executive, in extraordinary circumstances, to take any action deemed necessary to the nation's security and survival, even if such action is outside the written law. Consequently, prerogative powers are not necessarily actions that violate or dispense with the written law (although they may be, in particular cases). Executive privilege is a form of the presidential prerogative power. A presidential administration may withhold requested information when there is a compelling reason to do so. Lacking such a reason, the presumption must be in favor of openness.

As much as I disagree with Berger's interpretation of executive privilege, my analysis also diverges from the infatuation of many conservatives during the Reagan–Bush years with the broad-based exercise of presidential powers and prerogatives.[4] Given traditional conservatism's long-standing emphasis on individual liberty and fear of overbearing centralized governmental authority, it seems peculiar that during the Reagan–Bush years many conservatives became leading proponents of the strong presidency—a position more closely associated with pre-Watergate liberalism. Many defenses of the broad-based prerogative powers of the chief executive have been characterized by attacks on the very legitimacy of the coordinate branches—especially Congress—to constrain the exercise of such powers.[5] The following analysis finds much merit to the view that presidents have prerogative powers, but also recognizes the legitimacy of the coordinate branches of government to investigate, evaluate, and ultimately constrain the exercise of such powers. Executive privilege is no exception.

I am grateful for the support that I received from a number of individuals and organizations. My colleagues, Joseph Bessette and Michael Nelson, and my editor, Henry Y. K. Tom, read the manuscript and provided excellent suggestions. Dora Minor and Lisa Roark typed portions of the manuscript. Kathleen Gibby, Victoria Meador, and Dana Rickman provided research assistance. Maria E. denBoer copyedited the manuscript.

Jim Gottlieb, formerly the staff director and counsel to the Intergovernmental Relations and Human Resources Subcommittee of the House Committee on Government Operations, spoke with me on several occasions about this project and allowed me to review numerous letters, memoranda, and documents that he maintained on executive privilege controversies in the post-Watergate years. Jim now serves as staff director and chief counsel to the Senate Committee on Veterans' Affairs.

I appreciate the opportunity to have interviewed the following persons for this book: Sandy Harris, staff director to the Subcommittee on Environment, Energy, and Natural Resources of the House Energy and Commerce Committee; James Lewin, chief investigator to the House Judiciary Committee; Kevin Sabo, Republican general counsel to the House Committee on Government Operations; Morton Rosenberg, specialist in American public law at the Congressional Research Service; Kathryn Seddon, counsel to the Subcommittee on Information, Justice, Transportation, and Agriculture of the House Committee on Government Operations; Charles Tiefer, deputy general counsel to the clerk of the House of Representatives; Eric Thorson, staff member to the House Committee on Government Operations. I thank Rosenberg, Sabo, Seddon, and Monica Wrobelewski, the hearings coordinator of the Subcommittee on Investigations and Oversight of the House Committee on Space, Science and Technology, for sending me numerous materials on recent executive privilege controversies.

My coverage of modern executive privilege controversies also is based on archival research at presidential libraries. In particular, I examined White House documents from the Nixon Presidential Materials Project (Alexandria, Va.), the Gerald R. Ford Library (Ann Arbor, Mich.), and the Jimmy Carter Library (Atlanta, Ga.). I thank Leesa Tobin and David Horrocks of the Ford Library and Martin I. Elzy of the Carter Library for their assistance with the presidential documents.

The National Endowment for the Humanities provided a summer research grant for this project. A Lynde and Harry Bradley Foundation Fellowship supported a one-semester sabbatical from teaching to complete the manuscript.

My wife, Lynda M. Rozell, an attorney advisor with the Federal Trade Commission in Washington, D.C., proofread and commented critically on the manuscript. As always, I benefited from her many suggestions and cannot thank her enough for so much support and love.

EXECUTIVE PRIVILEGE

The Dilemma of Secrecy and Democratic Accountability

★————————————————————————————————————★

THE DILEMMA OF EXECUTIVE PRIVILEGE

The doctrine of executive privilege poses a complex dilemma: a presidential administration sometimes needs to conduct the duties of government in secret, yet the coordinate branches and the public need information about the executive branch so that they can fulfill their democratic responsibilities. This study proposes that the resolution to the dilemma of executive branch secrecy and democratic accountability is in the founders' theory of the separation of powers. That theory allows for a carefully exercised and properly constrained presidential power of executive privilege.

Not all will agree. In a political system predicated on democratic accountability, many analysts believe that there can be no legitimate basis at all for executive privilege. Raoul Berger certainly is not alone in the view that executive branch secrecy is indefensible. In his 1885 book *Congressional Government*, political scientist and future president of the United States Woodrow Wilson argued that representative government must be predicated on openness. He explained that Congress had the high responsibility of investigating administration activities. "It is the proper duty of a representative body to look diligently into every affair of government and to talk much about what it sees."[1] The Wilsonian view is echoed by David Wise, who maintains that executive privilege is a "dubious doctrine." Wise believes that executive privilege cannot be legitimate under a separation of powers system in which the legislative branch has extensive investigating powers.[2] Among the justifications given for withholding information, none is more prominent than national security concerns. Although most would agree there can be some reasonable limits to access to national security information, Wise argues that there are no acceptable limitations at all on access to executive branch information because "*all* information is of possible value to an adversary."

> It is impossible to arrive at a standard. . . . Moreover, "national security" is a term of political art, which can be defined by a given administration to coincide with its political interests. The men in power tend, sometimes unconsciously, to equate their own personal and partisan interests with the national interest, no matter how noble their motives.[3]

Wise is particularly concerned about freedom of the press issues. Democratic accountability cannot exist, he believes, in a society in which the press is limited in what it can investigate and report. Consequently, executive privilege cannot coexist with the Bill of Rights and accountable government.

> It is always possible to rationalize the case for curbing the press in particular circumstances. But who can say, once it begins, where it will end? Freedom to publish about government is either absolute, or it does not exist. Once qualified, it may be described as something else, but not as freedom of the press.[4]

Morton H. Halperin and Daniel N. Hoffman also argue that executive branch leaders use national security as a reason to withhold vital information from Congress, the bureaucracy, and the public, and thus destroy democratic accountability. In their view, secrecy often originates from "a domestic political need."[5] Furthermore, they maintain, secrecy threatens the basic liberties guaranteed by the Bill of Rights. "The Framers sought to design a structure for effective leadership that would not threaten liberty" (97). Halperin and Hoffman argue that the Framers—concerned with individual liberties—purposefully did not grant a presidential power of privilege in Article II of the Constitution. According to Halperin and Hoffman, secrecy fosters official "lying" and, consequently, public policy must be based on complete openness in governmental deliberations (101,104). They believe that openness is "constitutionally necessary" and that it protects citizens from those leaders who scheme to "prevent the American public from learning the truth" (104).

Halperin and Hoffman also admit that they are concerned with more than just protecting liberty and democratic accountability. They believe that open government will also ensure a number of policy changes that they desire, such as decreased defense budgets and less U.S. intervention in international affairs (105).

For our purposes, the major concerns about executive privilege are the rights of citizens and governmental accountability. Nearly four decades ago, James Wiggins wrote that "each added measure of secrecy measurably diminishes our freedom."[6] During the Watergate period, investigative reporter Clark Mollenhoff testified before Congress that executive privilege "would eventually destroy all of our freedom. . . . It is unfortunate that shortsighted editorial writers and superficial politically motivated legal scholars have occasionally given a degree of support to this so-called time-honored doctrine and this phony well-established precedent of executive privilege."[7]

A classic slippery-slope argument characterizes many critiques of executive privilege: allow any measure of withholding of information and ultimately all of our liberties will be undermined and democratic accountability destroyed. This argument is countered by the views of other analysts who believe that current limitations on secrecy policies are not in the public interest.

Michael A. Ledeen, former consultant to the Reagan administration National Security Council, criticizes the argument of Rep. Lee Hamilton (D-Ind.) that policies secretly arrived at are inferior to those formulated in full public view. Ledeen counters that "it is all wonderfully high-minded and unexceptionable; it is also unworkable. These abstract principles are in conflict with a world where secrecy makes its own demands. If secrets—of various sorts—cannot be kept, good policy and good relations are impossible."[8] Contrary to the arguments of the critics of executive privilege cited above, Ledeen maintains that our political culture is overly suspicious of secrecy. He believes that Americans are unimpressed with the "reason of state" concept as justification for government secrecy—a stark contrast to Great Britain in which the Official Secrets Act and libel laws render "the British government—and media—far more close-mouthed than ours."[9]

Former editor of the *Sunday Times* of London, Harold Evans, also finds the differences between U.S. and British secrecy policies telling. For example, under U.S. law it is a felony to lie to Congress, whereas in Great Britain there is no penalty for deceiving Parliament. Instead, "punishment is meted out to those who dare expose the deception."[10] In Great Britain, unauthorized disclosure of official information is a crime, whereas in the United States, as much official information as possible is made public or is at least guaranteed available through the Freedom of Information Act.[11]

Clearly no one has discovered exactly how to balance the competing and valid claims of freedom of information and governmental secrecy. As the former director of the Central Intelligence Agency, Stansfield Turner, has asked, "How much does a congressional committee need to know to be sure nothing illegal or immoral is being done? Can it know that much without exposing sensitive and necessary operations?" Turner correctly answers that there is no easy way to balance such competing needs to ensure both accountability and the capability of people who maintain secrets to do their jobs.[12]

The dilemma of executive privilege is made even more complex by several other factors explored in this study.

First, in our popular culture, journalism, and even scholarship, there is a long-standing glorification of the strong presidency. Presidents are encouraged from all of these venues to achieve "greatness" through activist policy agendas and bold leadership gestures. There is less admiration for presidents who exercise their powers cautiously. Nonetheless, presidents also are expected to conform to the letter of the law in exercising their powers. Those who attempt to achieve their goals through the use of prerogative powers often find that they come into conflict with legislators who themselves wish to share in the exercise of such powers or who have enacted legal restrictions on presidential authority. History is replete with examples of presidents who, out of some real or perceived necessity, acted beyond the strict letter of the law. Some got away with it and are honored by scholars as "great" presidents (e.g., Jefferson, Lincoln, the two Roosevelts); others did not and are scorned by scholars (e.g., Nixon, Reagan).

Second, even among those who agree that presidents possess independent prerogative powers, there is little agreement regarding the circumstances under which such powers legitimately can be exercised. As Daniel P. Franklin has written, "Prerogative powers are difficult to discuss, let alone define, in a society that cannot agree about how much liberty should be sacrificed for the sake of security."[13]

Third, the Constitution is silent on the question of executive branch secrecy. Does that mean that the Framers intended forever to exclude the exercise of that power? Or does it mean that secrecy in the executive is such an obvious necessity that no one thought of putting it into the Constitution?

Fourth, the Supreme Court has never recognized an absolute "right to know" or "right to receive information." At most, the First Amendment may recognize a right to receive ideas.[14]

Fifth, the issue of executive privilege concerns questions of both foreign and domestic policy. Nonetheless, the presumption in favor of executive privilege has always been strongest in areas of national security and foreign policy. Yet, if there is a necessity to hold leaders accountable for their actions, how can Congress and the public's need for information be less valid in some policy areas than in others?

Sixth, oftentimes there are demands that withheld information be released without delay. From the perspectives of those who claim a need to know, the issue of timeliness of information may be of utmost concern. Those who withhold information often make the case that the cause of democratic accountability is not necessarily better served by immediate disclosure of information as opposed to later disclosure when the need for secrecy is not so compelling.

Seventh, different views on executive privilege generally reflect different institutional perspectives. Presidents see themselves as imbued with worldwide responsibilities and as the representatives of the national interest. Oftentimes they perceive members of Congress who demand to play an active role in setting foreign policy or in scrutinizing executive branch foreign policy actions as meddling in areas where legislators do not belong. Members of Congress believe that they have the duty not only to play an active role in the policy process, but also to investigate all areas of executive branch activity. Louis Henkin observes that "if the Framers provided no guidance as to where to find the powers of the federal government in international matters, of course they provided no guidance as to how such unenumerated federal authority is allocated between Congress and the president."[15]

Different institutional perspectives may also be reinforced by different partisan ones. Certainly that often was the case in the era of divided government. During the Reagan–Bush years, Republicans most often defended presidential powers and prerogatives while Democrats vigorously challenged presidential authority. During the early stages of the Clinton presidency, the Democratic party majority has not been so eager to initiate investigations of executive branch activities. The Clinton White House has refused numerous requests from Republican members of the House of Representatives for executive branch information.

CHAPTER PLAN

Chapter 1 reviews the leading arguments against the legitimacy of executive privilege. The arguments are: (1) there is a lack of a constitutional grant of executive privilege; (2) the constitutional Framers' fear of tyranny prevented such a power from being granted; (3) the public and the coordinate branches of government have a right to know what the executive branch is doing; and (4) presidents have abused the power of executive privilege.

Chapter 2 argues for the legitimacy of executive privilege. The defense of a properly constrained executive privilege is based on (1) its theoretical and constitutional underpinnings; (2) the historical precedents for its exercise; (3) the demands of national security; (4) the need for candid, internal White House deliberations; (5) limitations on the congressional power of inquiry; (6) historical necessities; and (7) the widely accepted secrecy practices of the coordinate branches of government.

Chapter 3 looks at the most crucial period for the modern exercise of executive privilege—the Richard M. Nixon years. Nixon's abuses of presidential powers undermined the exercise of executive privilege by his successors and fundamentally changed the way that executive privilege is perceived and exercised. In brief, he gave executive privilege a bad name by invoking the doctrine to withhold embarrassing and incriminating—not vital—information. As far as executive privilege is concerned, the post-Watergate presidents consequently have had to operate in the shadow of Richard M. Nixon. This chapter examines (1) Nixon's official policy on the exercise of executive privilege; (2) Nixon's actual use of executive privilege; (3) Nixon's Watergate defense of executive privilege;

and (4) the implications of the abuses of executive privilege in the Nixon White House.

Chapters 4 and 5 review and analyze executive privilege controversies in the post-Watergate era. They use White House and congressional documents to analyze the development of the doctrine of executive privilege in the Ford, Carter, Reagan, and Bush administrations. These chapters examine each administration's official policy toward and use of executive privilege. Clearly the doctrine of executive privilege has fallen out of favor in the post-Watergate presidency, largely due to the successful efforts of opponents of executive branch secrecy to equate nearly every attempt to withhold information as a Nixonian effort to deceive or to conceal wrongdoing. No post-Watergate president has rejected the legitimacy of executive privilege. Nonetheless, because of the taint of Watergate, recent presidents have crafted strategies to withhold information without resorting to executive privilege.

Chapter 6 looks at a way to resolve the dilemma of executive privilege. The recent history of cases of presidents withholding information while denying the use of executive privilege and the efforts of members of Congress to impose ever-burdensome legalistic constraints on governmental secrecy point the way for a return to a pre-Watergate understanding of the role of executive privilege in our separation of powers system. Such an understanding rejects the view that executive privilege is a "myth" and an unqualified evil as well as the view that executive privilege is an unfettered presidential prerogative, and instead recognizes that executive privilege is a legitimate, though often controversial, presidential power, and that disputes over withholding of information can best be resolved by the political ebb and flow of the separation of powers system.

CHAPTER 1

The Arguments against Executive Privilege

★ ———————————————————————————— ★

Although numerous presidents have exercised executive privilege in one form or another, critics remain unconvinced of its legitimacy. An oft-cited analogy is that a criminal act does not become lawful after being committed many times: it is still a criminal act. That analogy highlights the most powerful criticisms of executive privilege: that it lacks any constitutional foundation; that the American constitutional Framers were too fearful of executive branch tyranny to have allowed for such a power; that Congress and the public have a "right to know" and a need to know what the executive is up to; and that the right to withhold information has become a convenient cloak for presidents who abuse their powers.

THE LACK OF A CONSTITUTIONAL FOUNDATION

The beginning point for any critique of executive privilege is the fact that our Constitution nowhere explicitly grants the executive the power to withhold information. Such critics as Raoul Berger maintain that to determine the scope of the executive power requires a strict reading of the Constitution. According to this view, there is no implied power of executive privilege.[1] The American constitutional Framers, therefore, excluded the executive power to withhold information on purpose. Quite simply, had the Framers intended there to be an executive privilege power, they would have granted it in Article II. Hence, Berger has proclaimed executive privilege "a constitutional myth."[2]

Perhaps the classic statement of the strict constitutional interpretation of the president's authority comes from William Howard Taft, former U.S. president and chief justice of the Supreme Court. Responding to former president Theodore Roosevelt's "stewardship theory" of the presidency—that the chief executive has a broad residuum of authority to act, as he sees fit, in the public interest[3]—Taft wrote the following:

> The true view of the executive function is, as I conceive it, that the president can exercise no power which cannot be fairly and reasonably traced to some specific grant of power or justly implied and included within such express grant as proper and necessary to its exercise. . . . There is no undefined residuum of power which he can exercise because it seems to him to be in the public interest.[4]

To make a convincing constitutional case against executive privilege requires much more than an assertion that such a power nowhere is explicitly granted in the Constitution. Throughout history, presidents have exercised formidable powers not explicitly granted by the Constitution (e.g., war powers, executive agreements). Congress has, too (e.g., creating independent regulatory agencies). The critics of executive privilege also must show that the Framers clearly intended that such a power not be exercised by the executive and in fact created impediments to such a power ever being adopted.

One constitutional argument against executive privilege is that the Framers assigned to Congress either coequal or "senior status in a partnership with the executive for the purpose of conducting foreign policy."[5] Because most claims of executive privilege center around national security and foreign policy concerns, this argument potentially undermines a frequently cited justification for executive withholding of information: that the executive has a compelling need for the full use of his authority, or even the exercise of extraconstitutional authority, vis-à-vis foreign nation-states.

A number of respected authorities reject the concept of extraordinary or prerogative executive powers. David Gray Adler maintains that "the president possesses no prerogative power" to act beyond what the Constitution allows.[6] Harold Hongju Koh writes that "the constitutional system of checks and balances is not suspended simply because foreign affairs are at issue."[7] Louis Henkin offers the following view:

> Constitutionalism implies limited government. For our subject, that means that the Constitution should be expounded so that there can be no extraconstitutional government, that, in principle and in effect, no activity of government is exempt from constitutional restraints, not even foreign affairs. . . . For us, as for the Framers, no branch of government has authority that is so large as to be essentially undefined and uncircumscribed, that is "plenary," that is not checked, not balanced, not even the President in foreign affairs.[8]

By implication, executive privilege—an independent, often unchecked presidential power—cannot be legitimate. To suggest that it is, therefore, would be tantamount to arguing that the executive has the authority, even under a system of separation of powers, to act without congressional consent or even knowledge.

Furthermore, some critics of executive privilege contend that the president is always accountable to Congress, yet Congress need not be accountable to the president. An 1860 report of the House of Representatives stated that "the conduct of the President is always subject to the constitutional supervision and judgment of Congress; while he, on the contrary, has no such power over either branch of that body."[9] According to Raoul Berger and Alan C. Swan, the Framers did recognize the need for secrecy in government, and constitutionally placed that power in the hands of Congress.[10] The evidence for this argument is found in Article I, Section 5(3) of the Constitution: "Each House shall keep a Journal of its proceedings, and from time to time, publish the same excepting such parts as may in their judgement require secrecy."

Because no such mention of the right of secrecy is made in the executive articles, Morton Halperin and Daniel N. Hoffman conclude that "the Framers gave the President no privilege to withhold information from Congress."[11] Berger adds that "in the Constitution the Framers provided for limited secrecy by Congress alone, thereby excluding executive secrecy from the public."[12]

A former special counsel to the U.S. attorney general, George C. Calhoun, attributes much of the interbranch conflict over executive privilege to the "belief of many in the government that each branch *owns* the information it develops."[13] According to Berger, Congress owns its own information *and* the executive's. He maintains that the Framers "patently modeled" the U.S. Congress after the British Parliament, thereby making Congress the nation's "Grand Inquest."[14] Consequently, the president has no constitutional authority to resist Congress's overtures in its demands for information. As Berger told a congressional committee, "There is no word in the Constitution that expresses any intention whatsoever to curtail the normal attribute of the legislative power . . . [and] there is not a single word in any one of the conventions expressing any intention to curtail the legislative power of investigation."[15]

Executive accountability to Congress also is guaranteed by the Article II, Section 4 provision for impeachment: "The President . . . shall be removed from Office on Impeachment for, and Conviction of, Treason, Bribery, or other high Crimes and Misdemeanors."

In order to properly conduct an impeachment proceeding, the House of Representatives must have complete access to executive branch information. An 1843 House report stated the following: "The House has the sole right of impeachment . . . a power which implies the right of inquiry on the part of the House to the fullest and most unlimited extent."[16]

President James K. Polk stated in 1846 that the House of Representatives has the right of access to "*all the archives and papers* of the Executive Department, public or private" in cases of inquiry into misspending of public funds by the executive. Polk added that the House's power of inquiry in such cases "*would penetrate into the most secret recesses* of the Executive Departments" (262–63). If this interpretation of the extent of the House's power of inquiry is correct, then the case for executive privilege appears substantially weakened. Obviously, the House cannot investigate the executive if the president can, for whatever reason, withhold any information that he chooses.

Berger argues that the Constitution's provision for a presidential delivery to Congress of information on the state of the Union also repudiates any claim to executive privilege. He believes that Article II, Section 3 is a legislative power, even though that provision is generally recognized as an executive one. "He shall from time to time give to the Congress information of the state of the Union, and recommend to their consideration such measures as he shall judge necessary and expedient."

Berger believes that this constitutional duty of presidents is yet another measure of Congress's absolute power of inquiry. The original provision presented at the Constitutional Convention allowed the president little discretion in determining the kinds of information he could provide to Congress. In the rejected version, the Framers established "his duty to inform the Legislature of the Condition of the U.S. so far as may respect his Department." The final, adopted version, Berger believes, did not limit the president's duty to supply information to Congress (37). In fact, the duty to provide information "from time to time," according to Berger, "is the reciprocal of the familiar legislative power to inquire" (38).

Finally, Berger cites the Article II, Section 3 provision that the president "shall take care that the laws be faithfully executed" as evidence that the executive must be accountable to the legislative. Berger asks, "Who has a more legitimate interest in inquiring whether a law has been faithfully executed than the lawmaker?" (3). Once again, executive privilege remains questionable to those who believe that Congress has the absolute right of inquiry under the Constitution.

THE FRAMERS' FEAR OF TYRANNY

Fearing that a strong executive might at some time be transformed into a tyrannical ruler, the Framers gathered at the Constitutional Convention sought to devise a governmental system of limited powers. Given the colonial experiences under the abuses of King George III, the Framers were determined that our constitutional system prohibit any chance of an arbitrary and tyrannical executive coming to power. Furthermore, the Framers made the legislature the supreme lawmaking branch of government. Our chief constitutional architect, James Madison, explained that "in republican government, the legislative authority necessarily predominates."[17] Roger Sherman characterized the executive as "nothing more than an instrument for carrying the will of Congress into effect."[18]

According to this view, the Framers so feared executive power that they made the legislative the supreme branch of government in all policy areas—even foreign affairs. David Gray Adler writes that "the Framers clearly granted the bulk of foreign relations powers to Congress. The president's constitutional authority pales by comparison."[19] Specifically, the Constitution grants to the president two exclusive powers: to receive ambassadors and to act as commander-in-chief of the armed forces. The president must share with the Senate the treaty-making power and the power to appoint ambassadors. Yet Congress has such formidable powers as declaring war and regulating commerce. These constitutional grants of authority lead Adler to conclude that, although the Constitution provides for a partnership between the president and Congress in foreign policy-making, "Congress is assigned the role of senior partner."[20]

Berger argues as well that the president cannot be the constitutional director of foreign policy.[21] Both Berger and Adler maintain that the foreign policy-making powers of the modern presidency are the result of a gradual usurpation of legislative authority. Although the past fifty years have been characterized by executive domination of foreign policy-making, such a state of affairs "represents a dramatic departure from the basic scheme of the Constitution."[22] Adler finds evidence for his argument from the *Federalist 75*, written by the ultradefender of a strong executive, Alexander Hamilton:

> The history of human conduct does not warrant that exalted opinion of human virtue which would make it wise in a nation to commit interests so delicate and momentous a kind as those which concern its intercourse with the rest of the world to the sole disposal of a magistrate, created and circumstanced, as would be a president of the United States.

According to Berger, a telling example of presidential usurpation of congressional authority is the treaty-making power. He cites a provision of Article II, Section 2 of the Constitution to substantiate the argument that presidents have been acting unconstitutionally: "He shall have power, by and with the advice and consent of the Senate, to make treaties."

The Senate, according to Berger, therefore should have the power to participate in the negotiation and formulation of treaties, as well as in their ratification. From his study of the Constitutional Convention, Berger concludes that the Framers intended the treaty-making power to have belonged to the Senate and that "it was the President . . . who was finally made a participant in the treaty-making process, which had been initially lodged—after the pattern of the Continental Congress—in the Senate alone."[23] Berger believes that there is no presidential privilege to withhold information on the development of treaties with foreign nation-states:

> How can you help "make" a treaty if you don't know a thing about how it is being negotiated? How can the Senate "advise" as to the "making" of a treaty if it is kept in the dark? That doesn't mean that you have to play strip poker in full view of the public. The alternative to operation in a gold fish bowl is not necessarily a darkroom.[24]

Despite the Framers' fear of a too powerful executive and their efforts to constrain presidential power, even in foreign policy, the ascendance of the president in foreign policy-making has become widely accepted. Nonetheless, former senator J. William Fulbright (D-Ark.) once countered that "usurpation is not legitimized simply by repetition, nor is a valid power nullified by failure to exercise it."[25] His comment was reminiscent of former justice Felix Frankfurter's statement that "illegality cannot attain legitimacy through practice"[26] and former chief justice Earl Warren's comment, "That an unconstitutional action has been taken before surely does not render that action any less unconstitutional at a later date."[27]

Indeed, the critics of executive privilege maintain that presidents have usurped such authority, in contravention of the constitutional scheme. How could the Framers—who sought to limit and control executive authority—have possibly accepted such a broad-based, independent power as the right to withhold information? Logically, a chief executive who is subservient to the will of the legislature has no such right.

THE "RIGHT" AND THE NEED TO KNOW

A democratic society places a premium on the values of open government and freedom of information. Critics of executive privilege are concerned with the need to foster, not hinder, those values. From their perspective, executive privilege is antithetical to core democratic values. It is, in a word, antidemocratic. More specifically, these critics maintain that, for our democracy to function properly, both Congress and the public must be fully informed of what the executive branch is doing. Congress must have adequate information to carry out its primary functions; and a well-informed citizenry cannot be kept in the dark about its government's actions.

Without a doubt, the executive branch is an essential source of information for Congress. In order to know best how to appropriate funds for the military and assistance to foreign governments, to oversee the bureaucracy, and to review treaties and executive agreements, Congress needs access to executive branch information. Without adequate information, members of Congress are unable to weigh alternatives, estimate costs and benefits, and develop strategies to improve government policies. As former senator Sam Ervin (D-N.C.) explains, "The refusal to make information available to the Congress *when needed for its legislative functions* is inimical to the power of the Congress to fulfill its legislative duties."[28]

Congress often must rely on executive branch information to determine whether public policies are faithfully being executed. To adopt Berger's language, the "Grand Inquest" of the nation can never legitimately be denied access to this information. Former senator Stuart Symington (D-Mo.) agrees: "The Executive Branch of our Government . . . is, or should be, the best source of information to which the Congress can turn if it is to know how and whether the laws and policies which it approved are, in fact, being carried out."[29] There is constitutional support for Symington's view. In one leading Supreme Court case, *McGrain v. Daugherty* (1927), Justice Willis Van Devanter offered the following judgment: "In actual legislative practice, power to secure needed information by such [investigatory] means has long been treated as an attribute of power to legislate. It was so regarded in the British Parliament and in the Colonial Legislatures before the American Revolution."[30]

From the perspective of some critics of executive privilege, congressional access to executive branch information not only is a practical necessity; it is legally required. Furthermore, Congress not only is entitled to all such information; its members are capable of maintaining secrets.[31] The assumption, therefore, is that the executive never really loses "control" over secretive information because: (1) it does not own that information; and (2) Congress can be trusted with secrets just as well as the executive.

Members of Congress make clear that executive branch information not only must be made available to them, but that they must receive such information in a timely fashion. Most legislators want timely information so that they can play a substantive role in the early stages of decision-making. To be precise, they prefer being "consulted" to merely being "informed."[32] Divulging previously withheld information after a decision has been made does little to advance Congress's role in the policy process. A 1981 House of Representatives report on Congress and foreign policy-making states the dilemma well: "Unless consultation is timely, it loses a good deal of its impact and 'effective' relations are of only symbolic value."[33]

From the congressionalist perspective, a particularly strong argument against executive privilege is that decision-makers benefit from being exposed to numerous viewpoints. Irving Janis's classic study, *Groupthink*, makes clear that from a policy-maker's perspective, it is important to avoid conformity, to seek out different opinions, and to resist isolation from outside viewpoints. Janis illustrates the disastrous consequences of decisions made by like-minded groups of individuals who resisted different points of view.[34] Consequently, an executive may at his peril withhold information from people who he knows would disagree with his position. Members of Congress believe that they are particularly well situated to provide the executive with diverse opinions. James MacGregor Burns agrees that leaders benefit from such outside input in that they can make more informed decisions than when secluded from opposing arguments:

> A more effective way to handle choice . . . is to use conflict deliberately to protect decision-making options and power, and, even more, to use conflict to structure [the] political environment so as to maximize "constructive" dissonance, thus allowing for more informed decision-making. Perhaps the chief means of doing this is to create a system of "multiple advocacy" around the decision-maker.[35]

The 1981 House report notes an important obstacle to the executive seeking out divergent viewpoints: a lack of trust in Congress. The report quotes a White House official who agreed that presidents need constructive advice from members of Congress. But the executive often keeps secrets because "even when the president has stressed the sensitivity of an issue Members of Congress have walked outside and talked to the press on the White House grounds."[36] Hence, members of Congress contend that they have a right to—and need for—all executive branch information, while the executive is often reluctant to agree to divulge certain kinds of information out of fear of public disclosure.

Many critics of executive privilege disregard the president's fears of public disclosure of sensitive information. The public, they believe, has a "right to know" everything about the operations of the executive branch in a democratic system of government. From this perspective, executive privilege hinders the free flow of information and ideas. Sam Ervin eloquently states that

> the practice of executive privilege . . . is clearly in contravention of the basic principle that the free flow of ideas and information and open and full disclosure of the governing process is essential to the operation of a free society. Throughout history, rulers have invoked secrecy regarding their actions in order to enslave the citizenry. When the government operates in secrecy its citizens are not informed and their ignorance breeds oppression. In contrast, a government whose actions are completely visible to all of its citizens is a government which best protects the freedom which the Founding Fathers attempted to embody in the Constitution.[37]

Executive privilege appears difficult to accommodate in a governing system based on the concept of accountability. How can leaders be held accountable for their actions when the public and Congress do not know what these leaders are doing? Bruce Miroff writes that "the American people cannot judge what they do not know."[38] He offers the following assessment of the problem: "Secret action . . . permits a president to persist in a course of policy even if that policy lacks support from, or is strongly opposed by, majorities in Congress and among the American people. . . . Secrecy also encourages contempt for democratic procedures and democratic values."[39]

Perhaps most ironic is the following quotation from former president Richard M. Nixon, just three months prior to the Watergate break-in: "When information which properly belongs to the public is systematically withheld by those in power, the people soon become ignorant of their own affairs, distrustful of those who manage them, and—eventually—incapable of determining their own destinies."[40]

Executive privilege appears to be contrary to the Freedom of Information Act (FOIA), passed by Congress in 1966 to allow for the fullest public disclosure possible of government actions.[41] Furthermore, executive privilege appears antithetical to the principle of a free press. Former *New York Times* writer Hanson W. Baldwin argues that government censorship or control of information "impairs the constitutional rights of a free press, and hence poses a potential danger to our form of democratic and representative government." Furthermore, "no free people can be really free if its press is spoon-fed with government pap, or if the news which provides a democracy with the rationale for its actions is so controlled, restricted, managed, or censored that it cannot be published."[42]

David Wise explains that many authorities believe that there must be a balancing test between national security claims and the principle of a free press. He rejects any such test in favor of an unfettered free press. In his view, because of the First Amendment guarantee of a free press, there can be no limits on the right to publish information about the government's activities, "no matter what the potential harm to an officially defined 'national security.' The risks of repression are greater."[43] As Wise maintains, "A democratic system requires a public informed about the decisions and actions of its political leaders."[44] That public cannot be so informed when the press is unable to obtain and report information about governmental activities.

MISUSES OF THE PRIVILEGE

Presidents and their staffs may invoke executive privilege to cover up illegal or unethical governmental activities. They may use executive privilege to hide embarrassing information or to maintain an advantage in policy debates with congressional opponents. Former congressman John E. Moss comments that executive branch officials withhold information "to avoid criticism rather than for reasons of national safety."[45] U.S. Sen. Edward M. Kennedy (D-Mass.) believes that

> government secrecy breeds government deceit, that executive privilege nurtures executive arrogance, that national security is frequently the cover for political embarrassment, and that the best antidote to official malfeasance, misfeasance, and nonfeasance is the sunshine and fresh air of full public disclosure of official activities.[46]

Underlying such arguments against executive privilege is a profound distrust of government power. Thomas I. Emerson writes that "to the extent that information is withheld from a citizen the basis for government control over him becomes coercion, not persuasion."[47] David Wise adds that "the secrecy system facilitates official lying."[48] In Wise's view, the president may use the excuse of secrecy in order to distort reality for self-serving purposes:

> Frequently the press and public, unable to check the events independently, can only await the appearance of the president on the television screen to announce the official version of reality, be it the Bay of Pigs, Tonkin Gulf, or Laos, or Cambodia, or Vietnam. . . . The government's capacity to distort information in order to preserve its own political power is almost limitless.
>
> If information is power, the ability to distort and control information will be used more often than not to preserve and perpetuate that power.[49]

Wise acknowledges a leading reason given for government secrecy: the need to conceal information from enemies abroad. Nonetheless, he concludes that there is no moral or philosophical basis for that reason and that the threat of enemies abroad merely is an untruthful justification for keeping people at home uninformed.[50]

Concerns about government misuse of such a power as executive privilege are certainly well founded. Indeed, there are numerous examples of executive branch officials concealing information of minimal security value to cover up governmental misconduct. Under the Nixon administration alone, the Securities and Exchange Commission in 1972 refused to provide pertinent information on the International Telephone and Telegraph investigation to the House Interstate and Foreign Commerce Subcommittee; the Department of Defense in 1972 refused to supply documents to the House Armed Services Committee during hearings on the firing of General John Lavelle, who was reported to have conducted unauthorized raids over Vietnam; the president refused to allow his secretary of state, William Rogers, to comply with an August 1971 Senate Foreign Relations Committee demand for information on foreign military assistance; and the president used executive privilege to cover up the Watergate scandal. Nixon believed that he had an absolute power of executive privilege—one that could be claimed on behalf of the entire executive branch of government.

Given Nixon's abuses of the executive privilege, it is no wonder that many critics perceive any such claim of presidential power as suspect.[51]

Such abuses, among others, compelled Morton H. Halperin and Daniel N. Hoffman to make the following assessment:

> Not only has secrecy undermined the constitutional prerogatives of Congress and the electorate, it has also led directly to substantial infringements of civil liberties. . . . We permitted our constitutional system of checks and balances to be eroded, our civil liberties to be infringed, because we believed that secrecy was necessary to our national security.[52]

For many critics of executive privilege, the evils of nondisclosure clearly outweigh any potential evil that may result from executive disclosure of sensitive information. For those who accept the need for a balancing test, in other words, the scale tips decisively in favor of candor and openness. Stuart Symington believes that "it is now clear that the risk of failure of executive branch policies and programs occasioned by their revelation to the Congress is much to be preferred as against the risk of vital damage inflicted on a democratic system because of failure to disclose the truth."[53] The leading critic of executive privilege, Raoul Berger, adds that "against the debatable assumption that fear of disclosure to Congress, may inhibit 'candid interchange' there is the proven fact that such exchanges have time and again served as the vehicles of corruption and malversation."[54] But perhaps none other than Richard Nixon stated the case against executive branch secrecy so clearly. In 1961 the then recently defeated presidential candidate criticized President John F. Kennedy's exercise of secrecy during the Bay of Pigs fiasco: "The concept of a return to secrecy in peacetime demonstrates a profound misunderstanding of the role of a free press as opposed to that of a controlled press. The plea for secrecy could become a cloak for errors, misjudgments, and other failings of government."[55]

Critics of executive privilege maintain that there is no constitutional support for the exercise of such a power. Furthermore, the frequent use of executive privilege in presidential administrations constitutes the repetition of a criminal act. Finally, these critics perceive executive privilege as antithetical to a democratic system, a convenient cloak to avoid accountability. For these reasons, they resolve the dilemma of executive privilege and democratic accountability in favor of complete openness in governmental activity.

CHAPTER 2

The Arguments in Favor of Executive Privilege

★————————————————————————————————★

The opponents of executive privilege persuasively argue that government secrecy is undemocratic and leads to abuses of power, but they often overstate their case. For example, it is true that the Framers wanted to preserve liberty by restricting power, but they certainly never set out to cripple executive power. Any power can be used to do right or to do wrong. The Framers sought to devise institutional mechanisms to counterbalance the abuse of power, but they never intended to destroy power altogether as a means of protecting our liberties.

The case for executive privilege is based on the view that such a presidential power has clear constitutional, political, and historical underpinnings. Unfortunately, many defenses of executive privilege are based on the false claim that this power is an absolute, unlimited prerogative of the chief executive. That claim clearly is as misguided as the belief that the Framers rejected for all times and under all circumstances any such exercise of presidential power. Rather, the Framers provided the president with a general grant of power that would enable him to take actions necessary to protect the national security.

THE UNDERPINNINGS OF EXECUTIVE PRIVILEGE

Theories of Constitutionalism

As part of their preparation for the Philadelphia Convention of 1787, the constitutional Framers studied political theory and history. James Madison, for example, prepared a history of republican governments. There is no doubt that the ideas of leading European philosophers weighed on the minds of the American constitutional Framers. An assessment of the Framers' intentions therefore requires an examination of the ideas of the most influential thinkers of modern constitutionalism: John Locke and Baron de Montesquieu.

The neglect, as well as the misunderstanding, of these leading constitutional thinkers has been a source of confusion over the Framers' intentions regarding executive branch secrecy. Archibald Cox, for example, argues that Locke's and Montesquieu's notions of the separation of powers are not germane to the executive privilege debate because "they had no need to concern themselves with problems involving two or more branches that required exact definition of the boundaries of each."[1] Harold Laski writes that our political system "in its ultimate foundation, is built upon a belief in weak government. It must never be forgotten that the Constitution is the child of the eighteenth century; that the influence of Locke and Montesquieu is written deeply into its clauses."[2] And Raoul Berger concludes from his reading of Montesquieu that "history delineates a virtually unlimited legislative power to demand information from the executive branch."[3]

A careful reading of Locke and Montesquieu reveals that neither of these thinkers advocated weak government or a subordinate executive power at all times. Certainly, they emphasized restrained governmental powers and individual rights more than their predecessors, which has much to do with the appeal of these two thinkers to the American constitutional Framers. Before we examine the views of Locke and Montesquieu on executive power, those views need to be placed in the proper context of modern political theory.

Political theorists today generally trace the origins of modern political thought to Niccolò Machiavelli. To simplify the distinction, the ancient philosophers focused on the need to create regimes that fostered citizen virtue and community. The modern thinkers, beginning with Machiavelli, concerned themselves with establishing regimes that controlled social and political strife and enabled people to cultivate their own interests without living in constant fear of one another.

The regimes envisioned by the modernists required some form of executive power. In *The Prince*, Machiavelli advised a ruler on the cruel necessities of executive power during the founding of a regime. In order to gain control over a principality and the respect of its subjects, Machiavelli believed, the ruler had to establish absolute authority through the exercise of often cruel measures. Only in such a way could order and authority be maintained, Machiavelli reasoned.[4] Machiavelli, therefore, did not advocate an overbearing executive power for its own sake. His masterly work, *The Discourses*, goes to great length to show that there should be inherent limits on the executive power in the post-founding era. Machiavelli feared that an executive given enormous powers during the founding period might resist forfeiting such authority during normal times.[5] Hence, he proposed the eventual establishment of a "mixed-regime" composed of aristocratic, democratic, and monarchic elements, where power checks power.[6]

Thomas Hobbes' *Leviathan* proposed that the sovereign power be granted extraordinary authority as the only means of overcoming civil strife. In Hobbes' regime, individuals sacrifice almost all of their liberties to the sovereign power in return for the relative comfort given them by the absolute dictator. The sovereign has absolute authority, but uses it to promote peaceful coexistence in the community.[7]

Machiavelli and Hobbes thus established the necessity of executive power to a stable regime. The chief task of the modern constitutionalists—Locke and Montesquieu—was to create the conditions for such a stable regime while moderating the harsher prescriptions of Machiavelli and Hobbes. Whereas Machiavelli and Hobbes imagined circumstances under which citizens had to forfeit basic liberties to the sovereign power, Locke and Montesquieu sought to create regimes characterized by both strength and liberty. They believed that the way to ensure such a regime was through a system of institutionally separated governmental powers.

John Locke, in his *Second Treatise of Government*, offers a three-fold distinction of governmental powers: the legislative, the executive, and the "federative."[8] Although on the surface Locke's emphasis on legislative supremacy seems unequivocal, he invests a considerable amount of power in the executive branch. For example, he places the "federative power"— the power to make war, peace, treaties, and alliances—solely within the realm of the executive.[9] Locke's chapter "Of Prerogative" is the most revealing. In times of emergency, when the legislature is not in session, or where the laws are silent, he proposes giving the executive "the power of doing public good without a rule."[10] For Locke, the "supreme law" of the land is preservation of society. Only the executive can act with power and "despatch" in times of emergency. Whereas the legislative branch has supreme lawmaking powers during normal times, the executive branch has the power to take extraordinary, even extralegal, actions in times of emergency.

Accordingly, it is not correct to argue that Locke advocated either weak government or a subordinate executive power. Locke's "executive" is, in many ways, equally as powerful as Hobbes' "sovereign." The most important difference is that Hobbes takes the exception—civil strife and the need to overcome that through extraordinary executive power—and makes it the rule.[11] Locke's unique contribution to the American experience is showing us how to maintain a strong executive, while moderating and checking this power at the same time.

Like his predecessors, Montesquieu also was concerned with the problem of reconciling freedom and coercion. Yet he more clearly formulated the proposition that power can only be checked by power. The liberty of the citizenry, he wrote, can best be protected by preventing any one power from holding the authority to formulate and to execute the laws. He devised a governmental triad—legislative, executive, and judicial powers—as a means of preventing any one arm of the government from becoming tyrannical:[12] "Constant experience shows us that every man invested with power is apt to abuse it, and to carry his authority as far as it will go . . . To prevent this abuse, it is necessary from the very nature of things that power should be a check of power."[13]

Although Montesquieu set forth a separation of powers system to limit governmental power as a means of enhancing individual liberty, he did not advocate weak government. Montesquieu empowered the executive—the "monarch"—to act with a degree of discretion necessary in times of emergency, even if such actions were not specifically granted by the legislature. In the end, Montesquieu allowed for a strong executive, independent of direct pressures from the "popular will," capable of acting with force and discretion.

This brief examination of major thinkers of modern constitutionalism points out the difficulties associated with the conclusion of many writers—that the Framers, taking their cues from Locke and Montesquieu, sought to devise a weak governmental system with a subordinated executive power. Laski and Berger are correct in asserting that earlier constitutional theorists profoundly influenced the Framers. The Laski and Berger interpretations of these thinkers are problematic. Berger and other critics of the privilege have looked to the founding as a time in which the Framers sought to preserve liberty to the exclusion of all other values. It cannot be emphasized enough that the Framers sought to preserve both liberty *and* power in devising our constitutional scheme. In fact, in the *Federalist Papers* Publius makes clear that efficient, effective government is most conducive to the maintenance of liberty. The notion of checks and balances, and the doctrine of separation of powers, were devices intended to enhance liberty, while maintaining "energy" in the executive. As Paul Peterson asserts, "The doctrines of separation of powers and checks and balances allowed the advocates of a strong executive to carry the day and allowed them to construct an energetic executive within a framework of republican liberty."[14]

Unlike Cox, Laski, and Berger, constitutional scholar Edward S. Corwin writes that Locke and Montesquieu understood executive power as "a broadly discretionary, residual, power which is available when other governmental powers fail."[15] Consequently, he concludes that "the Framers had in mind [their] idea of a divided initiative in the matter of legislation and a broad range of autonomous executive power or 'prerogative.'"[16] The Framers may have looked to earlier thinkers for guidance, yet these constitution-makers also wrote extensively about the role of executive power in republican government. The Framers, in fact, vested a broad range of discretionary authority in the president.

The Constitutional Period

Critics of executive privilege point to the Framers' fear of tyranny as proof that the Constitution provides for a subordinate executive power. These critics identify the colonial experiences under King George III as the key point of reference for the American constitutional Framers in creating the executive power.

The argument that the Framers sought to devise a regime characterized by liberty and weak executive power neglects the true point of reference for these Constitution-makers: the governing experiences under the Articles of Confederation. During that period, most of the states had extraordinarily weak governors with terms of office as brief as six or twelve months, no reeligibility, and no powers independent of the state legislatures. The most telling exception was New York, which had an independent executive with full administrative powers, a three-year term of office, and unlimited reeligibility. Of the state governments during the Articles of Confederation period, New York could claim the most efficient, competent administration.

At the national level, no single executive existed under the Articles of Confederation. A deliberative assembly, the Continental Congress, had authority for governing the separate states. The failures of governance under this system precipitated the 1787 Constitutional Convention in Philadelphia where the Framers set forth a new governing plan. Because of the inability of the separate sovereign states to raise a national militia, carry out interstate commerce, and conduct a coherent foreign policy, the Framers established a new constitutional system, which included an independent, single-member executive with substantial powers.

Before discussing the Framers' views of executive power—an important foundation for establishing the legitimacy of executive privilege—it is helpful to note that the delegates conducted the Constitutional Convention in secret. They did not officially record the debates of the convention. The official journal of the convention listed only the formal motions and roll-call votes by state. Only the delegates had access to that journal. Delegates had the windows of the building boarded up so no one could overhear the proceedings inside. The delegates wanted to maintain secrecy to protect the proceedings from outside pressures. James Madison later attested that "no Constitution would ever have been adopted by the Convention if the debates had been public."[17] Former chief justice of the Supreme Court Warren Burger echoed that statement years later when he noted that the convention delegates "were under a pledge to protect the secrecy of the proceedings without which, I think we must know now there would never have been a Constitution coming out of that meeting."[18] In fact, Burger's opinion for a unanimous Court in *U.S. v. Nixon* (1974)—the case that formally recognized the legitimacy of executive privilege—draws upon the fact that the convention delegates conducted their proceedings in secret as clear evidence of the Framers' recognition of the need for governmental secrecy.[19]

Contrary to Raoul Berger's argument, the fact that executive privilege nowhere is mentioned in the Constitution does not preclude the legitimate exercise of that presidential power. Recall Berger's interpretation that Article I, Section 5(3) of the Constitution provides for an exclusive legislative privilege to keep secrets. No comparable provision exists in Article II, leading Berger to conclude that the Framers intentionally excluded the president from exercising secrecy. This narrow reading of the Constitution is not well supported by the evidence.

First, Berger's interpretation fails to note important differences between the legislative and the executive articles of the Constitution. The legislative article, unlike the executive one, contains the words "herein granted" in referring to the legislature's powers and specifies that branch's most important duties (e.g., declaring war, raising and supporting armies, providing and maintaining a navy, regulating commerce, appropriating funds). The executive article provides a general grant of power with relatively few specifics. Many of the president's powers are not defined and enumerated, allowing the chief executive to exercise a broad scope of responsibilities under various circumstances. Under their general grant of authority—"The Executive Power shall be vested in a President of the United States of America"—presidents historically have exercised numerous powers not specified in the Constitution (e.g., issuing proclamations, making executive agreements with foreign nation-states, removing executive officials from office, adopting emergency measures in wartime).

Second, judging from the writings of the leading Framers who frequently stressed the needs for "secrecy" and "despatch" in government, it is hard to imagine that these same people believed that secrecy was such an unqualified evil that it had to be purposefully excluded from the executive article. It seems more plausible that the Framers understood secrecy as so obvious an executive power—and a judicial one, too—that there was no need for a specific grant of that power in the Constitution. Perhaps the Framers specified such a grant of power in Article I because secrecy could not be assumed to have resided in a legislature. Two passages from the *Federalist Papers* support executive branch secrecy. The classic statement is found in Alexander Hamilton's *Federalist 70*: "Decision, activity, secrecy and despatch will generally characterize the proceedings of one man in a much more eminent degree than the proceedings of any great number; and in proportion as the number is increased, these qualities will be diminished." John Jay, who had served as the secretary of foreign affairs under the Articles of Confederation, wrote in *Federalist 64* that "secrecy" and "despatch" were characteristic of the executive branch. He recognized the inability of a deliberative assembly to be entrusted with diplomatic secrets:

> There are cases where the most useful intelligence may be obtained, if the persons possessing it can be relieved from apprehensions of discovery. Those apprehensions will operate on those persons whether they are actuated by mercenary or friendly motives; and there doubtless are many of both descriptions who would rely on the secrecy of the President, but who would not confide in that of the Senate, and still less in that of a large popular assembly.

Jay's *Federalist 64* also contradicts Berger's interpretation of the Senate's role in treaties. From the Article II, Section 2 "advice and consent" clause, Berger concludes that the Framers precluded the exercise of executive privilege because the Senate cannot give advice on matters of which it is not informed. But Jay made clear that there are circumstances under which a president may have to resort to secret measures in the treaty-making process. Berger assigns the Senate the preeminent role in treaty-making. Jay portrayed the president and Senate as making substantial contributions of their own based on their particular institutional strengths:

> Although the president must in forming them [treaties], act by the advice and consent of the Senate, yet he will be able to manage the business of intelligence in such manner as prudence may suggest. . . . So often and so essentially have we heretofore suffered from the want of secrecy and despatch that the Constitution would have been inexcusably defective if no attention had been paid to those objects. . . . Thus we see that the Constitution provides that our negoti-

ations for treaties shall have every advantage which can be derived from talents, information, integrity, and deliberative investigations, on the one hand, and from secrecy and despatch on the other.

Hamilton's *Federalist 75* also appears to refute the belief that the Constitution assigns to the Senate the preeminent role in treaty-making. Hamilton wrote that "to have intrusted the power of making treaties to the Senate alone, would have been to relinquish the benefits of the constitutional agency of the president in the conduct of foreign negotiations."

Central to the opponents of executive privilege is the view that the Framers made Congress "senior partner" in the foreign policy-making process. Logically, the subordinate branch of government cannot keep secrets from the preeminent branch. A substantial body of evidence supports the opposite point of view. The key members of the Committee of Style at the Constitutional Convention—Alexander Hamilton, Rufus King, Governeur Morris—shaped the language of Article II to allow the executive to exercise vast powers. The vesting clause, the lack of any enumeration of duties in the commander-in-chief clause, and many silences about such powers as war, diplomatic powers, control over executive departments, all left the president with a vast reserve of unspecified authority. Political theorist Michael Foley explains that the U.S. Constitution contains many such silences—what he calls "constitutional abeyances"—which allow for the discretionary exercise of authority according to circumstances.[20] Constitutional scholar Jack W. Peltason writes that Article II "gives the president a power that has never been defined or enumerated and, in fact, cannot be defined since its scope depends largely on circumstances."[21]

Although not assigned to the Committee of Style, James Wilson played one of the most prominent roles in the drafting of Article II. He served on the Committee of Detail and wrote the final version of the first draft of Article II. When it came to the subjects of executive power and secrecy Wilson was unequivocal. He, too, recognized the necessity of an executive power characterized by the ability to act with secrecy and with dispatch. The following commentary from Wilson's law lecture notes is consistent with the view of the *Federalist Papers*:

In planning, forming, or arranging laws, deliberation is always becoming, and always useful. But in the active scenes of govt, there are emergencies in which the man . . . who deliberates is lost. Secrecy may be equally as necessary as dispatch. But, can either secrecy or dispatch be excepted, when, to every enterprise, mutual communication, mutual consultation, and mutual agreement, among men of perhaps discordant views, of discordant tempers, and discordant interests are indispensably necessary? How much time will be consumed, how little business will be done. . . . If, on the other hand, the executive power of government is placed in the hands of one person, who is to direct all subordinate officers of that department, is there not reason to expect, in his plans and conduct, promptitude, activity, firmness, consistency, and energy.[22]

Chief Justice of the Supreme Court John Marshall wrote in the famous *Marbury v. Madison* (1803) case that "the president is invested with certain important political powers, in the exercise of which he is to use his own discretion, and is accountable only to his country in his political character, and to his own conscience."[23] On another occasion Marshall commented that the president is the "sole organ of the nation in its external relations, and its sole representative with foreign nations."[24] In the early 1800s Justice Joseph Story acknowledged as well that the president "is compelled to resort to secret and unseen influences, to private interviews, and private arrangements, to accomplish his own appropriate purposes."[25]

Critics of executive privilege reject the argument that under certain circumstances, especially those pertaining to foreign policy, the president has vast discretionary authority. They often cite James Madison's comment that "in republican government, the legislative authority necessarily predominates."[26] Paul Peterson observes that this descriptive statement by Madison—as opposed to a prescriptive one—"is in fact a warning from Madison about the dangers of such supremacy and a warning that republican regimes are particularly susceptible to legislative tyranny."[27]

Because of what he perceives as a system based on legislative supremacy, Raoul Berger sees no constitutional basis for executive privilege. Recall that he cites the Article II, Section 4 provision for impeachment as proof of this position. Berger believes that the Framers "patently modeled" the U.S. Congress after the British Parliament. He points out that historically both the colonial legislatures and the British Parliament were able to compel disclosure of executive information.[28] For Berger, "history, the traditional index of constitutional construction, discloses that a sweeping power of legislative inquiry had been exercised by the Parliament and by the colonial legislatures."[29] Berger concludes that the modern Congress must have the same limitless power of inquiry as entrusted to the British Parliament.[30]

The problem with Berger's argument is the assumption that the power of the executive in a presidential system can be equated with that of a parliamentary system. As James W. Ceaser writes, "Under a presidential system the essential executive force is never extinguished or in doubt; under a parliamentary system the executive force cannot be guaranteed (and in practice has not been)."[31] Berger's argument also rests on the belief that the power of inquiry in a governmental system based on the separation of powers is as unquestioned and extensive as the power of inquiry in a system that rejects the concept of separation of powers. As Gary Schmitt argues, the Framers had established the separation of powers system "to help foreclose the possibility of legislative supremacy." Furthermore, this system resulted "in a more limited conception of the impeachment power" than Berger envisions.[32] Although Congress indeed needs information to conduct impeachment inquiries, the Supreme Court has ruled that the congressional power of inquiry has limits.[33] The Court also has determined that in cases of inquiry into possible criminal actions, the executive has to release pertinent information.[34] In no sense has Congress ever been granted a complete, unlimited power of inquiry that enables it to have access to all executive branch information.

Berger's interpretation of Article II, Section 3 of the Constitution—"He shall from time to time give to the Congress information of the state of the Union, and recommend to their consideration such measures as he shall judge necessary and expedient"—also is troublesome. Referring to the original version proposed at the Constitutional Convention, rather than the just recited adopted version, Berger argues that the Framers intended to limit the discretion of the president to present information in the State of the Union address. Berger's argument, therefore, rests on the dubious assumption that historians should look primarily to the original provision for Article II, Section 3 to understand the meaning of its adopted form. Clearly, the adopted version means the opposite of what Berger suggests. As Schmitt observes, the president "has the discretion both in determining what he shall say and when he shall say it."[35] In practice, presidents historically have used the State of the Union address to present information that they wanted to reveal to Congress, not information that Congress compelled them to present. Schmitt reports that in response to an 1808 congressional resolution requesting military information from the president, members of Congress agreed that they had "no power to coerce information" and that Article II, Section 3 of the Constitution had made the president the sole judge of what he could communicate.[36]

EXECUTIVE PRIVILEGE IN HISTORY

Although the philosophical and constitutional underpinnings of executive privilege are substantial, the legitimacy of that presidential power is strengthened by the evidence of its frequent historical exercise. It is true that a criminal act does not become legal through repetition. But there is much evidence to indicate that executive privilege is a legitimate, not usurped, power. Furthermore, the frequent exercise of presidential authority creates a strong presumption of validity, especially when such authority has been accepted, or not effectively challenged, by the coordinate branches of government.

Early Years of the Republic

The Framers' view of executive branch secrecy is best understood by examining governmental decision-making in the early republic. Undoubtedly, the intentions of the Framers are illuminated by what these men did when they put their constitutional principles into practice. As Raoul Berger writes, an analysis of the early years of the republic is "more nearly contemporaneous with the forging of the Constitution."[37]

The first presidential administration established the most important precedents for the exercise of executive power. George Washington understood the profound influence that the founders would have on future generations. As he wrote on 5 May 1783 to James Madison, "As the first of everything, *in our situation will serve to establish a precedent*, it is devoutly wished on my part, that these precedents may be fixed on true principles."[38] As president, Washington acted in accordance with a Hamiltonian view of executive power. Glenn A. Phelps offers the following perspective:

From the outside it is clear that Washington had a constitutional agenda as President—and that much of that agenda was predicated upon establishing a national government (and Presidency) independent of and superior to the states.

His administration was replete with attempts—some successful, some not—to circumvent the barriers of separation in the name of unity, energy, and efficiency.[39]

More specifically, several of Washington's actions established precedents for the exercise of what is now known as executive privilege. The first such action concerned a congressional request to investigate "public" information relating to the failure of a November 1791 military expedition by Gen. Arthur St. Clair against Native American Indians. The House of Representatives established an investigative committee on 27 March 1792, "to call for such persons, papers and records, as may be necessary to assist their inquiries."[40] The investigating committee requested from the president documents regarding St. Clair's expedition.

Washington convened his cabinet to determine how to respond to this first ever request for presidential materials by a congressional committee. The president wanted to discuss whether any harm would result from public disclosure of the information and, most pertinently, whether he could rightfully refuse to submit documents to Congress. Along with Hamilton, Knox, and Edmund Randolph, Thomas Jefferson attended the 2 April 1792 cabinet meeting. He later recalled the group's determination:

> We had all considered, and were of one mind, first, that the House was an inquest, and therefore might institute inquiries. Second, that it might call for papers generally. Third, that the Executive ought to communicate such papers as the public good would permit, and ought to refuse those, the disclosure of which would injure the public: consequently were to exercise a discretion. Fourth, that neither the committees nor House has a right to call on the Head of a Department, who and whose papers were under the President alone; but that the committee should instruct their chairman to move the House to address the President.[41]

Washington eventually determined that public disclosure of the information would not harm the national interest and that such disclosure was necessary to vindicate Gen. St. Clair. Although Washington chose to negotiate with Congress over the investigating committee's request and to turn over relevant documents to Congress, his administration had taken an affirmative position on the right of the executive branch to withhold information. Adam Breckenridge writes that "this beginning of the executive privilege indicates . . . the president could refuse documents because of their secret nature, a category insisted upon by subsequent presidents ever since."[42]

On 17 January 1794 the U.S. Senate advanced a motion directing Secretary of State Edmund Randolph "to lay before the Senate the correspondence which have been had between the Minister of the United States at the Republic of France, [Morris] and said Republic, and between said Minister and the Office of Secretary of State."[43] The Senate later amended the motion to address the president instead of Minister Morris. Significantly, the amended version also "requested" rather than "directed" that such information be forwarded to Congress (ibid.).

Believing that disclosure of the correspondence would be inappropriate, Washington sought the advice of his Cabinet as to how to handle the Senate's request. On 28 January 1794 three of Washington's cabinet members expressed their opinions:

> General Knox is of the opinion, that no part of the correspondence should be sent to the Senate. Colonel Hamilton, that the correct mode of proceeding is to do what General Knox advises; but the principle is safe, by excepting such parts as the president may choose to withhold. Mr. Randolph, that all correspondence proper, from its nature, to be communicated to the Senate, should be sent; but that what the president thinks is improper, should not be sent. (Ibid.)

Attorney General William Bradford wrote separately that "it is the duty of the Executive to withhold such parts of the said correspondence as in the judgment of the Executive shall be deemed unsafe and improper to be disclosed" (1320).

On 16 February 1794 Washington responded as follows to the Senate's request:

> After an examination of [the correspondence], I directed copies and translations to be made; except in those particulars, in my judgment, for public considerations, ought not to be communicated. These copies and translations are

now transmitted to the Senate; but the nature of them manifest the propriety of their being received as confidential. (Ibid.)

Washington allowed the Senate to examine some parts of the correspondence, subject to his approval. He believed that information damaging to the "public interest" could constitutionally be withheld from Congress. The Senate never challenged the president's authority to withhold the information.[44]

In 1796 John Jay completed U.S. negotiations with Great Britain over issues unsettled from the American Revolution. Because many considered the settlement unfavorable to the United States, Congress took a keen interest in the administration's actions in the negotiations. Not only did the Senate debate ratification of the Jay Treaty, the House set out to conduct its own investigation. On 24 March 1796 the House passed a resolution requesting from Washington information concerning his instructions to the U.S. minister to Britain regarding the treaty negotiations. That resolution raised the issue of the House's proper role in the treaty-making process. Washington refused to comply with the House request and explained his reasons for so deciding:

> The nature of foreign negotiations requires caution, and their success must often depend on secrecy; and even when brought to a conclusion a full disclosure of all the measures, demands, or eventual concessions which may have been proposed or contemplated would be extremely impolitic; for this might have a pernicious influence on future negotiations, or produce immediate inconveniences, perhaps danger and mischief, in relation to other powers. The necessity of such caution and secrecy was one cogent reason for vesting the power of making treaties in the President, with the advice and consent of the Senate, the principle on which that body was formed confining it to a small number of members. To admit, then, a right in the House of Representatives to demand and to have as a matter of course all the papers respecting a negotiation with a foreign power would be to establish a dangerous precedent.

Washington explained that "the boundaries fixed by the Constitution between the different departments should be preserved, a just regard to the Constitution and to the duty of my office . . . forbids a compliance with your request."[45]

Washington believed that sole authority over the substance of treaty negotiations resided constitutionally in the executive, not Congress. Alexander Hamilton also advised the president that not only did the House have no constitutional function to perform regarding the negotiation of treaties, but that it was the president's right to withhold sensitive materials from Congress.

The House of Representatives subsequently debated at length the propriety of Washington's refusal to disclose the documents. The House took no substantive action other than passing two nonbinding resolutions—one asserting that Congress need not stipulate any reason for requesting information from the executive; the other proclaiming that the House had a legitimate role in considering the speed at which a treaty was being implemented.[46] Our chief constitutional architect, Rep. James Madison, while disagreeing in part with Washington's action, proclaimed on the House floor "that the Executive had a right, under a due responsibility, also, to withhold information, when of a nature that did not permit a disclosure of it at the time."[47]

The Washington administration never included the Senate in the negotiation stage of the Jay Treaty. During the ratification stage, the Senate voted to keep the treaty secret, as Hamilton wrote, "because they thought it [the secrecy] the affair of the president to do as he thought fit."[48] The Senate minority opposed to ratification listed seven objections to the treaty. None cited Washington's decision to not seek advice from the Senate.[49]

President John Adams asserted a right to withhold information from Congress during the 1798 "XYZ Affair." In brief, Adams had secretly dispatched three diplomats to France to negotiate a treaty of international cooperation and trade. The French, through three agents of the *Directoire*, demanded a bribe from the United States as a condition for the negotiations. Republicans in the House demanded that the Federalist president make public the French correspondence. On 3 April 1798 Adams partially complied with the House request by making the XYZ correspondence public while omitting some information to protect his diplomats abroad.[50]

Executive Privilege in the Nineteenth Century

Even the ultradefender of popular sovereignty, Thomas Jefferson, recognized the legitimacy of executive branch secrecy. As president, he classified his correspondence as either public or secret. He withheld correspondence deemed secret from both the public and Congress.[51] For example, in 1807 President Jefferson denied a congressional request to provide information about the Aaron Burr conspiracy. Burr had been involved with a secessionist conspiracy, resulting in treason charges.[52] Most relevant to the executive privilege debate, a January 1807 House resolution requested that the president "lay before this House any information in the possession of the Executive, except such as he may deem the public welfare to require not to be disclosed."[53] Congress had clearly acknowledged the president's right to exercise secrecy. Jefferson replied to the congressional resolution by announcing Burr's guilt and asserting a need to withhold details about the other alleged conspirators: "In this state of the evidence, delivered sometimes, too, under the restrictions of private confidence, neither safety nor justice will permit the exposing names, except that of the principal actor, whose guilt is placed beyond question."[54] Jefferson also had written to the U.S. district attorney conducting the Burr prosecution that it was "the necessary right of the President of the United States to decide, independently, what papers coming to him as President, the public interest permit to be communicated, and to whom."[55]

Germane to the executive privilege controversy are Jefferson's views on presidential prerogative and foreign policy powers. Jefferson, who had conducted secret negotiations over the purchase of the Louisiana territory, wrote that "a strict observance of the written laws is doubtless *one* of the high duties of a good citizen, but it is not the *highest*. The laws of necessity, of self-preservation, of saving our country when in danger, are of a higher obligation."[56] Jefferson also said that "the transaction of business with foreign nations is executive altogether. It belongs, then, to the head of that department except as to such portions of it as are strictly submitted to the Senate. *Exceptions are to be construed strictly.*"[57]

The subsequent exercises of presidential secrecy in the nineteenth century are so numerous as to preclude an analysis of each one. Nonetheless, it is possible to provide a concise historical overview in order to convey the point that numerous presidents exercised what later became known as executive privilege, lending credibility to the constitutionality of that power.

The leading author of the Constitution, James Madison, withheld information from Congress during his presidency. Madison purposefully withheld information about French trade restrictions against the United States, which eventually led to widespread support for war against Great Britain.[58] Madison, and then later President James Monroe, withheld information from Congress regarding the U.S. takeover of the Florida territory.[59] On 16 February 1816 the Senate Committee on Foreign Relations issued a report stating the following:

> If it be true that the success of negotiations is greatly influenced by time and accidental circumstances, the importance to the negotiative authority of acquiring regular and secret intelligence cannot be doubted. The Senate does not possess the means of acquiring such intelligence. It does not manage the correspondence with our ministers abroad nor with foreign concerns here. . . . The President . . . manages our concerns with foreign nations and must necessarily be most competent to determine when, how and upon what subjects negotiation may be urged with the greatest prospect of success.[60]

In 1825 the House of Representatives requested from President Monroe information concerning the "Steward incident," except any details that the president determined it was not in the public interest to disclose.[61] Monroe refused to comply and responded that submitting the requested materials "might tend to excite prejudices" and "would not comport with the public interest nor with what is due to the parties concerned."[62]

Although President Andrew Jackson established for his time an unprecedented close relationship with the public, he did not shy away from exercising, on numerous occasions, the presidential power to withhold information. In 1832 the House requested from Jackson information pertaining to U.S. negotiations with the Republic of Buenos Aires. Jackson responded that it would "not be consistent with the public interest to communicate the correspondence and instructions requested by the House so long as the negotiation shall be pending."[63] In 1833 he refused to divulge information to the Senate pertaining to negotiations with Great Britain over the northeastern boundary of the United States.[64] Later that year, when the Senate requested from Jackson documents pertaining to the removal of money from the Bank of the United States, the president refused and replied that Congress could not "require of [him] an account of any communication, either verbally or in writing, made to the heads of Departments acting as a Cabinet council." Jackson protested that the Senate could not compel him to reveal "the free and private conversations I have held with those officers on any subject relating to their duties and my own" (3:1255). In 1835 the president refused to provide to the House certain requested documents pertaining to U.S.-French correspondences (3:1348). Jackson refused a Senate request for information about the removal of U.S. Surveyor General Gideon Fitz and stated that "this is another of those calls for information made upon me by the Senate which have, in my judgment, either related to the subjects exclusively belonging to the executive department or otherwise encroached on the constitutional powers of the Executive" (3:1351).

President John Tyler also frequently asserted a presidential discretion to withhold information. In February 1842 he wrote to Congress that he could not divulge any details regarding the U.S.-British negotiations over the northeastern boundary because "in my judgment no communication could be made by me at this time on the subject of its resolution without detriment or danger to the public interests" (4:1954). The following month Tyler refused a House request for information about applicants to executive branch offices on the ground that such information was confidential and strictly an executive branch matter (4:1958–59). In June of that year the House requested from Tyler, "so far as may be compatible with the public interest," information regarding a European treaty on the suppression of the slave trade. Tyler responded that divulging the information "would not be compatible with the public interest" (5:2011). Two months later Tyler refused a Senate request for information about possible U.S. efforts to get Mexico to recognize claims of U.S. citizens (5:2031–32). In December of that year, Tyler told the Senate he "did not deem it consistent with the public interest" to reveal details about U.S. negotiations with Great Britain over the northwest boundary (5:2064).

The most celebrated case of executive branch secrecy in the Tyler administration concerned the government's investigation into fraud against the Cherokee Indians. Tyler refused to divulge such information to the House because of ongoing negotiations to settle the Indian claims and because the investigative reports contained possibly incriminating statements by implicated individuals. The president made clear his right to assert a discretion over executive branch documents:

> The injunction of the Constitution that the President "shall take care that the laws be faithfully executed," necessarily confers an authority, commensurate with the obligation imposed to inquire into the manner in which all public agents perform the duties assigned to them by law. To be effective, these inquiries must often be confidential. They may result in the collection of truth or of falsehood, or they may be incomplete and may require further prosecution. To maintain that the President can exercise no discretion as to the time in which the matters thus collected shall be promulgated . . . would deprive him at once of the means of performing one of the most salutary duties of his office. . . . To require from the Executive the transfer of this discretion to a coordinate branch of the Government is equivalent to the denial of its possession by him and would render him dependent upon that branch in the performance of a duty purely executive. (5:2075)

President James K. Polk refused an 1846 House request for information pertaining to the foreign policy expenditures of his predecessor, John Tyler. Polk asserted his duty to uphold his predecessor's determination of confidentiality. Polk also believed that "it might become absolutely necessary to incur expenditures for objects which could never be accomplished if it were suspected in advance that the items of expenditure and the agencies employed would be made public" (5:2285). In 1848, in response to a House request for documents pertaining to the return of President General López de Santa Anna to Mexico, Polk released those deemed "compatible with the public interests to communicate" (5:2415). Polk then elaborated a strong defense for confidentiality in diplomatic endeavors, based on precedent and necessity. As precedent, he cited George Washington's 30 March 1796 message to the House of Representatives in which Washington refused to release to Congress certain documents considered "improper to be disclosed" (5:2416–17). Furthermore, Polk maintained that his own case for protecting confidentiality was particularly compelling, given the fact that full disclosure of diplomatic correspondence during a war would have resulted in "serious embarrassment in any future negotiation between the [United States and Mexico]." Polk concluded that "I regard it to be my constitutional right and my solemn duty under the circumstances of this case to decline a compliance with the request of the House contained in their resolution" (5:2417).

In July 1848 Polk refused a House request for documents concerning his instructions to diplomats who had negotiated the U.S. treaty with Mexico. He reported that "as a general rule applicable to all our important negotiations with foreign powers, it could not fail to be prejudicial to the public interest to publish the instructions of our ministers until some time had elapsed after the conclusion of such negotiations" (5:2454). Several months later, Polk released the requested documents to the House, but also iterated his earlier position that he had the right to withhold information when deemed in "the public interest" to do so (6:2529–37).

President Millard Fillmore withheld diplomatic information from the Senate on several occasions in 1851–52 when he believed that transmitting such information was not in the public interest (6:2675–76, 2687, 2695). President James Buchanan refused an 1859 Senate request for law enforcement documents regarding the illegal landing of a slave ship on the Georgia coast.[65]

President Abraham Lincoln exercised the most extensive prerogative powers of any U.S. president. Given the extraordinary actions Lincoln adopted to prosecute the federal war effort, it is hardly surprising that he exercised a discretion to withhold information when deemed to be in the public interest. In 1861 Lincoln refused a House request for information about the arrests of Baltimore police commissioners at Fort McHenry.[66] In 1862 Lincoln refused a Senate request for information pertaining to the arrest of Brig. Gen. Stone (7:3275). In 1863 the House requested from the secretary of state, "if not in [his] judgment incompatible with the public interest," information on U.S. negotiations with New Grenada. Lincoln replied that it would not be in the "public interest" to comply with the request (7:3350).

Lincoln's successor, Andrew Johnson, refused on several occasions in 1866 to release requested information to Congress (8:3575, 3576, 3583). In 1876 Ulysses S. Grant refused a House request for information about his presidential actions away from the nation's capital on the basis that such information had no bearing on Congress's constitutional duties (9:4315–18). In 1887 President Grover Cleveland refused a Senate request for information regarding the sale of an American schooner and resignation of the U.S. minister to Mexico.[67] In April 1892 President Benjamin Harrison replied to a Senate request for information about actions regarding a proposed international conference on silver that "it would not be compatible with the public interest" to divulge the information at that time.[68] In his second, nonconsecutive, term, President Cleveland refused an 1896 House request for all details pertaining to U.S. affairs in Cuba, but did release selected information (13:6098). That same year, Cleveland withheld from the Senate some requested information about official U.S. correspondence with the government of Spain (13:6101).

Executive Privilege in the Twentieth Century

In 1901 President William McKinley refused to divulge to the Senate information on a War Department investigation of expenditures of Cuban funds (14:6458). President Theodore Roosevelt replied to a January 1909 Senate resolution requesting documents from the attorney general on whether proceedings had been instituted against a company for possible Sherman Antitrust Act violations:

> I have instructed the Attorney General not to respond to that portion of the resolution which calls for a statement of his reasons for nonaction. I have done so because I do not conceive it to be within the authority of the Senate to give directions of this character to the head of an executive department, or to demand from him reasons for his action. Heads of the executive departments are subject to the Constitution, and to the laws passed by the Congress in pursuance of the Constitution, and to the directions of the President of the United States, but to no other direction whatever.[69]

The Senate Judiciary Committee cleverly responded by issuing a subpoena for the same documents to the head of the Bureau of Corporations. Roosevelt secured the papers for himself and then told Congress that it would only get the documents by impeaching him.[70] The president explained that "these facts . . . were given to the government under the seal of secrecy and cannot be divulged, and I will see to it that the word of this government to the individual is kept sacred."[71]

In April 1924 President Calvin Coolidge refused a Senate request for details on companies being investigated by the Bureau of Internal Revenue. Coolidge maintained that the information was confidential and not germane to Congress's constitutional duties.[72]

In July 1930 the Senate Foreign Relations Committee requested from President Herbert Hoover's secretary of state copies of correspondence concerning the London Naval Treaty. The president responded that many communications had been provided in confidence and that he had a duty not to violate the trust that negotiators had placed in him. The president did not divulge all of the requested documents.[73]

President Franklin D. Roosevelt withheld documents requested by Congress on a number of occasions. For example, in 1941 FDR instructed his attorney general to withhold certain Federal Bureau of Investigation (FBI) papers from a House committee. In 1943 FDR's director of the Bureau of the Budget refused a House investigative committee subpoena to testify. The president had instructed that Bureau files remain confidential. That same year, the president directed the acting secretary of war not to divulge to Congress documents pertaining to the departments of War and Navy. In 1944 a House investigating committee requested information from the FBI director and issued to him a subpoena to testify. The director refused to testify and would not divulge the contents of a presidential memorandum requiring him not to testify. The attorney general wrote to the committee that communications between the president and department heads were privileged.[74] That same year, the chairman of the Select House Committee investigating the Federal Communications Commission (FCC) acknowledged that "for over 140 years" an exemption from testifying before Congress "has been granted to the executive departments, particularly where it involves military secrets or relations with foreign nations."[75]

President Harry S Truman also asserted on numerous occasions a discretion to maintain secrecy. In 1948 the House Un-American Activities Committee attempted to probe allegations of disloyalty in the Truman administration. The president issued an executive order insuring the confidentiality of loyalty files in the administration.[76] The president also made clear that he would not turn papers over to the committee.[77] That same year Truman would not permit a presidential assistant who had been subpoenaed by the House Committee on Education and Labor to appear before the committee.[78] The committee wanted to obtain information about the assistant's conversations with the president, resulting in the committee minority report assertion that "I cannot believe that any congressional committee is entitled to make that kind of investigation into the private conferences of the president with one of his principal aides."[79] In 1950 the president directed his secretary of state, attorney general, and chairman of the Civil Service Commission not to comply with a Senate subcommittee subpoena of files pertaining to the loyalty of State Department employees. Truman cited his 1948 executive order,[80] but eventually backed down after learning that the same documents had once before been made available to Congress.[81] During Senate hearings in 1951 over Truman's firing of Gen. Douglas MacArthur, Gen. Omar Bradley refused a request to testify on conversations he had as an adviser to the president. Truman considered his conversations with Bradley to be confidential.[82] The chairman of the Senate Committee on Armed Services and Foreign Relations, Sen. Richard Russell (D-Ga.), ruled that Bradley had the right to hold confidential conversations with the president. The committee subsequently upheld Russell's ruling by a vote of eighteen to eight.[83] In 1952 the chairman of a special subcommittee of the House Judiciary Committee requested of government agencies any information on "cases referred to the Department of Justice or U.S. Attorneys for either criminal or civil action."[84] Truman instructed agency and department heads not to comply with the request, which he considered too broad—"a dragnet approach to examining the administration of the laws"—and extremely costly to the government.[85] Finally, that same year Truman defended his decision to maintain the confidentiality of the activities of the Loyalty Security Program.[86]

The Dwight D. Eisenhower administration represents an important development in the doctrine of executive privilege. The actual use of the term "executive privilege" originated in the Eisenhower administration. President Eisenhower's administration invoked that doctrine on more than forty occasions. The most important controversy over executive privilege during the Eisenhower years concerned the army–McCarthy hearings. During testimony the army counsel John Adams mentioned that he had had a conference with top White House aides in the attorney general's office. Congressional investigators sought information on what transpired in those conversations among high-ranking officials. Eisenhower intervened with a letter on 17 May 1954 to Secretary of Defense Charles Wilson instructing department employees not to testify.

> Because it is essential to efficient and effective administration that employees of the Executive Branch be in a position to be completely candid in advising with each other on official matters, and because it is not in the public interest that any of their conversations or communications, or any documents or reproductions, concerning such advice be disclosed, you will instruct employees of your Department that in all of their appearances before the Subcommittee of the Senate Committee on Government Operations regarding the inquiry now before it they are not to testify to any such conversations or communications, or to produce any such documents or reproductions. This principle must be maintained regardless of who would benefit by such disclosures.[87]

Other executive branch officials used Eisenhower's letter as the justification for their refusals to testify before Congress. United Nations ambassador Henry Cabot Lodge, for example, refused to testify to Congress on the army–McCarthy affair on the basis that he was a White House adviser. Eisenhower replied affirmatively: "The position you propose to take is exactly correct. I would be astonished if any of my personal advisors would undertake to give testimony on intimate staff counsel and advice. The result would be to eliminate all such offices from the presidential staff. In turn, this would mean paralysis."[88]

Eisenhower adopted an uncompromising stand on executive privilege. He told a group of Republican legislative leaders that "any man who testifies as to the advice he gave me won't be working for me that night." Eisenhower elaborated his position: "Those people who have a position here in this government because of me, those people who are my confidential advisors are not going to be subpoenaed. . . . Governor Adams's official job is really a part of me and he's not going up on the Hill."[89] Sen. Joseph McCarthy (R-Wisc.) denounced Eisenhower's order as an "iron curtain" and exclaimed that "this is the first time I've ever seen the executive branch of government take the fifth amendment."[90] Despite some other criticism of the president for defining executive privilege too broadly—possibly allowing every executive branch officer to assert that prerogative—the *Washington Post* agreed that the president's constitutional authority to withhold information from Congress "is altogether beyond question."[91]

There are too many other cases of executive privilege in the Eisenhower administration to cover here. It is most important to recognize that Eisenhower's 17 May 1954 letter established a precedent for the exercise of executive privilege in the modern presidency. Indeed, Eisenhower's immediate Democratic successor, John F. Kennedy, did not shy away from executive privilege.

Kennedy's view of executive privilege fit comfortably within his understanding of presidential power. As a presidential candidate in 1960, Kennedy told the National Press Club that a president "must be prepared to exercise the fullest powers of his office—some that are specified and some that are not."[92] In his first presidential press conference, Kennedy responded to a reporter's question on executive privilege: "But I must say that I do not hold the view that all matters and all information which is available to the Executive should be made available at all times, and I don't think any member of the press does."[93] Kennedy explained his view of executive privilege as follows:

> Since the early days of the Republic, Americans have also recognized that the Federal Government is obliged to protect certain information which might otherwise jeopardize the security of the country. That need has become particularly acute in recent years as the United States has assumed a powerful position in world affairs, and as world peace has come to depend in large part on how that position is safeguarded. We are also moving into an era of delicate negotiations in which it will be especially important that governments be able to communicate in confidence.
>
> Clearly, the two principles of an informed public and of confidentiality within the Government are irreconcilable in their purest forms, and a balance must be struck between them.[94]

In 1962 a special Senate subcommittee investigated military Cold War education and speech review policies. The president wrote letters to his secretary of defense instructing the secretary not to comply with a request for the names of individuals who wrote or edited speeches. Kennedy specifically instructed the secretary "not to give testimony or produce any documents which would disclose such information." Kennedy's letter further stated that "it would not be possible for you to maintain an orderly Department and receive the candid advice and loyal respect of your subordinates if they, instead of you and your senior associates, are to be individually answerable to the Congress, as well as to you, for their internal acts and advice."[95] The chairman of the subcommittee, Sen. John Stennis (D-Miss.), ruled in favor of Kennedy's claim of executive privilege. The subcommittee upheld that ruling.[96]

Although in practice Kennedy permitted administrative officers to exercise executive privilege, in principle he supported a less expansive use of that prerogative than did the Eisenhower administration. The chairman of the House Subcommittee on Government Information, Rep. John E. Moss (D-Calif.), vigorously opposed the use of executive privilege by presidential administrations. When Moss requested clarification of Kennedy's official policy toward executive privilege, the president emphasized that such authority "can be invoked only by the president and will not be used without specific presidential approval." Kennedy expressed agreement with the need for Congress to have "the widest public accessibility to governmental information."[97] Nonetheless, Kennedy used executive privilege to prevent legislative oversight of foreign policy. The president ordered his military adviser, Gen. Maxwell Taylor, to refuse to testify before a congressional committee examining the Bay of Pigs fiasco.[98]

Rep. Moss later requested clarification of President Lyndon B. Johnson's policy on executive privilege. The president replied that, following Kennedy's policy, "the claim of 'executive privilege' will continue to be made only by the president."[99] Again, this presidential policy was not followed. In 1968 the Department of Defense refused a request of the Senate Foreign Relations Committee for a copy of the Command Control Study of the Gulf of Tonkin incident.[100] That same year, the Senate Judiciary Committee requested that Treasury Undersecretary Joseph W. Barr, Associate Special Counsel to the President DeVier Pierson, and Secretary of Defense Clark Clifford testify in the hearings on the nomination of Abe Fortas for chief justice of the Supreme Court. Barr refused to testify and conveyed the following explanation:

> In the development of this legislation, I participated in meetings with representatives of the White House and discussed the matter directly with the President. Based on long-standing precedents, it would be improper for me under these circumstances to give testimony before a Congressional committee concerning such meetings and discussions. Therefore, I must, with great respect, decline your invitation to appear and testify.[101]

Clifford requested to be excused from testifying due to other pressing responsibilities.[102] Pierson did not testify for the following reasons:

> As Associate Special Counsel to the President since March of 1967, I have been one of the "immediate staff assistants" provided to the President by law. (3 U.S.C. 105, 106.) It has been firmly established, as a matter of principle and precedents, that members of the President's immediate staff shall not appear before a Congressional committee to testify with respect to the performance of their duties on behalf of the President. This limitation, which has been recognized by Congress as well as the Executive, is fundamental to our system of government. I must, therefore, respectfully decline the invitation to testify in these hearings.[103]

Although the Kennedy and Johnson administrations did not exercise executive privilege as extensively as the Eisenhower administration, they clearly accepted the validity of this presidential power. The modern exercise of executive privilege, however, reached its most expansive stage during the Nixon administration. The Nixon years also represent a major stage in the development of the executive privilege controversy. Nixon attempted to transform executive privilege from a widely accepted constitutional prerogative into an absolute, unfettered presidential power. Nixon's excesses served eventually to partially discredit the doctrine of executive privilege. Nixon's successors accordingly have been cautious about making claims to a presidential power of executive privilege.

Because Nixon's presidency represents such a crucial turning point in the executive privilege controversy, the following chapter will deal with the Nixon years in some detail. For now, it is important to recognize that presidents historically have exercised what is now known as executive privilege. The very widescale use of this power by presidents lends validity to the claim that executive privilege clearly is a constitutional doctrine. But beyond an examination of the uses of executive privilege, it is necessary to present the various justifications for this presidential power.

IN DEFENSE OF EXECUTIVE PRIVILEGE

Although numerous presidents have exercised executive privilege, not all have done so judiciously. As with all other grants of authority, the power to do good is also the power to do bad. The only way to avoid the latter—

and consequently eliminate the ability to do the former—is to strip away authority altogether. Chief Justice William Rehnquist has defended the need for executive privilege:

> While reasonable men may dispute the propriety of particular invocations of executive privilege by various presidents during the nation's history, I think most would agree that the doctrine itself is an absolutely essential condition for the faithful discharge by the executive of his constitutional duties. It is, therefore, as surely implied in the Constitution as is the power of Congress to investigate and compel testimony.[104]

The historical evidence for executive privilege is convincing and the reasons for its exercise compelling. Critics of executive privilege not only take a too narrow view of the Constitution; they have an unrealistic understanding of how America's governing system should work. The case for executive privilege is based on national security needs, the need for candid advice, the limits on congressional inquiry, historical necessities, and secrecy in other branches.

National Security Needs

Congress and the public's "right to know" must be balanced with the requirements of national security. Although the Constitution Framers recognized well enough the importance of secrecy, unity, and dispatch to governing, the need to enhance those values in the modern era, particularly with regard to foreign policy-making, is even more compelling than it was two centuries ago. Many, if not most, of the crises faced by modern governments cannot be dealt with through open, lengthy, national deliberations. The heightened pace of contemporary international events places a premium on rapid and decisive decision-making. The presidency possesses the institutional capacities uniquely suited to responding to crisis situations. The leading Framers recognized that, being one, rather than many, the president is much more capable than Congress of acting with unity, secrecy, dispatch, and resolve. As Paul Peterson has written, "It is the executive power that most lends itself to energy. . . . To speak of energy in the legislative or judicial branches would be something akin to an oxymoron."[105] The courts have recognized the executive's preeminence in national security and foreign policy-making on a number of occasions.[106] A. Stephen Boyan, Jr., writes that, in the area of national security concerns, a review of cases shows that

> while the courts rhetorically support the separation of powers, in varying degrees they accept presidential characterization of the disputed matter without challenge and they permit the president to act without clear legislative authorization. . . . Moreover, while national security cases typically involve civil liberties issues, the courts have refused to apply the constitutional doctrines which they would apply if the same issue arose in a non-national security context.[107]

Foreign policy typically has been conducted on less democratic principles than domestic policy-making. The classic constitutional statement of that position is Justice George Sutherland's controversial opinion written for the Court majority in *U.S. v. Curtiss-Wright Corporation* (1936).[108] Sutherland noted that it is important to "consider the differences between the powers of the federal government in respect of foreign or external affairs and those in respect of domestic or internal affairs. That there are differences between them, and that these differences are fundamental, may not be doubted."[109] This Court opinion lends credibility to the argument that the chief executive has a "discretion" in foreign affairs to act beyond what the realm of the law allows.[110] Sutherland went so far as to declare the "very delicate, plenary and exclusive power of the president as the sole organ of the federal government in the field of international relations a power which does not require as a basis for its exercise an act of Congress, but . . . must be exercised in subordination to the applicable provisions of the Constitution."[111]

In any discussion of governmental secrecy, the different institutional orientations of the executive and legislative branches must be acknowledged. Congress usually deliberates in public; official actions behind closed doors are the exception. The executive branch deliberates outside public view; open deliberations are the very rare exception.

In the realm of national security, an important matter of concern is the potential effect of public revelations of policy discussions. Such openness, for example, could lead to demands for the executive branch to act before it is prepared to do so. Consequently, the ability to deliberate carefully over time and to weigh options before making decisions could be compromised. In national security policy-making, it often is important to be somewhat removed from time and partisan pressures that may affect policy decisions.

The courts have generally provided broad discretionary authority to the president in national security and foreign affairs. In *Zemel v. Rusk* (1965) the Supreme Court decided that "Congress—in giving the president authority over matters of foreign affairs—must of necessity paint with a brush broader than that it customarily wields in domestic affairs."[112] In a more recent case, *Department of Navy v. Egan* (1988), the Court offered a broad defense of presidential discretion in foreign affairs, explaining that the president's "authority to classify and control access to information bearing on national security and to determine whether an individual is sufficiently trustworthy to occupy a position in the Executive Branch . . . flows primarily from [the president's commander-in-chief power] and exists quite apart from any explicit congressional grant."[113] The courts have agreed that it is neither constitutionally proper nor prudent for Congress to tie the hands of the president in foreign affairs during an emergency situation.[114] The Supreme Court recently struck down important legislative control devices, further expanding the scope of the president's powers.[115] Finally, the Court has determined that secrecy is a necessary condition for the president to carry out many constitutional duties, especially in foreign affairs. In *Chicago and Southern Airlines v. Waterman Steamship Corporation* (1948), the Court held the following:

> The president, both as Commander-in-Chief and as the nation's organ for foreign affairs, has available intelligence services whose reports are not and ought not to be published to the world. It would be intolerable that courts, without the relevant information, should review and perhaps nullify actions of the Executive taken on information properly held secret.[116]

The strongest judicial defense of executive branch secrecy in national security affairs is *U.S. v. Reynolds* (1952). The Supreme Court held that "it may be possible to satisfy the Court, from all the circumstances of the case, that there is a reasonable danger that compulsion of the evidence will expose military secrets which, in the interest of national security, should not be divulged."[117] The *Reynolds* case also held that department heads could exercise a discretion to withhold information.[118]

Executive privilege can be defended on the grounds that Congress, as an institution, is ill-suited to handling sensitive national security information and also is not capable of decisive foreign policy-making. Under U.S. law, the power to classify information is given to the executive, not the legislative, branch, for good reason. The congressional decision-making process is purposefully slow and indecisive. Congress is sometimes out of session when foreign policy problems arise. Much of Congress's problem in national security decision-making stems from the inability to maintain secrets. In a large, diverse group of individuals it is highly unlikely that sensitive information, once disclosed, will not be disseminated more broadly. Once sensitive information is turned over to members of Congress there is no guarantee that some member will not divulge materials for policy or partisan reasons. The large majority of members are responsible public officials. Yet there may be just one who, at the wrong time, seeks to gain from his or her access to secret information. Joseph W. Bishop makes the following point: "There is no guarantee that information coming into the hands of Congress or the whole membership of one of its major committees will long remain secret. . . . There is no assurance . . . that so large a body of men will not include a percentage, on statistical grounds, of subversives, alcoholics, psychopaths and other security risks."[119]

Although Bishop's characterizations are less than tactful, the general point that there are, at least, a few untrustworthy individuals in any large group of persons is well taken. ABC-TV's Brit Hume reports that a member of the Senate Intelligence Committee, Sen. Joseph Biden (D-Del.), "twice threatened to go public with covert plans by the Reagan administration that were harebrained."[120] Former speaker of the House, Jim Wright (D-Tex.), exclaimed that "the fact that a matter is classified secret, doesn't mean it's sacrosanct and immune from criticism. . . . It is not only my right but my responsibility to express publicly my opposition to policies I think are wrong."[121] Former Rep. Leo Ryan (D-Calif.) told Richard Cheney in 1975 that an appropriate way for a member of Congress to block an "ill conceived operation" was to leak a state secret.[122] In 1982 Rep. Buddy Roemer (D-La.) declared of secret information during a congressional hearing that "I will tell you as one member of this subcommittee, we ought to do and encourage you to do everything possible not just to amass the information, but to turn it over to the public."[123] In 1974 Rep. Michael Harrington (D-Mass.) released secret testimony of CIA Director William Colby given before the House Armed Services Committee concerning the CIA's "destabilization" policy in Chile. Harrington was not a member of the committee but he was able to secure the transcript of the Colby testimony under a congressional rule that allows any member of the House or Senate access to any records of a committee of the legislative chamber in which he or she serves. The House Ethics Committee dropped the censure charges against Harrington.[124]

Part of the problem of maintaining secrets in the legislature is that Congress lacks a central figure with ultimate control over the institution. Members of the institution are individual entrepreneurs in a place where generally no one exerts discipline on the membership. Numerous committees now claim the right of access to sensitive information, resulting in continual requests and struggles for executive branch information.[125] Furthermore, the Constitution's speech and debate clause protects Congress from encroachment on legislative business by the executive or judicial branch. George C. Calhoun, former special counsel to the U.S. attorney general, explains that "if members of Congress decide to make secret information public during a congressional debate, a court will not order them to stop and the speech and debate clause forecloses prosecution by the executive branch."[126]

There is, therefore, a compelling case that national security often requires secrecy and that the right to exercise executive privilege is a necessary precondition for the chief executive to achieve national security aims. Additionally, the chief executive needs sound staff advice, and the quality of counsel depends ultimately on the degree of candor.

The Need for Candid Advice

Michael A. Ledeen, former consultant to the National Security Council, distinguishes between two kinds of openness: "One refers to candor, the other to the number of participants. We need candor, but we do not need large meetings or a large number of participants, or a full public debate *at every stage* of the policy process, or even of every aspect of the policy.[127]

The president's constitutional duties necessitate his being able to consult with advisers, without fear of public disclosure of their advice. If officers of the executive branch believed that their confidential advice could eventually be disclosed, the quality of that advice would suffer serious damage. Indeed, it would be difficult for advisers to be completely honest and frank in their discussions if their every word might someday be disclosed to partisan opponents or the public. Averell Harriman testified before Congress that "the president is entitled to receive the frank views of his advisers and therefore must be able to protect the personal or confidential nature of their communications with him."[128] William P. Bundy also testified that "if officers of an administration should come to feel that their confidential advice would be disclosed, short of a period of many years, I do believe that the consequences in terms of honesty, candor, courage, and frankness within the executive branch could be very serious indeed."[129] And Leonard G. Ratner writes the following:

> The presidential claim of executive privilege clearly is grounded in the Constitution. The president's constitutional functions necessitate consultation with advisers, and the possibility of disclosure may well inhibit the candor of their advice. In addition, disclosure of diplomatic, military, or national security secrets may prejudice national interests.[130]

The White House Office, created in 1939, established a presidential enclave of advisers and assistants in whom the chief executive had personal confidence. Then, as now, many considered it commonsensical that the president should be able to have candid interchanges with his closest advisers. The doctrine of executive privilege recognizes this commonsense notion. Unfortunately, because President Nixon invoked executive privilege to protect incriminating candid interchanges, he gave the constitutional doctrine, for many people, a bad name. Theodore H. White makes an important distinction:

> Executive privilege is a matter of vital importance to the conduct of the American Presidency. Unless the President can talk frankly, and listen to frank advice, he cannot think clearly enough to act effectively. Whoever invades this privacy weakens the Presidency. It was Richard Nixon's misfortune and guilt to invoke executive privilege, not to protect the Presidency, but to protect himself.[131]

Indeed, in the *U.S. v. Nixon* case, the Supreme Court not only recognized the constitutionality of executive privilege, but the necessity of executive branch secrecy to the operation of the presidency. Consider the following passage from the Court's unanimous opinion:

> The valid need for protection of communications between high government officials and those who advise and assist them in the performance of their manifold duties . . . is too plain to require further discussion. Human experience teaches that those who expect public dissemination of their remarks may well temper candor with a concern for appearances and for their own interests to the detriment of the decision-making process. . . . The confidentiality of presidential communications . . . has constitutional underpinnings. . . . The privilege is fundamental to the operation of government and inextricably rooted in the separation of powers under the Constitution.[132]

In 1979 the Court iterated its support of executive privilege based on the need for candid interchange among advisers: "Documents shielded by executive privilege remain privileged even after the decision to which they pertain may have been effected, since disclosure at any time could inhibit the free flow of advice, including analysis, reports and expression of opinions."[133]

The Court, therefore, has recognized that the need for candid interchange is an important basis for the constitutional doctrine of executive privilege. Although it is well recognized that Congress needs access to executive branch information to carry out its oversight and investigative duties, it does not follow that Congress must have full access to the details of every executive branch communication.

Limits on Congressional Inquiry

Congress's power of inquiry, though broad, is not unlimited.[134] Raoul Berger's claim that the Constitution grants to Congress power as the "Grand Inquest" of the nation is unfounded. There is nothing in Article I, or in any part of the Constitution, which substantiates the claim that Congress possesses such a power. The debates at the Constitutional Convention and at the subsequent ratifying conventions provide little evidence that the Framers intended to confer such authority on Congress. Although historic precedent and case law establish the legitimacy of the congressional power of inquiry,[135] the argument that this power is unlimited is not supported by the evidence.

Although opponents of executive privilege argue that Congress has an absolute right of inquiry into the workings of the executive branch, a distinction must be drawn between sources of information generally and those the legislative branch needs to perform its functions.[136] There is generally a strong presumption of validity to a congressional request for information clearly relevant to its investigatory function. There is no such presumption in the case of a congressional "fishing expedition"—a broad, sweeping quest for any and all executive branch information that might be of interest to Congress for one reason or another.

Congress itself has recognized that there are limitations on its power of inquiry. In 1879 the House Judiciary Committee issued a report stating that neither the legislative nor executive branch has compulsory power over the records of the other.[137] Congress has given statutory authority to executive branch withholding of information. In particular, Congress recognized the necessity of protecting intelligence sources when it enacted the "sources and methods proviso" of the 1947 National Security Act and when it enacted the 1949 implementing provision of the CIA Act. The judicial branch has ruled that the proviso is a proper basis for the secrecy agreement of CIA employees.[138] The proviso and the implementing provision are recognized as nondisclosure statutes in cases of Freedom of Information Act requests.[139] In passing the 1966 Freedom of Information Act, Congress once again provided statutory authorization for executive branch withholding of information. The FOIA stipulates nine conditions under which access to government documents may be denied.

The argument for executive branch secrecy in cases of congressional inquiry is stronger in foreign than in domestic affairs. Congress is not equipped to investigate and play a central role in every executive branch foreign policy action. The case against an absolute congressional inquiry power is made all the more compelling by the problem of leaks of information. But the problem of leaks is not merely that sensitive information is made public. There is also the complicated nature of maintaining the trust of allies abroad. Michael Ledeen notes that foreign leaders purposely withhold vital information from the United States when they believe that the U.S. government is unable to keep secrets. He maintains that exposure of secrets by Congress has deprived the United States "of the honest thoughts of foreign leaders, and their knowledge as well." Ledeen concludes that "secrecy actually encourages the free flow of information and candid expression, while exposure limits the flow of knowledge and forces top officials to speak guardedly, if at all."[140] Benjamin R. Civiletti presents a similar perspective:

> Unless we possess current, accurate knowledge about the actions a foreign power is likely to take, our information base is limited; and the more limited our information base, the more speculative are our analyses, and the greater the danger to our security. Secrecy, however, is an essential element of effective intelligence gathering. . . . If we reveal the information obtained, we will not only lose our advantage and risk changes in the required plans, but we will also jeopardize or perhaps destroy our sources and methods of gathering information.[141]

Despite this evidence, some scholars and members of Congress believe that Congress has an absolute, unlimited power, as the "Grand Inquest" of the nation, to compel disclosure of all executive branch information. Rep. John Dingell (D-Mich.) asserts that members of Congress "have the power under the law to receive each and every item in the hands of the government."[142] This expansive view of congressional inquiry is equally as wrong as the belief that the president has the unlimited power to withhold all information from Congress, regardless of his reasons for nondisclosure. This quest for constitutional absolutes obscures the fact that there are inherent constitutional limits on the powers of the respective governmental branches. The common standard for legislative inquiry has been whether the requested information was vital to Congress's lawmaking and oversight function. It is ironic that leading critics of executive privilege maintain that such a power lacks validity because it is not specifically granted by the Constitution, and then argue that Congress possesses an absolute, unlimited inquiry power despite a similar lack of such a constitutional grant.

Historic Necessities

Numerous historic incidents—far too many to cover here—have confirmed that there are many good reasons for withholding information. For example, the Second World War, the crises over Berlin and Cuba, the long Cold War, and the war against Iraq have all confronted the United States with situations requiring rapid responses, as well as secret negotiations, thereby precluding full disclosure to Congress of military and diplomatic plans. William Rehnquist offers a commonsensical view:

> The need for extraordinary secrecy in the field of weapons systems and tactical military plans for the conducting of hostilities would appear to be self-evident. At least those of my generation and older are familiar with the extraordinary precaution taken against revelation of either the date or the place of landing on the Normandy beaches during the Second World War in 1944. The executive branch is charged with the responsibility for such decisions, and has quite wisely insisted that where lives of American soldiers or the security of the nation is at stake, the very minimum dissemination of future plans is absolutely essential. Such secrecy with respect to highly sensitive decisions of this sort excludes not merely Congress, but all but an infinitesimal number of the employees and officials of the executive branch as well.[143]

Prior to U.S. involvement in the Second World War, due to an increasingly unstable international environment, President Franklin D. Roosevelt frequently overrode the legislative decision-making process. Through the use of the executive agreement (which does not require congressional consent),[144] the president effectively bypassed the isolationist majority in Congress on a number of occasions. Roosevelt concluded an alliance with Great Britain in 1940, ignoring the congressional neutrality laws. As Richard Pious writes, the president "was wise to bypass Congress."[145] In the end, presidential discretion was vindicated and congressional performance discredited. Three months prior to the bombing of Pearl Harbor, Congress nearly repealed the Selective Service Act. Congress blocked funds for the construction of vital naval facilities. Congress turned down administration requests for the procurement of advanced arms. Not until the end of 1941 did Congress repeal neutrality legislation. Pious concludes that "Congress demonstrated no foresight, courage, or common sense."[146]

Congressional decision-making during the emergence of the nation's gravest crisis proved to be wholly inadequate. Therefore, a major defense of executive privilege rests on the proposition that Congress often does not discharge its duties in the national security realm with wisdom, and that legislative interference in international negotiations may have deleterious effects on the nation's security in crisis situations. In his concurring opinion in *New York Times v. United States* (1971), Justice Potter Stewart expresses this view:

> Yet it is elementary that the successful conduct of international diplomacy and the maintenance of an effective national defense require both confidentiality and secrecy. Other nations can hardly deal with this Nation in an atmosphere of mutual trust unless they can be assured that their confidences will be kept. And within our own executive departments, the development of considered and intelligent international policies would be impossible if those charged with their formulation could not communicate with each other freely, frankly, and in confidence. In the area of basic national defense the frequent need for absolute secrecy is, of course, self evident.[147]

The Other Branches' Exercise of Confidentiality

Finally, executive privilege can be defended on the basis of accepted practices of secrecy in the other branches of government. Members of Congress receive candid, confidential advice from committee staff and legislative assistants.[148] Congressional committees meet on occasion in closed sessions to "mark up" legislation. Congress is not obligated to disclose information to another branch. A court subpoena will not be honored except with a vote of the legislative chamber concerned. Congress has also exempted itself from disclosing information under the Freedom of Information Act. Members of Congress enjoy a constitutional form of privilege that absolves them from having to account for their official behavior, particularly regarding speech, anywhere but in Congress. As with the executive, this privilege does not extend into the realm of criminal conduct.

Secrecy also is found in the judicial branch. It is difficult to imagine more secretive deliberations than those that take place in Supreme Court conferences. David M. O'Brien refers to secrecy as one of the "basic institutional norms" of the Supreme Court. "Isolation from the Capitol and the close proximity of the justices' chambers within the Court promote secrecy, to a degree that is remarkable. . . . The norm of secrecy conditions the employment of the justices' staff and has become more important as the number of employees increases."[149] Members of the judiciary claim immunity from having to respond to congressional subpoenas. The norm of judicial privilege also protects judges from having to testify about their professional conduct.

It is inconceivable that such a practice as secrecy, common to the legislative and judicial branches, should not be exercised by the executive.[150] The executive branch is regularly engaged in a number of activities that are secret in nature. George C. Calhoun explains that the executive branch

> presents . . . matters to grand juries; assembles confidential investigative files in criminal matters; compiles files containing personal information involving such things as census, tax, and veterans information; and health, education and welfare benefits to name a few. All of these activities must, of necessity, generate a considerable amount of confidential information. And personnel in the executive branch . . . necessarily prepare many more confidential memoranda. Finally, they produce a considerable amount of classified information as a result of the activities of the intelligence community.[151]

In the cases of legislative, judicial, and executive branch secrecy, a common purpose is being served: to arrive at more prudent policy decisions than those that would be arrived at through an open, deliberative process. And in each case, the end result is what will be subjected to public scrutiny. Indeed, accountability is built into secretive decision-making processes. The elected public officials must justify the end result at some point.

Executive privilege clearly has substantial constitutional underpinnings, historic precedents, and compelling arguments in its favor. Despite the evidence, executive privilege remains a constitutional doctrine mired in controversy. Much of the controversy can be attributed to the fact that, as with other constitutional powers, not every president has exercised executive privilege prudently or properly. The doctrine of executive privilege became most controversial during the Watergate era. Regarding President Nixon's actions, Raoul Berger explains that "'confidentiality' was the vehicle for the cover-up of criminal acts and conspiracies by his aides, an instrument he repeatedly employed to the obstruction of justice."[152]

Berger's description of governmental secrecy in the Nixon White House is indisputable. Nonetheless, it is important not to generalize from the abuses of one administration that all "secrecy in the operations of government is an abomination."[153] It is no more valid to argue against the legitimate exercise of executive privilege because of the abuses of that power by President Nixon than it is to dismiss the legitimate exercise of legislative inquiry because of the abuses of that power by Sen. Joseph McCarthy. Nonetheless, the Nixon years are important in the debate over government secrecy because those years represent a turning point in the perceptions and uses of executive privilege.

CHAPTER 3

Undermining a Constitutional Doctrine

★ ——————————————————————————————————————— ★

Richard Nixon and the Abuse of Executive Privilege

Although executive privilege is a legitimate power with constitutional "underpinnings," it is not an unlimited, unfettered presidential power. Traditionally, presidents who have exercised executive privilege have done so without rejecting in principle the legitimacy either of Congress to conduct inquiries or of the judiciary to question presidential authority. For the most part, presidents have recognized the necessity of a balancing test to weigh the importance of legitimate competing institutional claims. Presidents have weighed in favor of executive privilege to protect the nation's security, the public interest, and the candidness of internal White House deliberations.

President Richard M. Nixon went beyond the traditional defenses of executive privilege in the cases of national security needs, protecting the public interest, and encouraging candid staff advice. Although Nixon claimed, like his predecessors, to have used executive privilege for the public good, his actions did not demonstrate public-interest motivations. He invoked executive privilege for purposes of political expediency and used the doctrine as a vehicle to withhold embarrassing—not vital—information.

The Nixon era brought about a fundamental change in the way that executive privilege is perceived and exercised. Prior to Nixon, many presidents confidently asserted this authority and generally the coordinate branches of government accepted the legitimacy of executive privilege. In the post-Watergate era, presidents have been most reluctant to assert executive privilege and many members of Congress have characterized all exercises of executive branch secrecy as Nixonian attempts to conceal and deceive.

Because Nixon's exercise of executive privilege has had such a profound, lasting impact on the status of that constitutional doctrine, it is necessary to identify and analyze the thirty-seventh president's contribution to the debate over executive privilege.

NIXON'S POLICY ON EXECUTIVE PRIVILEGE

Although President Nixon now is remembered for his unremitting defense of an absolute executive privilege power during Watergate, he did not always hold this view. Ironically, as a member of the House of Representatives in 1948, Nixon vigorously objected to President Harry S Truman's refusal to release the text of an FBI letter concerning a prominent scientist accused of disloyalty by the House Un-American Activities Committee. A member himself of that committee, Nixon rose on 22 April 1948 to protest the president's assertion of a right to withhold information from Congress:

> The point has been made that the President of the United States has issued an order that none of this information can be released to the Congress and that therefore the Congress has no right to question the judgment of the President in making that decision.
>
> I say that the proposition cannot stand from a constitutional standpoint or on the basis of the merits for this very good reason: that would mean that the President could have arbitrarily issued an Executive order in the Meyers case, the Teapot Dome case, or any other case denying the Congress of the United States information that it needed to conduct an investigation of the executive department and the Congress would have no right to question his decision.
>
> Any such order of the President can be questioned by the Congress as to whether or not that order is justified on the merits.[1]

During the 1968 presidential campaign, Nixon made a statement pledging to conduct an "open" administration in which there would be a free flow of information from the executive branch to Congress, the media, and the public. Nixon iterated that pledge early in his first term. Barely one week after Nixon had taken the oath of office, the chairman of the House Subcommittee on Government Information, Rep. John E. Moss (D-Calif.), wrote a letter to the president urging that the new administration reaffirm the Kennedy and Johnson administrations' official policy of allowing only the president—not White House staffers or subordinate officers of the executive branch—to assert executive privilege. Moss previously had solicited, and received, assurances from Nixon's two most recent predecessors that executive privilege would only be asserted by the president.[2] In a 7 April 1969 letter to Moss, Nixon responded affirmatively and attached a copy of a memorandum outlining administration policy on executive privilege that the president had issued to heads of executive agencies. First, Nixon explained to Moss the administration's position on executive privilege:

> I believe, and I have stated earlier, that the scope of executive privilege must be very narrowly construed. Under this Administration, executive privilege will not be asserted without specific Presidential approval.
>
> I want to take this opportunity to assure you and your committee that this Administration is dedicated to insuring a free flow of information to the Congress and the news media—and, thus, to the citizens. You are, I am sure, familiar with the statement I made on this subject during the campaign. Now that I have the responsibility to implement this pledge, I wish to reaffirm my intent to do so. I want open government to be a reality in every way possible.[3]

Second, Nixon enclosed with his letter to Moss the memorandum of 24 March 1969, "Establishing a Procedure to Govern Compliance with Congressional Demands for Information." The Nixon memorandum stated the following:

> The policy of this Administration is to comply to the fullest extent possible with Congressional requests for information. While the Executive branch has the responsibility of withholding certain information the disclosure of which would be incompatible with the public interest, this Administration will invoke this authority only in the most compelling circumstances and after a rigorous inquiry into the actual need for its exercise. For those reasons Executive privilege will not be used without specific Presidential approval.[4]

The memorandum outlined the procedure to be used whenever a question of executive privilege was raised. To summarize, under the official procedure, if a department head believed that a congressional request for information might concern privileged information, he would consult with the attorney general. In consultation, the department head and attorney general then would decide whether to release the information to Congress, or to submit the matter to the president through the counsel to the president. At that stage, the president either would instruct the department head to claim executive privilege with presidential approval, or request that Congress give some time to the president to make a decision.[5]

Nixon's official policy on the use of executive privilege did not diverge fundamentally from those of his predecessors. Executive privilege, under Nixon's policy, could only be invoked for the most compelling reasons and only the president could decide whether it was appropriate to assert executive privilege.

Nonetheless, Nixon's exercise of executive privilege became controversial when many critics charged that the administration had used the constitutional doctrine to shield White House officials from testifying before Congress and to conceal wrongdoing. At an impromptu press conference near the beginning of his second term, the president promised that he later would further clarify his administration's policy on executive privilege. Several weeks later, on 12 March 1973, the president issued a statement to the press doing just that: "Executive privilege will not be used as a shield to prevent embarrassing information from being made available but will be exercised only in those particular instances in which disclosure would harm the public interest."[6] Nixon's statement addressed specifically the question of congressional demands for testimony from executive branch officials. The 1969 Nixon memorandum did not address that question. Consequently, Nixon issued further guidelines on the use of executive privilege in the cases of congressional requests for testimony. To summarize the additional guidelines, an agency official confronted with a congressional request for information or testimony must follow the 1969 guidelines. The same procedure applies to Cabinet officers and members of the president's personal staff. Finally, members and former members of the president's personal staff "normally shall follow the well-established precedent and decline a request for formal appearance before a committee of the Congress."[7]

On 10 April 1973 Nixon's attorney general, Richard Kleindienst, effectively expanded the doctrine of executive privilege by stating that the president had the authority to prevent any federal employee from testifying before Congress, for whatever reason.[8]

Nixon's official policy on executive privilege granted that prerogative to the entire executive branch of the federal government. Nonetheless, the president emphasized in his policy that "reasonable" congressional requests for documents or testimony would be accommodated. He left the ultimate determination of reasonableness to the attorney general and the president. Under this policy, the president's determination is final and cannot be challenged by another branch of government.

On the surface, Nixon's guidelines on executive privilege appear unusually broad-based in that they apply to all executive branch officials. Yet the Nixon guidelines are carefully crafted to appear consistent with the approaches of his predecessors, mandating presidential approval of any use of executive privilege and making clear that, in the normal course of events, Congress's requests for information and testimony will be honored.

Nixon's formal guidelines on the use of executive privilege do not tell the whole story of his administration's exercise of that power. To understand properly the nature of the executive privilege controversy during the Nixon years, it is necessary to examine the administration's actual use of that power and other statements and actions justifying its approach toward withholding of information.

NIXON'S EXERCISE OF EXECUTIVE PRIVILEGE

In his 12 March 1973 statement, President Nixon maintained that he had asserted executive privilege on only three occasions, whereas "hundreds of administration officials spent thousands of hours freely testifying before committees of the Congress." Nixon added that "these facts speak not of a closed administration but one that is pledged to openness and is proud to stand on its record."[9]

The former president's claims were misleading. Prior to Watergate, Nixon exercised the executive privilege, directly and indirectly, on more than three occasions. Furthermore, on numerous occasions, Nixon administration agency heads refused requests either to provide information or to testify before Congress.

National Security Adviser Henry Kissinger refused numerous requests to appear before congressional committees. Members of Congress believed that the Nixon White House had gone to extraordinary lengths in permitting agency heads to decide for themselves not to provide information or to testify before Congress. In fact, Congress held a number of hearings on the matter of whether "agency" or "departmental privilege" was a legitimate exercise of executive branch power. The invocation of executive privilege by numerous subordinate officials in the Nixon administration prompted legislation to curtail such claims of privilege. For example, H.R. 6228, introduced by Rep. John N. Erlenburn (R-Ill.), proposed that all executive branch information be made available to Congress and the comptroller general of the United States "except in cases where the president himself invokes the claim of executive privilege."[10] The purpose of this proposal was to make the president alone accountable for all the claims of executive privilege. However, the legislation was successfully opposed by advocates of a broad definition of the privilege as well as strict opponents of the privilege, who claimed that the proposal effectively would legitimize executive privilege. What is telling is the fact that members of Congress thought it necessary to place a limitation on executive privilege, restricting the doctrine exclusively to presidential use, when the official policy of the Nixon administration was to impose a similar limitation.

Nixon cleverly sought to restrict information and testimony from agency heads by giving many of them dual responsibilities: in addition to their Cabinet positions some of the agency heads were members of the president's personal staff. Recall that Nixon's 12 March 1973 statement emphasized that members of the president's personal staff could not be compelled to divulge information or to testify before Congress because a president must be entitled to confidential interchanges among his most trusted personal advisers. On several occasions, agency heads refused congressional requests for information or testimony based on their responsibilities as White House advisers to the president, even though the issues raised by Congress clearly involved matters of agency responsibility.[11]

The president did not always make clear whether he, or someone within his White House, actually made the decision in particular cases whether to allow an assertion of executive privilege. For example, in 1973 a former air force secretary refused to testify at a Civil Service Commission investigation into his firing of a civilian cost analyst for revealing confidential information about cost overruns on the C-5A aircraft. The air force secretary asserted executive privilege as the basis for not testifying. When asked whether executive privilege had been properly used in this case, President Nixon responded as follows: "In this case, as I understand it—and I did not approve this directly, but it was approved at my direction by those who have the responsibility within the White House—in this case it was a proper area in which the executive privilege should have been used."[12]

Nixon either asserted or approved the use of executive privilege on other occasions as well. In June 1970 the Intergovernmental Relations Subcommittee of the House Committee on Government Operations requested information on certain scientists who had been nominated for, and then excluded from serving on, advisory board positions in the Department of Health, Education, and Welfare (HEW). Specifically, members of Congress sought access to Federal Bureau of Investigation (FBI) files used by HEW that allegedly showed that some of the individuals prevented from serving on the advisory panels had been active members of the Communist Party, U.S.A. The secretary of HEW, Robert Finch, responded that the department could only make the files available with authorization from the investigative agency for the files, in this case the Department of Justice. The president approved an assertion of executive privilege by his attorney general, John Mitchell, to withhold the requested documents on the basis that it would not be in the public interest to release confidential FBI reports.[13]

In August 1971 Sen. J. William Fulbright (D-Ark.), the chairman of the Senate Foreign Relations Committee, requested from Secretary of State William P. Rogers specific information on the administration's military assistance programs. On 31 August 1971 the president asserted executive privilege, consequently denying Fulbright's request for that information. Neither Fulbright nor members of the committee raised this difference of opinion on access to information to the level of a constitutional dispute. Rather, they emphasized that Congress needed the information to be more financially responsible by scrutinizing government spending carefully.[14]

In 1972, while considering the nomination of Richard Kleindienst to the position of attorney general, the Senate Committee on the Judiciary began to look into accusations that the Justice Department had settled three antitrust lawsuits against the International Telephone and Telegraph Company in return for an agreement that ITT would cover $400,000 in expenses for the 1972 Republican National Convention. The committee requested the testimony of White House adviser Peter Flanagan, who had been accused of knowing about ITT's efforts to gain the settlement. The Nixon White House claimed executive privilege and refused to allow Flanagan to testify. The justification for this use of executive privilege stemmed from the president's policy of not allowing members of his immediate staff to testify before Congress regarding their official duties. The White House and the committee did eventually compromise on the issue, allowing Flanagan to provide limited testimony on an agreed upon topic pertaining to the Kleindienst nomination, but not the ITT controversy.[15]

Another controversy raised the issue of executive privilege, although the president did not invoke that power at the time. The controversy surrounded availability of information on recommendations made to the president on the proposed Amchitka underground nuclear tests. Some members of the House of Representatives had already unsuccessfully tried to block the tests through budgetary means. When House members learned that the president had received conflicting advice on whether to carry out the tests, some of them sought access to the agency reports to the president. The president refused, claiming national defense and foreign policy reasons for withholding the information. Thirty-three House members joined as private individuals to take legal action against the president's decision, using the Freedom of Information Act to compel disclosure. The case, *Environmental Protection Agency v. Mink* (1973), eventually reached the Supreme Court.[16]

Germane to the executive privilege controversy is the fact that the Nixon administration claimed that it could withhold any information that it deemed in the national interest not to divulge, and that such a claim cannot be examined by another branch of the government. The president even denied that the courts had any authority to review the disputed materials *in camera* because such review constituted actual disclosure of privileged information. Ultimately, the Supreme Court held in the

Mink case that, although the doctrine of executive privilege limits what documents Congress can demand, the courts can require *in camera* inspection of documents, and that such inspection is not tantamount to revealing vital secrets.[17]

The Watergate scandal stands as the most celebrated case in history of the executive privilege controversy. During the course of that scandal, the president used executive privilege as a shield to prevent the disclosure of embarrassing, legally damaging information as opposed to national security information. Nonetheless, in his attempts to cover up the scandal, the president cited national security concerns as a reason for withholding information vital to the Watergate inquiries.[18]

Throughout much of the Watergate investigations, the president tried to convey a reasonable posture on the question of executive privilege. He claimed to be willing to make unprecedented concessions to demands for information. He waived executive privilege for staff aides to testify before the Senate Watergate Committee on issues of possible criminal conduct. Nixon instructed White House staff only to assert the privilege as follows:

> In connection with the appearance of witnesses before grand juries, judicial proceedings, and congressional committees, I direct that executive privilege be waived in all matters except those involving national security, those involving direct communication to or from the president in any form, written or oral, and those involving communication given or received in any form, written or oral on behalf of the president.[19]

On 16 July 1973 former assistant to H. R. Haldeman, Alexander Butterfield, testified before the Senate Watergate Committee that the president had tape recorded conversations in the Oval Office and in the Executive Office Building. The Senate Watergate Committee subsequently requested the tapes, as did the Watergate special prosecutor, Archibald Cox. Nixon claimed executive privilege and consequently refused to turn over the tapes either to the committee or to Cox. After a number of efforts to secure the tapes, Cox went to a federal court to have a subpoena issued for recordings of specific conversations. Judge John Sirica issued the subpoena, which Nixon refused to comply with, again claiming executive privilege. Nixon appealed Sirica's ruling to the U.S. Court of Appeals in the District of Columbia. The court upheld Sirica's ruling. Nixon responded by having Cox fired (the notorious "Saturday night massacre")—an event that set off such a firestorm of protest that Nixon had to turn the disputed tapes over to Sirica.

In April 1974 the new Watergate special prosecutor, Leon Jaworski, requested sixty-four additional White House tapes. Nixon again claimed executive privilege to withhold the tapes. This time Sirica demanded on 20 May 1974 that the tapes be released to him for *in camera* inspection. Four days later, Nixon attorney James St. Clair appealed the Sirica order to the court of appeals and Leon Jaworski requested from the Supreme Court a *writ of certiorari* prior to the court of appeals' ruling.

In *U.S. v. Nixon*[20] the Supreme Court issued its historic, unanimous decision on the Nixon tapes controversy. During oral argument of the case, St. Clair presented the president's position in favor of an absolute executive privilege. St. Clair maintained that the president did not have to comply with the special prosecutor's subpoena. Jaworski responded that executive privilege could not be used to shield criminal conduct. The special prosecutor further posed a question that addressed the essence of this executive privilege controversy. "Shall the evidence from the White House be confined to what a single person, highly interested in the outcome, is willing to make available?"[21]

The Court rejected the claim of an absolute presidential power of executive privilege. The Court rejected the claim that the president had the ultimate authority over all executive branch information. Furthermore, the Court reaffirmed the right of the judicial branch to resolve disputes between the political branches of the government. In this particular controversy, the Court ruled that the president's claim of executive privilege had to be balanced against the Court's need for information in a criminal case. Regarding executive privilege, the Court stated that "to the extent that this interest in confidentiality relates to the effective discharge of the president's powers, it is constitutionally based."[22] Nonetheless, the Court ruled that the need for information in this criminal case overruled the president's claim to executive privilege.[23] The Court determined that to permit a claim of executive privilege that effectively resulted in the withholding of vital evidence "would cut deeply into the guarantee of due process of law and gravely impair the basic function of the courts."[24] With that decision, the president had no recourse but to turn over the incriminating tapes that ended his presidency.

Nixon continued to press his claim to executive privilege, even out of office. As ex-president, he sought control over his presidential materials, including the White House tapes. The Court acknowledged in *Nixon v. Administrator of General Services* (1977) that ex-presidents do have authority to claim executive privilege in particular circumstances. Nonetheless, the Court ruled that, in this particular case, the balancing test weighed in favor of the public's right of access to presidential materials.[25] Despite this decision, Nixon continued to press claims for control over his presidential materials.

NIXON'S DEFENSE OF EXECUTIVE PRIVILEGE

President Nixon offered the most far-reaching, comprehensive definition of the executive privilege imaginable under our constitutional system. He argued that (1) the president has an unlimited power of executive privilege; (2) under the separation of powers system, no other branch of government can question the president's constitutional authority in this area; (3) executive privilege belongs to all executive branch officials; (4) he had to strongly assert executive privilege during Watergate to protect the office of the presidency, but not himself; and (5) any breach of the president's absolute power of executive privilege would threaten the national security.

Unlimited Power of Executive Privilege

Nixon tried to make the case that there can be no limitations on the president's use of executive privilege except those established by the president himself. In *Senate Select Committee on Presidential Campaign Activities v. Nixon* (1973) the president's defenders adopted such an absolute executive privilege claim in their statement that "such a privilege, inherent in the constitutional grant of executive power, is a matter of presidential judgment alone."[26] In the brief in opposition to the special prosecutor's demand for White House tapes, Nixon's defenders maintained that "the privilege is not confined to specific kinds of subject matter . . . nor to particular kinds of communications. Reason dictates a much broader concept, that the privilege extends to all of the executive power vested in the president by Article II and that it reaches any information that the president determines cannot be disclosed consistent with the public interest and the proper performance of his constitutional duties."[27]

After leaving office, Nixon went so far as to argue that there are no limits on presidential power generally. Nixon most clearly presented that view in his televised interviews with journalist David Frost. When questioned on 19 May 1977 by Frost about the limits on presidential power Nixon replied that "when the president does it, that means it is not illegal."[28] Such a statement implies that there are no limits on presidential authority, including the power to withhold information. All that is required is presidential approval of an action. In a clear refutation of the more common constitutional view that no person is above the law, Nixon argued that presidential actions had higher standing than the law itself. For example, Nixon justified the burglary of Daniel Ellsberg's psychiatrist's office as a legitimate presidential action, not subject to limitation. While asserting that he did not know of the burglary in advance, Nixon responded that, if told, "I would have said, 'Go right ahead.'" Nixon added that "I didn't want to discredit the man as an individual. I couldn't care less about the punk. I wanted to discredit that kind of activity, which was despicable and damaging to the national interest."[29] Nixon added that such normally illegal activities become lawful when sanctioned by the president. The causes for sanctioning such activities are varied and may, Nixon asserted, include the "national interest" or "national security."

Separation of Powers

During his presidency, Nixon adopted the view that Congress and the courts lack the legitimacy to question or contest executive claims of privilege. In Nixon's conception of the separation of powers the president reigns supreme and may unilaterally determine the scope and limits of his own powers. Nixon claimed that whenever a dispute between the political branches over executive privilege occurs, the president's claim of privilege resolves the dispute. In a sense, this view of the president in the separation of powers system elevates the role of the chief executive to that of participant *and* referee in a political struggle. Even the judiciary cannot referee disputes over executive privilege. In a revealing quote President

Nixon stated during the Watergate controversy that "the manner in which the president exercises his assigned executive powers is not subject to questioning by another branch of the government."[30]

In the president's brief in opposition to the special prosecutor's demand for White House tapes, Nixon's attorneys offered the following view:

> In the exercise of his discretion to claim executive privilege te president is answerable to the Nation but not to the courts. The courts, a co-equal but not a superior branch of government, are not free to probe the mental processes and the private confidences of the president and his advisers. To do so would be a clear violation of the constitutional separation of powers. Under that doctrine the judicial branch lacks power to compel the president to produce information that he has determined it is not in the public interest to disclose.[31]

The president personally responded in the same vein to Judge Sirica. In expressing his reasons for refusing to comply with the subpoena of White House tapes, Nixon stated that "the president is not subject to compulsory process from the other branches of government." He provided the following reasons: "The independence of the three branches of our government is at the very heart of our constitutional system. It would be wholly inadmissible for the president to seek to compel some particular action by the courts. It is equally inadmissible for the courts to seek to compel some particular action from the president."[32] During oral argument in *U.S. v. Nixon*, President Nixon's attorney candidly rejected the right of the judiciary to contest presidential claims of privilege. The following exchange between the Court's justices and James St. Clair reveals the president's view that, although the Court could declare the law, the president still had the final word.

> *Question:* You are submitting this matter to the Court . . .
>
> *St. Clair:* To this Court under a special showing on behalf of the president . . .
>
> *Question:* And you are still leaving it up to this Court to decide it.
>
> *St. Clair:* Yes, in a sense.
>
> *Question:* In what sense?
>
> *St. Clair:* In the sense that this Court has the obligation to determine the law. The President also has an obligation to carry out his constitutional duties.

Question: Well, do you agree that this is what is before this Court, and
you are submitting it to this Court for decision?

St. Clair: This is being submitted to this Court for its guidance and
judgment with respect to the law. The President, on the other hand,
has his obligations under the Constitution.

Question: Are you submitting it to this Court for this Court's decision?

St. Clair: As to what the law is, yes.[33]

During testimony before Senate committees, Kleindienst argued that
Congress had no right even to seek information on criminal activities in
the executive branch if the president claimed executive privilege. Furthermore, he asserted that the attorney general alone determined what
information Congress could receive from the Department of Justice.[34]
Kleindienst also maintained that the doctrine of executive privilege could
be used to withhold information sought by Congress in an impeachment
hearing.[35]

In the Nixon view of executive privilege, the president's authority to
exercise such power is absolute, unfettered by any actions that the other
branches of government might take to compel disclosure or settle disputes
over withheld information. Nixon also extended this vast power to members of his staff and, effectively, the entire federal bureaucracy.

Staff and Departmental Privilege

Nixon not only argued that the president's actions to protect the national
interest cannot be unlawful; he also said that the activities of members of
the executive branch are exempted from normal legal limitations if conducted on the president's behalf: "If the President, for example, approves
something, approves an action because of the national security or . . . because of a threat to internal peace and order of significant magnitude,
then the President's decision in that instance is one that enables those
who carry it out to carry it out without violating a law."[36]

For President Nixon executive privilege was not a right possessed only
by the president and selected White House insiders. Rather, in Nixon's
view executive privilege could be invoked by the president on behalf of
all executive branch officials. Nixon claimed that the president's exercise
of power could not be questioned by the other branches of government.

The president's aides also could not be questioned. Nixon maintained that "if the president is not subject to such questioning, it is equally inappropriate that members of his staff not [sic] be so questioned, for their roles are in effect an extension of the president."[37]

Nixon applied this reasoning not only to his White House staff but also to the entire executive bureaucracy. Nixon's attorney general, Richard Kleindienst, asserted on behalf of the president that Congress lacked authority to call any employee of the federal government to appear before Congress if the president decided to bar such testimony.[38] Kleindienst further maintained that the president could invoke executive privilege to bar congressional testimony by White House staff in an impeachment proceeding: "If you are conducting an impeachment proceeding based upon high crimes and misdemeanors and you want to subpoena someone from the president's staff to give you information, I believe that, based upon the doctrine of separation of powers, the president would have the power to invoke executive privilege with respect to that information."[39]

Nixon initially tried to prevent the counsel to the president, John Dean, from testifying before the Senate Watergate Committee. In a 15 March 1973 news conference the president maintained that it was proper to prevent Dean from testifying because "he has, in effect, what I would call a double privilege." The so-called double privilege included the lawyer-client relationship as well as "the presidential privilege."[40] Dean maintained that he could testify because he would not be discussing matters of national security. Although on the surface the lawyer-client privilege appears to be a sound reason to prevent the counsel to the president from testifying before Congress, in this case Dean would testify regarding a criminal conspiracy between the attorney and the client. The lawyer-client privilege and the presidential privilege cannot be used to shield criminal conspiracies.

By extending executive privilege to White House staff, the president had defined the constitutional doctrine in a way compatible with historical precedent. What made Nixon's action extraordinary was his use of executive privilege to shield wrongdoing by himself and his staff. When Nixon effectively extended executive privilege to the entire federal bureaucracy, he acted without precedent. Because of this unprecedented broad use of executive privilege, debates arose in Congress over the exercise of "agency" and "departmental privilege." Congress and the courts also tried to subpoena information from the Nixon White House to investigate criminal conspiracy charges, and both met with resistance. Nixon claimed that he had to take these actions to protect the presidency given his "constitutional responsibility to defend the principle of separation of powers."[41]

Protecting the Presidency

In refusing to disclose information to Congress and the judiciary during Watergate, Nixon argued that in no sense was he acting merely to protect himself. Instead, he insisted, he was obligated to protect the presidency from improper encroachments on its constitutional prerogatives. During a question and answer session at a 17 November 1973 conference of the Associated Press Managing Editors Association in Orlando, Florida, the president responded to a query about his view of executive privilege. Nixon asserted that he had waived executive privilege for himself and his staff only "voluntarily" so as "to avoid a precedent that might destroy the principle of confidentiality for future presidents." The president then cited what he called the "Jefferson rule" of presidential refusal to disclose information to the courts and Congress so as to protect the powers of the presidency. Referring to the Burr conspiracy case, Nixon explained the "rule" as follows:

> Now why did Jefferson do that? Jefferson didn't do that to protect Jefferson. He did that to protect the presidency. That is exactly what I will do in these cases. It isn't for the purpose of protecting the President; it is for the purpose of seeing that the presidency, where great decisions have to be made, and great decisions cannot be made unless there is very free flow of conversation, and that means confidentiality, I have a responsibility to protect that presidency.[42]

On 26 November 1973 Nixon submitted seven of the presidential tapes to Judge Sirica. The president included a number of claims of executive privilege over certain materials in the tapes, presumably to protect the confidentiality of certain White House deliberations. Although presented as a conciliatory gesture to try to end the demands for more White House tapes, the tactic merely fueled the controversy and led to demands for more of the White House tapes.

In the brief in opposition to the special prosecutor's demand for the

White House tapes, Nixon's defenders asserted that the president refused the order to protect the president's constitutional powers and ability to provide the nation with "informed and vigorous leadership."[43] The president's brief made the following argument for protecting the presidency:

> If the Special Prosecutor should be successful in the attempt to compel disclosure of recordings of presidential conversations, the damage to the institution of the presidency will be irreparable. The character of that office will be fundamentally altered and the total structure of government—dependent as it is upon the separation of powers—will be impaired.
>
> The consequence of an order to disclose recordings or notes would be that no longer could a president speak in confidence with his close advisers on any subject. The threat of potential disclosure of any and all conversations would make it virtually impossible for President Nixon or his successors in that great office to function. Beyond that, a holding that the president is personally subject to the orders of a court would effectively destroy the status of the Executive Branch as an equal and coordinate element of government.
>
> There is no precedent that can be said to justify or permit such a result. On the contrary, it is clear that while courts and their grand juries have the power to seek evidence of all persons, including the president, the president has the power and thus the privilege to withhold information if he concludes that disclosure would be contrary to the public interest.[44]

The president articulated similar arguments in two letters to the chairman of the Senate Watergate Committee, Sen. Sam J. Ervin (D-N.C.). First, in response to a letter from Ervin requesting personal testimony from the president as well as access to presidential papers, on 6 July 1973 Nixon wrote the following comments:

> In this letter I shall state the reasons why I shall not testify before the committee or permit access to presidential papers.
>
> I want to strongly emphasize that my decision, in both cases, is based on my constitutional obligation to preserve intact the powers and prerogatives of the presidency and not upon any desire to withhold information relevant to your inquiry. . . . The pending requests . . . would move us from proper presidential cooperation with a Senate Committee to jeopardizing the fundamental constitutional role of the presidency. This I must and shall resist.

Nixon went on to say that the president cannot function in an environment in which the candor of his staff becomes threatened by public disclosure of presidential papers and materials. Nixon added that "the duty of every president to protect and defend the constitutional rights and powers of his office is an obligation that runs directly to the people of this country."[45]

Second, in response to the Senate Committee subpoena of presidential materials, Nixon responded in a 4 January 1974 letter to Ervin:

> To produce the material you now seek would unquestionably destroy any vestige of confidentiality of presidential communications, thereby irreparably impairing the constitutional functions of the office of the presidency. Neither the judiciary nor the Congress could survive a similar power asserted by the executive branch to rummage through their files and confidential processes. Under the circumstances, I can only view your subpoena as an overt attempt to intrude into the executive to a degree that constitutes an unconstitutional usurpation of power. . . . I take this position to protect the office of the president against incursions by another branch, which I believe, as have my predecessors in office, is of utmost constitutional importance. Accordingly, in order to protect the fundamental structure of our government of three separate but equal branches, I must and do respectfully decline to produce the materials called for in your subpoenas.[46]

In addition to protecting the constitutional prerogatives of the presidency, Nixon maintained that he used executive privilege to preserve the national security.

Preserving the National Security

Finally, President Nixon asserted traditional national security concerns as justification for his use of executive privilege during Watergate. He argued that without the protection of executive privilege, "our military security, our relations with other countries, our law enforcement procedures, and many other aspects of the national interest could be significantly damaged and the decisionmaking process of the executive branch could be impaired."[47]

Once again, the president's brief in opposition to the special prosecutor's demand for information stated the argument in favor of executive privilege:

> Disclosure of information allegedly relevant to this inquiry would mean disclosure as well as [sic] other information of a highly confidential nature relating

to a wide range of matters not related to this inquiry. Some of these matters deal with sensitive issues of national security. Others go to the exercise by the president of his constitutional duties on matters other than Watergate.[48]

In announcing the security classification Executive Order 11652 on 8 March 1972, Nixon stated that "the federal government is obliged to protect certain information which might otherwise jeopardize the security of the country. The need has become particularly acute in recent years as the United States has assumed a powerful position in world affairs, and as world peace has come to depend in large part on how that position is safeguarded. We are also moving into an era of delicate negotiations in which it will be especially important that governments be able to communicate in confidence." Ironically, Nixon declared the need for a balance between the public's right to know and government secrecy and argued that the security classification system should not be used to conceal mistakes "or to prevent embarrassment to [government] officials." Nixon offered a view much in contrast to the arguments in favor of an absolute executive privilege power: "Fundamental to our way of life is the belief that when information which properly belongs to the public is systematically withheld by those in power, the people soon become ignorant of their own affairs, distrustful of those who manage them, and—eventually—incapable of determining their own destinies."[49]

ABUSING THE CONSTITUTIONAL DOCTRINE

President Nixon's defenses of his view of executive privilege lack constitutional and historical validity. In the unanimous *U.S. v. Nixon* decision, the Supreme Court made abundantly clear that executive privilege is not an unlimited, unfettered presidential power. The Court strongly rejected the argument that, under the separation of powers system, the president's exercise of power cannot be questioned by the coordinate branches of government. Indeed, the Court reaffirmed its own authority to say what the law is and to challenge the presidential exercise of power. Nixon's claim that only the president can determine the scope and limits of his constitutional authority was indefensible.

There is no doubt that national security is a sound basis for defending executive privilege. The trouble is that Nixon used the national security argument to further cover up White House wrongdoing. In a 21 March 1973 conversation among Nixon, H. R. Haldeman, and John Dean, the president proposed using national security concerns as a Watergate defense:

> *President:* What is the answer on this? How can you keep it out?
> I don't know. You can't keep it out if Hunt talks. You see the point
> is irrelevant. It has gotten to this point . . .
> *Dean:* You might put it on a national security basis . . .
> *President:* With the bombing thing coming out and everything coming
> out, the whole thing was national security.
> *Dean:* I think we could get by on that . . .
> *President:* Bud [Krogh] should just say it was a question of national
> security, and I was not in a position to divulge it. Anyway let's don't
> go beyond that.[50]

Nixon persisted in his claim that his actions were motivated by national security—even after publication of the White House transcripts and the *U.S. v. Nixon* case revealed the sham, even after he had been forced to resign the presidency. In his 19 May 1977 televised interview with David Frost, Nixon recited Abraham Lincoln's words as supportive of the view that normally unconstitutional actions become constitutional when undertaken by the president to preserve the nation. Frost inquired that "there was no comparison was there between the situation you faced and the situation Lincoln faced?" Nixon didn't back down. "This nation was torn apart in an ideological way by the war in Vietnam, as much as the Civil War tore apart the nation when Lincoln was president." Nixon insisted that his actions must "be understood in the context of the times. The nation was at war. Men were dying." Furthermore, he argued that "keeping the peace at home and keeping support for the war was essential in order to get the enemy to negotiate." Nixon defended the infamous Huston Plan, which advocated infiltration of antiwar groups through wire tappings, burglaries, mail openings, and other techniques.[51] The president defended FBI wiretaps in 1969 of staff members of Henry Kissinger's National Security Council and White House wiretaps of news reporters on the basis of national security. Nixon told John Dean that the wiretaps were legal and covered by the doctrine of executive privilege.[52]

The facts make it unarguably clear that Nixon did not use executive privilege during Watergate to protect the presidency; he did so to protect himself. Like his predecessors, Nixon claimed that he had to exercise executive privilege for the public good. His actions betrayed that claim. The major result of Nixon's abuse of executive privilege has been largely to politically discredit a legitimate, necessary constitutional power of the presidency. Even though the *U.S. v. Nixon* case was a defeat for Nixon and a victory for the doctrine of executive privilege, that doctrine has not recovered from Nixon's abuses of power. Nixon's actions in part undermined the ability of his successors to exercise a perfectly defensible constitutional power. His actions lent credibility and stature to such antiexecutive privilege absolutists as Raoul Berger. Presidents Ford, Carter, Reagan, Bush, and Clinton have had to deal with this particular legacy of Watergate.

President Nixon and the opponents of executive privilege have something important in common: they all believe in absolute, unambiguous answers to a complex constitutional controversy. One group argues that the president has an absolute, unlimited power of executive privilege that cannot be challenged by the other branches of government. The other group maintains that the president never, under any circumstance, has the authority to assert executive privilege, and that Congress can compel the executive branch to hand over any information that it wants, without limitation.

Before looking at the argument for a properly limited presidential power of executive privilege, it is necessary to examine the more recent history of that constitutional doctrine. The doctrine of executive privilege has been in decline since Watergate, largely due to the effective tactics by opponents of the doctrine to characterize every use of presidential secrecy as a Nixonian attempt to conceal or deceive. Although post-Watergate presidents, Republican and Democrat alike, have accepted the constitutional legitimacy of executive privilege, they have all been reluctant to exercise this power and generally unwilling, and perhaps unable, to stake political capital and congressional relations on making a case for executive privilege.

CHAPTER 4

The Post-Watergate Years

★————————————————————————————★

The "Open" Presidencies of Gerald R. Ford and Jimmy Carter

The Watergate crisis brought the executive privilege controversy to the forefront of public discourse in the United States. Although the constitutional doctrine had been a matter of some controversy for many years, no single event had ever brought executive privilege to such a prominent place in national political discussion.

The Nixon administration's actions discredited a constitutional doctrine that had been used judiciously by many previous administrations. Nixon's successors subsequently have had to deal with this legacy of his presidency. Congress has become much more aggressive in challenging presidential exercise of executive privilege. Presidents have become very reluctant to exercise, or make a case for, executive privilege.

Although executive privilege has fallen out of favor, the post-Watergate presidents have not neglected the perceived need to keep secrets or to withhold information. In some cases, they have adopted strategies of withholding information without citing executive privilege as authority for so doing, but relying, instead, on statutory or some other authority for such actions. Despite the creative efforts of presidents to maintain secrecy and confidentiality, Congress generally has been able to compel disclosure of executive branch information by various political and legal maneuvers. When disputes over executive privilege have taken place in the post-Watergate years, presidential administrations generally have backed down from their claims in the face of congressional challenges. Even the

Reagan administration, which adopted unprecedented government secrecy measures, never made a strong case for the president's right to assert
executive privilege, choosing instead to accommodate its short-term political needs by conceding to Congress disputed information.

The ways in which successive presidents have handled the issue of executive privilege in the years after Watergate have weakened the doctrine
substantially, resulting in (1) creative presidential efforts to achieve the
ends of executive privilege, without citing that constitutional doctrine as
authority; (2) congressional attempts, largely successful, to demean
every use of executive privilege as automatically an attempt to deceive or
to conceal wrongdoing; and (3) the undermining of a legitimate presidential power that often is necessary to the conduct of the presidency.

The following evidence makes it clear that executive privilege—an important power that presidents need to carry out many of their constitutional duties—needs to be reestablished in the political branches as a necessary executive power. None of the post-Watergate presidencies has
taken the proper steps to reestablish the viability of this constitutional
doctrine.

GERALD R. FORD, 1974–1977

The Ford years represent an important transitional stage in the modern
presidency. As the first post-Watergate president, Ford experienced vigorous challenges to his authority and veracity—challenges certainly
more suited to his predecessor—by Congress and the media. To be sure,
his candor and efforts to lead an "open" presidency did much to move the
nation beyond the cynicism and rancor of the Nixon years. Nonetheless,
many members of Congress and political commentators then believed
that an important lesson of the Nixon years was that power in the hands
of the executive leads to abuses of authority. Congress embarked upon an
unprecedented reform effort to invigorate its own authority in the separation of powers system and to limit the exercise of presidential powers.
Congress also undertook unprecedented investigations into the activities
of the U.S. intelligence community.

It was against this backdrop that a number of executive privilege controversies arose during the Ford years. President Ford never adopted a for-

mal policy on executive privilege, but he did exercise that power on several occasions, with varying degrees of success.

Ford's "Policy" on Executive Privilege

Unlike his predecessor, President Ford never issued a formal memorandum or executive order specifying his administration's policy on executive privilege. A review of White House documents reveals that certain members of the Ford administration raised the subject of developing a set of procedures for handling executive privilege controversies. Certain members of Congress sent letters to the president requesting that such guidelines be issued. The White House even composed a draft executive order on executive privilege, but Ford never issued the order. If there was any Ford White House strategy on executive privilege, it was to avoid controversy as much as possible by not issuing a formal policy, avoiding the use of the term "executive privilege" in favor of other descriptions for decisions to withhold information, and, when possible, citing statutory authority to deny requested information. Ford did say that he believed that the president had the right of executive privilege. Ford exercised that power on a few occasions to protect what he considered vital national security information.

Within one week of the Ford inauguration, Rep. John E. Moss (D-Calif.) sent a letter to the president requesting that Ford, like Nixon, adopt a formal policy on executive privilege in which the constitutional doctrine could be "invoked only by the president or with specific presidential approval in each instance." Moss noted that he had received commitments from presidents Kennedy, Johnson, and Nixon to limit the use of executive privilege to personal claims by the president. Consequently, Moss expected a similar response to this request from Ford.[1]

Unlike his three predecessors, Ford never directly responded to the letter. Only the deputy assistant to the president, Max L. Friedersdorf, responded to Moss's letter, assuring the congressman that the letter would be shared with the president's advisers.[2]

Ford also received a letter on executive privilege from Reps. John N. Erlenborn (R-Ill.) and William S. Moorhead (D-Pa.) on 13 August 1974, and another jointly written letter on executive privilege from Sens. Sam

Ervin (D-N.C.), William V. Roth (R-Del.), and Edmund S. Muskie (D-Maine) on 22 August 1974. Friedersdorf acknowledged the Erlenborn–Moorhead letter and assistant to the president, William E. Timmons, acknowledged the senators' letter.[3] No formal action was taken on the matters raised in these letters.

The White House continued to receive pressure to adopt some policy on the use of executive privilege. On 19 September 1974 the general counsel to the Office of Management and Budget (OMB), Stanley Ebner, expressed his concern to the counsel to the president, Philip W. Buchen, that "President Ford has taken no public position on the issue of executive privilege." Ebner noted that the OMB had to deal with numerous "requests for information or records from the Congress and from outside government." He recalled President Nixon's memorandum on executive privilege and concluded that "you will no doubt want to give some consideration to the question of a possible reaffirmation or modification of this policy by the president on his own initiative."[4]

William E. Timmons advised Buchen on 23 September 1974 to "research the issue [of executive privilege] and get guidance from the president on how he plans to handle this ticklish problem when it is raised." Timmons wrote that members of Congress would press for disputed information on Watergate, the Nixon pardon, and other matters, making it imperative that the president set some guidelines on the use of executive privilege.[5]

That same day Timmons and Friedersdorf proposed a meeting between the president and Reps. Erlenborn and Moorhead to discuss pending legislation on executive privilege.[6] The meeting was held for fifteen minutes on 10 October 1974 at the Oval Office. There is no record of what was said in the meeting, but a White House background paper for the meeting identified "talking points" for the president. The talking points noted that Ford would emphasize his desire to run an open administration and that he would value the "views and recommendations" of the congressmen on the topic of executive privilege.[7] The legislative proposal on executive privilege that provided the basis for the meeting failed to pass Congress.

The Ford White House continued to use an *ad hoc* group, formed in the Nixon administration, to make recommendations on information policy issues, including those pertaining to the Freedom of Information Act and executive privilege. A 24 September 1974 memorandum from the executive director of the Domestic Council on the Right of Privacy, Doug Metz, to Philip W. Buchen, outlined several recommendations and presidential options on the topic of executive privilege. The memorandum made clear that Ford's options on executive privilege were limited because that subject was "inextricably bound up with Watergate." The memorandum advised Ford to meet with members of Congress on the subject, to affirm the intention to conduct an "open" presidency, to avoid an outright defense of the constitutional prerogative of executive privilege, and to issue an executive order on the subject "affirming the traditional commitment to prudence in the exercise of the privilege." The memorandum was accompanied by a discussion draft of an executive order entitled "Establishing a Procedure for Determining Whether Executive Privilege Should Be Invoked." Also included was a proposed draft letter on executive privilege for the president to issue to all federal employees.[8] The intention of the executive order and the letter was to formalize a presidential position on executive privilege. Ford never issued the proposed executive order and letter.

A 25 September 1974 memorandum from Associate Counsel Dudley Chapman to Philip W. Buchen summarized executive privilege issues before the administration and offered recommendations for handling the subject. Echoing the Metz memorandum, Chapman stated that "the unfavorable connotations of executive privilege and the present mood of Congress dictate a sharp break from traditional practice." Chapman, too, recommended that Ford adopt a formal policy on executive privilege rather than try to deal with each controversy on a case-by-case basis. Chapman believed that Ford needed to acknowledge the legitimacy of Congress's various requests for information and to meet with the congressmen who had written letters to the president urging the adoption of legislation to limit the use of executive privilege.[9]

In November, Chapman followed up with another executive privilege memorandum. This memorandum noted the difficulty posed by the new personalities in Congress who were requesting executive branch information and who "no longer give up when they are told no." Chapman maintained that "many of the requests we are now getting cannot be resolved through traditional compromise because the purpose of the request is to test the principle." Chapman offered suggestions for getting around executive privilege controversies: (1) cite exemptions from the

FOIA as the basis for withholding information "rather than executive privilege"; (2) use executive privilege as a last resort—even avoid the use of the term in favor of "presidential" or "constitutional privilege," "confidential working papers," and so forth; and (3) issue formal guidelines on the use of executive privilege. Chapman noted that congressional requests for a formal presidential declaration on executive privilege remained unanswered.[10]

The issue of how the White House should treat executive privilege controversies remained unresolved throughout the Ford years. On 4 April 1975 a discussion on how to handle executive privilege controversies was held at the office of the deputy counsel to the president. The discussion summary makes clear that the administration lacked guidelines for handling executive privilege controversies.[11]

In late November 1975 Buchen sent a memorandum to all senior White House staff and members of the Cabinet summarizing access to information controversies before the administration. The memorandum cited the use of statutory bases for refusing information in some cases, compliance with congressional requests in a number of cases, and the use of executive privilege as a basis to withhold information in a few cases. Part III of the memorandum was entitled "Procedures for Asserting Executive Privilege." That section summarized the procedures adopted by some of Ford's predecessors. It identified no such procedures for the Ford administration. In fact, the only mention of Ford in this section was the fact that the president, in response to a question, had told Congress that he believed in the principle of executive privilege and in the right of confidentiality for each branch of government.[12]

A November 1975 memorandum on executive privilege from the office of the attorney general noted the need to approach the subject when it should arise "in a systematic fashion." The memorandum was "intended to facilitate the construction of a framework for future actions." The memorandum further suggested categories of areas in which executive privilege could be asserted and the levels of priority to be granted to the stated purposes for withholding information.[13]

What is most telling about all these memoranda and letters is the amount of effort the Ford administration devoted to discussing how to handle the controversial issue of executive privilege. Despite all of this discussion, the president never adopted a formal policy on the use of executive privilege. His administration dealt with executive privilege controversies on a case-by-case basis.

To understand Ford's handling of this subject, the political context of that period must be acknowledged. To have adopted a formal, and hence public, position on executive privilege would have invited an avalanche of public protest and congressional condemnation of Ford's action, even if the president had adopted a reasonably restricted policy on the exercise of such a presidential power. To many citizens and members of Congress, "executive privilege" and "Watergate" were intertwined. Ford's decision not to adopt a formal policy on executive privilege—when only one that would have severely weakened the constitutional doctrine could have been conceivable at that time—was prudent, given the difficult environment in which he governed.

Ford's Exercise of Executive Privilege

In the wake of Watergate, President Ford projected a willingness to accommodate the needs of Congress. On 12 August 1974, three days after taking the presidential oath of office, Ford addressed members of Congress from the House chambers. He made clear that he intended to be very different than his predecessor:

> As president . . . my motto toward the Congress is communication, conciliation, compromise and cooperation. This Congress, unless it has changed, will be my working partner as well as my most constructive critic. I am not asking for conformity. . . . I do not want a honeymoon with you. I want a good marriage. . . . My office door has always been open, and that is how it is going to be at the White House. . . .
>
> There will be no illegal tapings, eavesdropping, buggings or break-ins by my administration. There will be hot pursuit of tough laws to prevent illegal invasion of privacy.[14]

Ford's speech drew an enormously favorable response from the legislators. In retrospect, it seems remarkable that members of Congress would feel moved to applaud with such enthusiasm a presidential pledge not to break the law or abuse power. Members of Congress were delighted to be rid of Nixon and they saw in Ford—a former House member—hope for the beginning of an era of presidential-congressional cooperation. A

New York Times reporter wrote that the legislators were so overjoyed with Ford that "they probably would have cheered if he had read them a page from the telephone book."[15]

Ford's pledge of cooperation along with his promise to run an "open" presidency certainly created high expectations among members of Congress. Nonetheless, regarding the doctrine of executive privilege, some members of Congress wanted to test the limits of how far Ford would go in exercising this presidential power. And despite his pledge to cooperate with Congress, Ford never conceded that the legislature had the right of access to all executive branch information.

The Nixon Pardon

The unpopular presidential pardon of Richard M. Nixon on 8 September 1974 set back much of the progress Ford had made in establishing a relationship with members of Congress based on trust. Many members of Congress reacted angrily not only to the decision itself, but to the secretive manner in which Ford considered and then issued the pardon. The way that Ford handled the pardon decision, dropping it on an unsuspecting country one Sunday morning, "like Pearl Harbor," as Deputy Press Secretary John W. Hushen described it, also fueled speculation that Nixon and Ford had struck an unseemly deal: the White House for a pardon.[16]

To determine whether any such deal had taken place, some members of Congress sought to compel testimony from Ford's legal counsel Philip W. Buchen and other White House staffers. These requests for congressional testimony from the White House staff led to the first executive privilege controversy during Ford's presidency. The president ended the controversy on 30 September 1974, when he agreed to appear before Congress to answer questions about his decision to pardon Nixon.[17] During the 17 October 1974 nationally televised appearance before the House Subcommittee on Criminal Justice, Ford said that "the right of executive privilege is to be exercised with caution and restraint." Furthermore, he explained that "I feel a responsibility, as you do, that each branch of government must preserve a degree of confidentiality for its internal communications."[18] In effect, Ford projected a conciliatory tone while affirming presidential authority to assert executive privilege.

Aid to South Vietnam

During his brief term in office, Ford went to unusual lengths to provide information to Congress in areas where previous presidents had been reluctant to cooperate with legislative inquiries. The president agreed to furnish Congress with requested information on the activities of the Central Intelligence Agency (CIA) and the Federal Bureau of Investigation (FBI). For example, Ford turned over to Congress previously withheld information that was relevant to inquiries into alleged CIA complicity in assassination schemes.

Nonetheless, Ford did draw the line with Congress over certain requests for information. In 1975 the Senate Judiciary Subcommittee on Separation of Powers requested from Ford the release of information on correspondence between President Nixon and South Vietnamese President Nguyen Van Thieu regarding promises of U.S. aid to South Vietnam in the event that North Vietnam did not honor the Paris Peace Accords. On 1 May 1975 Ford declared that he would not release any of the disputed documents and letters. The subcommittee described Ford as "adamant in his refusal" to release the materials, but could do little more than hold hearings on the issue of congressional access to executive branch information.[19]

In some cases, information disputes between the president and Congress did not result in an explicit claim of executive privilege. Because of the controversial nature of the constitutional doctrine in light of Nixon's actions, the Ford White House adopted a strategy of occasionally citing statutory authority to withhold information, thereby getting around the need to raise the issue of, and to defend, executive privilege.[20] Two cases in particular show that the strategy to substitute statutory law for executive privilege as the basis for withholding information from Congress did not work.

Request for Survey of Hospitals

On 23 October 1975 Rep. John Moss, chairman of the Subcommittee on Oversight and Investigations of the Committee on Interstate and Foreign Commerce, requested from Secretary of the Department of Health, Education, and Welfare (HEW) F. David Mathews information on surveys of hospitals conducted by the Joint Commission on Accreditation of Hospitals. On the advice of counsel, Mathews refused the request and cited as the basis for refusal the Social Security Act's confidentiality provision (Section 186a). The subcommittee challenged Mathews and issued a subpoena for the information. On 12 November 1975 Attorney General Edward Levi advised Mathews that the confidentiality provision of the Social Security Act was not a strong enough basis for an executive branch official to withhold information requested by Congress. The provision only pertained to not making information public. Subsequently, Mathews ended the controversy by turning the requested information over to Congress.[21]

Confidential Export Reports[22]

On 10 July 1975 Chairman Moss requested from the Department of Commerce's director of the Office of Export Administration copies of all quarterly reports filed by exporters under the Export Administration Act of 1969. Moss's subcommittee was investigating the extent to which U.S. companies had been requested by Arab countries not to do business with Israel. On 24 July 1975 Secretary of the Department of Commerce Rogers C. B. Morton sent to Moss a summary of Israel boycott information reported by U.S. companies. Morton refused to submit the requested quarterly reports and based his authority for such a refusal on Section 7(c) of the Export Administration Act:

> No department, agency, or official exercising any functions under this Act shall publish or disclose information obtained hereunder which is deemed confidential or with reference to which a request for confidential treatment is made by the person furnishing such information, unless the head of such department or agency determines that the withholding thereof is contrary to the national interest.[23]

The subcommittee responded on 28 July 1975 by issuing a subpoena for the documents. On 4 September 1975 Attorney General Levi issued an opinion to Morton that Section 7(c) of the Export Administration Act applied to Congress and that it was therefore proper to withhold the disputed documents. Morton appeared before the subcommittee on 22 September 1975, and informed the subcommittee members of the attorney general's opinion that it was proper to withhold the reports. Morton did offer to provide Congress with summaries of information in the reports, but that failed to satisfy the subcommittee members who insisted on having access to the actual reports that contained the names of companies participating in the boycott of Israel.[24]

The subcommittee held hearings on this controversy on 11 and 12 October 1975, and heard testimony from legal scholars on executive branch withholding of information from Congress. On 11 November 1975, the subcommittee passed a resolution to hold Morton in contempt of Congress. The Interstate and Foreign Commerce Committee scheduled a meeting to discuss the contempt resolution. The day before the meeting was scheduled to be held, Morton agreed to show the disputed documents to Chairman Moss, with the understanding that the information would not be made public. The committee dropped the contempt of Congress proceedings against Morton, as Congress finally achieved the result that it had desired.

House Select Committee on Intelligence Subpoenas[25]

On 6 November 1975 the House Select Committee on Intelligence, chaired by Rep. Otis Pike (D-N.Y.), issued seven subpoenas to the Ford administration—five of them to the National Security Council (NSC). On 11 November 1975 Lt. Gen. Brent Scowcroft, deputy assistant to the president for national security affairs, responded to the subpoenas by forwarding the available requested documents to the committee and promising to furnish the remaining materials when available. The NSC did not claim executive privilege over any of the documents.

The committee issued one subpoena to the Central Intelligence Agency (CIA). On 11 November 1975 the special counsel to the CIA, Mitchell Rogovin, responded to the subpoena with a letter to the committee providing the requested information. The CIA also did not claim executive privilege in this case.

Finally, the committee issued a subpoena to Secretary of State Henry Kissinger, to compel disclosure of all documents pertaining to Department of State recommendations to the NSC on covert activities drafted since 20 January 1965. In this case, President Ford formally directed Kissinger to assert executive privilege over the documents. On 14 November 1975 the Department of State legal adviser informed the committee of Ford's decision. That same day, the committee cited Kissinger for contempt and recommended that the Speaker of the House "certify the report of the Select Committee as to the contumacious conduct of Henry A. Kissinger, as Secretary of State, in failing and refusing to produce certain pertinent materials in compliance with a subpoena duces tecum of said Select Committee . . . , under the seal of the House of Representatives to the United States Attorney for the District of Columbia, to the end that Henry A. Kissinger, as Secretary of State, may be proceeded against in the manner and form provided by law."[26] In a 19 November 1975 letter to Pike, the president wrote that "in addition to disclosing highly sensitive military and foreign affairs assessments and evaluations, the documents revealed to an unacceptable degree the consultation process involving advice and recommendations to Presidents Kennedy, Johnson and Nixon, made to them directly or to committees composed of their closest aides and counselors."[27] A White House memorandum from Philip W. Buchen, counsel to the president, reveals a number of bases for the assertion of executive privilege in this case. In particular, the memorandum cited *U.S. v. Nixon* and instances in the Eisenhower and Kennedy administrations of "presidential directives to Cabinet members not to release certain information to Congress."[28] Eventually the administration and Congress reached a compromise in which committee members and staff would attend an oral briefing on the information contained in the disputed materials. The committee recommitted its report recommending a citation of contempt for Kissinger before the House of Representatives had an opportunity to vote on the measure.

Electronic Surveillance Controversy[29]

The most controversial case of presidential withholding of information during the Ford administration occurred in 1976 and resulted in a complex series of interbranch negotiations as well as legal disputes over a two-year period into Jimmy Carter's term of office. This controversy involved the use of warrantless wiretaps on citizens for national security purposes. In brief, the FBI had sent letters to the American Telephone and Telegraph Company (AT&T) requesting that certain individuals be placed under electronic surveillance. The House Committee on Interstate and Foreign Commerce subpoenaed the letters and other documents on behalf of the Subcommittee on Oversight and Investigations. The subcommittee wanted to investigate the extent of wiretapping activity, the names of individuals subject to surveillance, whether the wiretaps truly were for national security reasons, and whether these activities were being carried out in accordance with existing laws.

The president refused to divulge the requested letters and documents. He claimed national security concerns as the basis for this refusal. Ford did offer a compromise in which he would supply the committee with the attorney general's memoranda citing the reasons for the surveillance, as well as a sample list of surveillances with the names of the objects of wiretaps deleted. The subcommittee rejected the compromise, maintaining that Ford had not offered enough information to determine whether abuses had actually taken place.

AT&T decided that it should comply with the congressional subpoena and supply the requested materials to the subcommittee. The Department of Justice sued AT&T to prohibit the company from turning over the materials. Ford maintained that the company had an obligation "as an agent of the United States" not to comply with the subpoena.[30] The district court sided with Ford and enjoined AT&T from releasing the disputed materials. The district court determined that because the controversy concerned a national security matter and that disclosure of the disputed materials to the subcommittee possibly could lead to public disclosure of sensitive information, there must be deference to the executive.[31]

The subcommittee chairman, Rep. John Moss, appealed the case on behalf of the House of Representatives. The court of appeals rejected the district court decision to defer to the executive branch but nonetheless upheld the injunction against AT&T. The court of appeals remanded the dispute to the district court for further negotiation between the political branches.[32] Negotiations failed to resolve the dispute and the case again went to the court of appeals.[33] Again the court of appeals refused to side with either branch and encouraged further interbranch negotiation and compromise. The court of appeals did suggest procedures for sampling disputed materials and *in camera* inspection by the district court.[34] Eventually, the executive and legislative branches agreed on a procedure by which committee counsel received certain intelligence memoranda. The committee decided that it had achieved its goal in gaining access and determined that there had been no abuse of surveillance authority. In December 1978 both parties to the dispute agreed to dismiss the case.

In this dispute over information, the judicial branch served as a facilitator of negotiations between the political branches. The court of appeals acknowledged the executive's legitimate national security claims and the legislature's legitimate need for information in order to conduct investigations. Rather than decide completely in favor of either claim, the court of appeals worked to get the two parties to compromise. Although the resolution to this controversy does not stand as an affirmation of either the executive or legislative position, it does stand as testimony to Congress's ability to get disputed information from the executive when motivated to do so.

Executive Privilege in the Ford Administration

The above review illustrates just how sensitive an issue executive privilege had become immediately after Watergate. Ford never rejected the legitimacy of that constitutional doctrine. But given the nature of the post-Watergate environment, he was in no position politically to make a vigorous defense of executive privilege. Ford never issued any formal policy on his administration's use of executive privilege. He avoided personally responding to congressional inquiries regarding his administration's policy on executive privilege. In the spirit of the "open" administration Ford gave Congress unprecedented access to information about the activities of the CIA and the FBI. To the extent possible, his White House purposefully avoided the use of the phrase "executive privilege" and used other legal bases for withholding information (e.g., statutory law, separation of powers doctrine). Although Ford's White House held extensive discussions on how to handle executive privilege controversies, the president avoided taking any public position on the issue that was more specific than support in principle for the doctrine. Ford understood well enough the nature of the post-Watergate environment and did not wish to unnecessarily stir up any controversy over an issue so closely linked to the Nixon presidency.

JIMMY CARTER, 1977–1981

Although Jimmy Carter successfully sought the presidency in 1976 as a candidate committed to "open" government and fundamental change from the Nixon era, as president he never rejected the right of executive privilege. Nonetheless, Carter did not make much use of that constitutional power, even when circumstances appeared to justify such action. Carter never issued any formal policy on his administration's use of executive privilege. He avoided personally responding to congressional inquiries on the subject. When his administration sought to withhold information, it did so generally without raising executive privilege as a constitutional basis for such action.

Carter's response to executive privilege is very similar, in fact, to Ford's actions. The thirty-ninth president often avoided the phrase "executive privilege" and his administration frequently couched decisions to withhold information in terms of "separation of powers" or the need to protect "free and open" exchanges within the White House. Clearly, Carter's advisers understood that, because of his promise to run an "open" presidency, the use of executive privilege would result in substantial criticism of the administration.

An examination of the Carter administration's handling of executive privilege makes clear just how controversial this constitutional doctrine had become as a result of Watergate. As with the Ford years, during Carter's tenure Congress displayed an aggressive posture toward gaining access to executive branch information. The Carter White House tried to protect confidentiality, not break the pledge of an "open" presidency, and satisfy congressional demands for information at the same time.

Carter's "Policy" on Executive Privilege

Like his predecessor, President Carter never issued a formal memorandum or executive order specifying his administration's policy on executive privilege. A review of White House documents reveals that certain members of the Carter administration raised the subject of developing a formal policy on executive privilege on a number of occasions. Certain members of Congress had sent inquiries to the Carter White House requesting a commitment from the president that only he would assert executive privilege, if such a power had to be exercised at all. And certain Carter White House staffers had written a proposed executive order on executive privilege that met congressional resistance and that the president subsequently never issued.

Carter's approach to executive privilege controversies must be considered within the context of his promise to conduct an "open" presidency. Carter believed in the presidential power of executive privilege, although he exercised that authority sparingly.

In keeping with the precedent established by Rep. John E. Moss, the chairman of the Government Information and Individual Rights Subcommittee of the House Committee on Government Operations, Rep. Richardson Preyer (D-N. C.), and the Ranking Minority Party member, Rep. Paul N. McCloskey, Jr. (R-Calif.), wrote a letter to Carter on 13 June 1977 requesting a formal presidential statement of policy on the use of executive privilege. The congressmen noted that presidents Kennedy, Johnson, and Nixon had personally responded to previous such requests and all had affirmed that "executive privilege can be invoked only by the president and would not be used without specific presidential approval." Preyer and McCloskey explained that a Carter deputy attorney general already had shown reluctance to turn over to the Senate Rules Committee a requested internal Department of Justice memorandum and had seemed confused over whether executive privilege had been invoked. The controversy, they wrote, had "underscored the confusion among new administration officials about the guidelines for such a claim."[35]

Carter followed the post-Watergate precedent established by Ford—he never responded to the letter. Preyer and Richardson nonetheless persisted in their efforts to get Jimmy Carter to commit, in some manner, to an official policy limiting executive privilege to presidential use only. In May 1978 Preyer and members of his staff met with Counsel to the President Robert J. Lipshutz, and members of his staff, to discuss a variety of issues germane to the work of the Subcommittee on Government Information and Individual Rights. Although there is no White House record of what transpired in that meeting, apparently Lipshutz told Preyer and the others in response to a question that the White House policy on executive privilege was that the president must assert that authority. Preyer sought more than a verbal assurance of Carter's policy and wrote the following to Lipshutz soon after the meeting:

> I was especially encouraged to learn that it is your policy that only the president can invoke a claim of "executive privilege" and that so far this administration has been able to negotiate successfully all the disputes in regard to conflicts over requests for information between Congress and the Executive branch. Such accommodation encourages a lasting comity between co-equal branches of government.
>
> In this regard I think it would be helpful both to Congress and to the Executive branch if the president would publicly reaffirm his policy of openness. Traditionally this has taken the form of a letter to this subcommittee briefly stating the president's intention in this area.[36]

Preyer added that he planned to write a letter once again to Carter, to remind the president of the earlier request for a policy statement on executive privilege and to iterate that request. Nearly four months later, Preyer and McCloskey wrote another letter to Carter:

> On June 13, 1977, this subcommittee, following a long tradition dating back to the presidency of John Kennedy, requested from you a statement of your administration's policy regarding the use of the claim of "executive privilege." Since writing we have been in contact with your Counsel, Robert F. [sic] Lipshutz, on this matter and were happy to discover that it is your practice that only the president is authorized to invoke a claim of "executive privilege." We also were pleased to ascertain that thus far your administration has been able to negotiate successfully all of the disputes between Congress and the Executive branch without the use of this concept.
>
> The members of our subcommittee, however, still believe it would be helpful if you would publicly affirm this policy. In the past this has been accomplished by a letter to the subcommittee briefly stating the president's intentions in this area. Such a public affirmation, we believe, would materially aid both the Congress and the Executive branch in its day-to-day relationships.[37]

Preyer and McCloskey merely received acknowledgments of their request from Assistant to the President for Congressional Liaison Frank Moore.[38] The president did not respond and consequently never issued any statement of policy on executive privilege.[39]

In the first year of Carter's term, there were many internal administration discussions and correspondences concerning the issue of executive privilege.[40] Those discussions and correspondences focused on the need to establish a formal administration policy on executive privilege.[41] The office of counsel to the president developed a draft executive order on the use of executive privilege by departmental agencies. Heads of the various executive departments then had the opportunity to respond to the proposed order.[42] The draft emphasized the administration's goal of cooperation with congressional requests for information, belief in the use of executive privilege under only the most compelling circumstances, and requirement of "specific presidential approval" for any use of executive privilege. The draft also stated formal procedures for the use of executive privilege.[43]

Rep. John E. Moss reviewed the proposed executive order and wrote to Carter urging that the directive not be issued. Moss vigorously objected that the proposed order would "create an imbalance" of power between the executive and legislative branches. Moss argued that the proposal was too broad. He believed that it would allow certain executive branch personnel "to play a substantive role in determining the application of executive privilege to congressional requests for information."[44]

Because Carter never issued the proposed executive order and never conveyed to administration personnel how to handle executive privilege controversies, members of the administration lacked guidance on how to respond to such controversies. As late as 1979 a controversy arose over requested congressional testimony from White House staff prompting a memorandum from Counsel to the President Robert J. Lipshutz. The memorandum made clear that "the personal staff of the president is immune from testimonial compulsion by Congress." Lipshutz further emphasized the importance of "frank and candid discussions between the president and his personal staff."[45]

It was not until the week before election day in 1980 that the Carter administration established some official procedures for the use of executive privilege. In early 1980 the new counsel to the president, Lloyd Cutler, requested an intradepartmental memorandum on the use of executive privilege. Doug Huron and Barbara Bergman of the office of counsel to the president produced an executive privilege memorandum summarizing the history of the doctrine, legal principles, congressional enforcement mechanisms, and procedures for invocation. The memorandum made clear that under Carter no official procedures on the use of executive privilege had been established and that the administration had adopted *de facto* the procedures of the Nixon administration.[46]

Because of a trade conflict with Mexico that resulted in a White House debate over how to handle certain internal documents, Cutler wrote to the special trade representative, Reubin Askew, on 22 October 1980: "I am concerned that a uniform policy regarding assertion of executive privilege be applied throughout the Executive Office of the President." Cutler explained that presidential advisers could not waive executive privilege without presidential approval. This memorandum constituted the first official statement of procedures on executive privilege in the Carter White House.[47] Cutler further developed the procedures with a 31 October 1980 memorandum to all White House staff and heads of units within the Executive Office of the President.

The 31 October 1980 memorandum established that the concurrence of the office of counsel to the president must be sought by those considering the use of executive privilege. The memorandum also emphasized that only the president had the authority to waive executive privilege. Cutler expressed concern that the decision by senior officials to waive executive privilege over disputed information would "significantly affect the successful assertion of privilege by other advisers to the president and by the president himself."[48] These procedures only applied to the White House staff and the heads of units within the Executive Office of the President. Cutler also wrote a memorandum on that day to the attorney general requesting some input as to whether "a similar consultation arrangement throughout the executive branch" should be adopted.[49]

Ronald Reagan's election to the presidency made moot the Carter White House deliberations over developing uniform executive privilege procedures throughout the executive branch. The discussions turned to outlining for the incoming administration "the pending matters raising executive privilege problems."[50]

Carter's Exercise of Executive Privilege

President Carter did not make extensive use of executive privilege. He did accept the legitimacy of that presidential prerogative and he asserted it on a few occasions.

The first such case concerned the president's controversial decision not to support funding many water dam projects while allowing certain such projects to be completed. The White House refused a congressional request for access to internal White House memoranda on discussions relating to this decision on the basis that such materials were privileged. The Audubon Society then filed suit against the administration to compel release of the memorandum. The Audubon Society believed that the president approved of the completion of one dam project and construction of another in arbitrary fashion without the benefit of an environmental impact statement. In a 30 April 1977 memorandum Robert J. Lipshutz and Margaret McKenna outlined three policy options for the president: produce the documents, claim executive privilege, or negotiate a continuance of the lawsuit. The president approved the claim of executive privilege in this case.[51] The president's claim soon was withdrawn, however, because the Audubon Society and the Department of the Interior reached an agreement to end the litigation.[52]

The issue of executive privilege arose in White House deliberations later that year when the chairman of the Subcommittee on Commerce, Consumer, and Monetary Affairs of the House Committee on Government Operations, Rep. Benjamin S. Rosenthal (D-N. Y.), requested on 1 November 1977 access to documents relevant to the antiboycott amendments to the Export Administration Act. Secretary of Commerce Juanita M. Kreps wrote a memorandum to the president explaining that certain requested documents were submitted to Rosenthal and other documents—considered too sensitive—were not. She noted that although executive privilege constituted the only legal grounds for withholding information, "because of the connotations this term has acquired since Watergate, it is preferable for us to couch our response in other terms, such as separation of powers."[53] Kreps wrote to Rosenthal to advise him that the Department of Commerce would make certain documents available to the subcommittee and would provide only summaries of information contained in the more sensitive documents.[54] The subcommittee completed its hearings without requesting a subpoena of the disputed documents and merely reviewed the materials submitted by the Department of Commerce. Nonetheless, the subcommittee—not wishing to set a precedent unfavorable to Congress—formally rejected Kreps's proposal for handling disputed documents.[55] Although the president had been advised that the only legal basis for withholding the documents was executive privilege, the administration resolved the dispute to its favor without asserting the controversial doctrine.

Rosenthal separately had requested a broad range of documents from the Department of Treasury regarding the income tax treatment of payments made by U.S. oil companies to foreign nation-states. On 23 November 1977 Robert Lipshutz wrote a memorandum to Domestic Policy Adviser Stuart Eizenstat explaining the sensitive nature of the documents. Apparently, if the income payments were reclassified as royalties—not as foreign taxes—domestic oil companies would be subjected to much higher tax liability. Lipshutz believed that public disclosure of documents regarding the possible reclassification would disrupt Middle East negotiations, possibly influence the deliberations of the Organization of Petroleum Exporting Countries (OPEC), and jeopardize the administration's energy legislation.[56] Rosenthal decided not to pursue the documents while the Internal Revenue Service (IRS) was in the process of advising the Department of Treasury on how to handle the matter of classifying income payments. Rosenthal advised the White House that he might raise the access issue again after Congress reconvened the following January. Lipshutz conveyed to Carter that "the 'executive privilege' question has been finessed successfully at least for the next seven weeks."[57]

On 12 July 1978 Rosenthal requested from James Griffin, the director of the Office of International Investments at the Department of Treasury, "access to all documents, records and papers relating to the Committee on Foreign Investment in the United States . . . including all letters, memoranda, minutes of meetings and all other documents . . . and to have copies of any of these materials necessary to the conduct of our investigation."[58] Because this request had, once again, raised the sensitive matter of foreign investment in the United States, members of the Department of Treasury met with Rosenthal to work out some agreeable compromise on the documents. Notes from the meeting indicate that Rosenthal received most of the requested documents from Treasury, but some documents and materials had been withheld and portions of others "had been deleted for foreign policy purposes." Rosenthal refused to accept any limitation at all on congressional claims to executive branch information and proceeded to pursue his request for all of the documents.[59]

Assistant Secretary of the Treasury C. Fred Bergsten wrote to Rosenthal to explain that the withheld documents concerned either communications with foreign governments or confidential policy deliberations. Furthermore, "discussions leading to policy formulation must be free from outside scrutiny lest the full and candid consideration of policy alternatives be harmfully chilled."[60] After a series of negotiations and reconsiderations of decisions to withhold certain documents, Rosenthal gained access to many more disputed materials and did not press claims on certain documents thought to be unimportant to his subcommittee's investigation. In the end, there remained a dispute over only one document, prompting the general counsel to the Department of the Treasury, Robert H. Mundheim, to recommend that, if necessary, the president approve the assertion of "a governmental privilege" if Congress subpoenaed the document.[61] The president never used executive privilege in this case, as Congress never issued a subpoena for the document.

In a separate controversy in 1978, a House subcommittee issued a subpoena for disputed administration documents and cited a cabinet secretary for contempt of Congress. In brief, the Subcommittee on Oversight and Investigations of the House Committee on Interstate and Foreign Commerce sought from the Department of Health, Education and Welfare (HEW) certain documents concerning the processing methods of drug manufacturers. The Department of Justice ruled that the requested documents could not be disclosed to Congress because they contained trade secrets. The subcommittee subpoenaed the documents and HEW secretary Joseph A. Califano refused to comply. The subcommittee subsequently voted to cite Califano in contempt of Congress and informed the full committee of this action. Before further action could be taken, Califano worked out a compromise agreement whereby Congress received edited versions of the disputed documents. The White House chose to refrain from asserting executive privilege over the documents.[62]

In 1979 a controversy arose over whether Congress could compel testimony from White House personal aides to the president. Sen. Harrison A. Williams (D-N. J.) had invited Special Assistant to the President Sarah Weddington to testify at hearings on "Women in the Coming Decade" held by the Senate Human Resources Committee. Unaware of any White House prohibition against personal aides to the president testifying on Capitol Hill, Weddington accepted the invitation and then had to cancel her scheduled appearance on 31 January 1979, on the advice of the counsel to the president.[63] The late cancellation angered Williams and prompted press inquiries into whether the White House had adopted the use of executive privilege to prevent congressional testimony by White House staff. Illustrative of the sensitive nature of the issue was a news conference exchange between a reporter and Press Secretary Jody Powell. The reporter asked if executive privilege had been invoked to prevent Weddington's testimony, to which Powell replied: "Oooh, executive privilege! [Laughter] That always scares the hell out of the White House when anybody raises executive privilege. [Laughter] I don't know anything about the thing. I do know that historically that senior advisers to the president are not compelled to appear, cannot be compelled to appear."[64]

This controversy prompted Lipshutz to request a draft of proposed guidelines on how the White House staff should respond to future requests from Congress.[65] On 8 February 1979 Lipshutz issued the guidelines to the White House staff. The memorandum articulated the traditional arguments against compulsory testimony to Congress by White House advisers (i.e., need for "frank and candid discussions," personal advisers are agents of the president). Significantly, Lipshutz did not mention executive privilege as the legal basis for preventing the testimony of White House staff but stated instead that "this immunity is grounded in the Constitutional doctrine of separation of powers."[66]

Two years before, a U.S. senator had requested a copy of a draft testimony to Congress by an assistant secretary in the Department of Commerce. The draft testimony contained advice to the president that the White House did not want publicly released (the actual testimony differed substantially from the draft form). The president agreed to refuse to release the draft testimony to Congress and a memorandum from Lipshutz and McKenna to Carter stated that "we hope to find a sound legal basis to answer the subpoena without using the term executive privilege."[67]

Nonetheless, in late 1980 the counsel to the President, Lloyd Cutler, wrote a letter to the chairman of the Subcommittee on Investigations of the House Committee on Armed Services, Rep. Samuel S. Stratton (D-N.Y.), to inform the congressman that the president had directed Deputy Assistant to the President for National Security Affairs David Aaron not to testify before the subcommittee. Cutler's letter defended the president's position: "The Congress has always respected the privilege of

the president to decline requests that the president himself or his immediate White House advisers appear to testify before congressional
committees."[68]

A 1980 controversy over access to administration documents illustrates
the extent to which Carter sought to avoid the use of executive privilege,
yet considered that power a possible last resort in a battle with Congress.
On 3 April 1980 Carter issued a proclamation establishing a fee on im-
ported crude oil and gasoline.[69] This unpopular decision led to a request
on 8 April 1980, by the Subcommittee on the Environment, Energy, and
Natural Resources of the House Committee on Government Operations,
for all of the Department of Energy documents relevant to Carter's decision. The department refused the request on the ground that the White
House needed time to review the documents before deciding *not* to invoke executive privilege.[70] The subcommittee responded on 22 April
1980, by voting to subpoena the documents (35). Department of Energy
secretary Charles Duncan responded the next day by forwarding to the
subcommittee only some of the requested documents while withholding
others to protect free and open deliberations within the administration
(96–101). The subcommittee voted on 24 April 1980 to subpoena Duncan to appear before the subcommittee with the disputed documents
(116–17). Duncan appeared on 29 April 1980, but explained that he
planned to continue withholding the disputed documents without resorting to the use of executive privilege. Nonetheless, he explained that
executive privilege would be used as a last resort, if necessary (146). The
subcommittee voted to hold Duncan in contempt of Congress (134–39).
The controversy effectively was ended when on 13 May 1980 a district
court voided Carter's proclamation and on the following day the administration agreed to the subcommittee's offer to review the documents in
executive session.[71]

Executive Privilege in the Carter Administration

Following his predecessor Gerald R. Ford, Jimmy Carter never issued a
formal presidential directive defining his administration's policy on the
use of executive privilege. It was not until near election day 1980 that the
counsel to the president issued a set of procedures on the use of executive

privilege to White House staff and the heads of units within the Executive Office of the President.

Also in the spirit of the actions of the Ford administration, the Carter administration tried, to the extent possible, to avoid the use of executive privilege while still defending the presidential right to withhold information through other sources of authority. White House memoranda reveal that, because of the taint of Watergate, the administration tried to avoid the use of the phrase "executive privilege" and made concerted efforts to accommodate requests for information without resorting to executive privilege, even when there appeared to be a compelling reason for withholding information. Nowhere in the White House files does any member of the Carter administration suggest that executive privilege should be avoided because it is of dubious constitutionality. Carter officials accepted the legitimacy of that presidential power, but sought, to the extent possible, to avoid its use—or, at least to avoid the use of the phrase "executive privilege"—merely for what they perceived to be politically necessary reasons.

CHAPTER 5

The Post-Watergate Years

★————————————————————————★

Ronald Reagan, George Bush, and the
Era of Divided Government

Although presidents Ford and Carter pledged to conduct "open" administrations, neither of these chief executives rejected the legitimacy of executive privilege. Both of them sought to avoid informational disputes
while protecting the institutionalized secret presidency. Their successors,
Ronald Reagan and George Bush, were somewhat more aggressive at
pursuing governmental secrecy, although not successful at reestablishing
the viability of executive privilege.

RONALD REAGAN, 1981–1989

To its partisans, the Reagan administration brought about a revival of effective presidential leadership after a sequence of "failed" presidencies.
According to this view, Reagan refuted the political science theories of the
"imperiled" presidency and restored workable, active leadership to the
executive branch.

In contrast, Reagan's critics maintain that his administration abused
power and sacrificed substantive accomplishment for the image of leadership. From this perspective, Reagan's notion of leadership is one in
which little credence is given to the legitimate interests of the coordinate
branches or of private citizens.

Central to this debate over the Reagan legacy is the controversy over
executive branch secrecy. Reagan's partisan defenders and critics alike

certainly can agree that his leadership differed substantially on issues of government secrecy from the "open" presidencies of Gerald R. Ford and Jimmy Carter. To be sure, Ford and Carter mistakenly assumed after the Watergate scandal that a policy of openness best suited the demands of presidential leadership. Reagan perhaps better understood that information control, not openness, enhances presidential power.

The Reagan years provide telling commentary on just how far the constitutional doctrine of executive privilege has fallen into disrepute and, hence, disuse. The Reagan administration—accused by many critics of being overly prone to secrecy and deception—showed great reluctance to fully exercise executive privilege. When the administration did invoke the privilege on a few occasions, it eventually backed down in the face of congressional citations for contempt and threats to delay confirmation proceedings. Unsure of his own authority in this area, President Reagan—who had championed proposals for unprecedented strict classification, cumbersome impediments on Freedom of Information Act requests, lie-detector tests for potential leakers, lifetime censorship for over one hundred thousand current and former government employees, and numerous other forms of information control—waived executive privilege for all administration officials called to testify at the Iran-contra hearings and refused advice to assert executive privilege over his personal diaries.

The Reagan administration experiences reveal two important facts about executive privilege. First, executive privilege lacks the political support necessary to withstand congressional demands for full disclosure of information. That is, it lacks support in Congress, so much so that members of the legislature are unrestrained in their efforts to seek compliance with requests for information. Presidents, too, appear to have lost the will to do battle with Congress over executive privilege to protect their constitutional powers. Furthermore, it is now inherently difficult for presidents who challenge congressional demands for information to make an appealing public case for governmental secrecy, especially given the media's natural bias in favor of complete openness in public affairs. A legitimate, often necessary presidential power has become the victim of the post-Watergate trend toward greater impediments on the chief executive's authority. Second, Congress clearly has the means by which to compel executive disclosure of information. Any attempt to provide a statutory definition of executive privilege, as a way of limiting this presidential power, would be frivolous. As the Reagan experiences so clearly demonstrate, the traditional separation of powers system provides Congress all of the necessary means by which to combat executive privilege claims.

Reagan's Policy on Executive Privilege

Reagan's predecessors, Jimmy Carter and Gerald R. Ford, did not officially change the policy on executive privilege set out in Richard Nixon's 24 March 1969 memorandum to department heads. On 4 November 1982 President Reagan issued a redraft of the Nixon memorandum. The Reagan memorandum to the heads of executive departments and agencies—"Procedures Governing Responses to Congressional Requests for Information"—did not fundamentally change the Nixon guidelines.

The Reagan guidelines stated the administration policy "to comply with congressional requests for information to the fullest extent consistent with the constitutional and statutory obligations of the executive branch." Furthermore, the memorandum upheld the need for "confidentiality of some communications" and added that executive privilege would be used "only in the most compelling circumstances, and only after careful review demonstrates that assertion of the privilege is necessary." The memorandum emphasized the importance of negotiation with Congress to settle any differences of opinion between the branches and assured that "executive privilege shall not be invoked without specific presidential authorization."

The Reagan memorandum asserted that there are "legitimate and appropriate" uses of executive privilege and established procedures to be followed by agencies in cases of congressional requests for confidential or sensitive information. The procedures stated that congressional requests for information would be complied with unless "compliance raises a substantial question of executive privilege." Such a question is raised if the information "might significantly impair the national security (including the conduct of foreign relations), the deliberative process of the executive branch or other aspects of the performance of the executive branch's constitutional duties." Under the Reagan procedures, if a department head believed that a congressional request for information might concern privileged information, he would notify and consult with both the attorney general and the counsel to the president. The department head, attorney general, and counsel to the president would then decide whether to release the information to Congress, or to have the matter submitted to the president for a decision (the matter goes to the president if any one of the three believes that an invocation of executive privilege is necessary). At that stage, the department head requests that Congress await a presidential decision before taking any additional action. If the president chooses to use executive privilege, he instructs the department head to inform Congress "that the claim of executive privilege is being made with the specific approval of the president."[1]

The Reagan memorandum allowed for the protection of various forms of executive branch information, even if that information originated from staff levels far removed from the president. Nonetheless, under Reagan's procedures, the president himself had to approve the use of executive privilege. The Reagan memorandum states more clearly than the 1969 Nixon memorandum the purposes for which executive privilege might be invoked.

The fact that Reagan issued such a memorandum—when presidents Ford and Carter avoided so doing—in itself is a measure of the importance that his administration attached to the need for secrecy in certain executive branch activities. The Reagan administration adopted a number of measures to enhance secrecy in government. Nonetheless, the administration, despite such measures, did not vigorously employ or defend executive privilege.

Executive Branch Secrecy under Reagan

The lack of a vigorous use of executive privilege by the Reagan administration cannot be attributed to reticence toward promoting executive branch secrecy. Given the administration's expansive efforts to promote secrecy, its inability to make a sustained case for a broad executive privilege power stands out.

For example, in issuing Executive Order 12356 in 1982, President Reagan became the first chief executive in four decades to mandate tighter access to information and more classification. Whereas President Jimmy

Carter had mandated (Executive Order 12065) that there be a balancing test to weigh security interests against the public's need to know when classifying documents, Reagan ensured that all such questions be resolved in favor of secrecy. Reagan's executive order eliminated the requirement that "identifiable damage" to security interests be demonstrated before restricting materials. His executive order also extended the classification period, eliminated automatic declassification of documents after a specified period, and authorized executive branch agencies to reclassify previously declassified documents.[2]

Reagan issued National Security Directive 84 on 11 March 1983 as an "addendum" to Executive Order 12356. Again, as a measure to promote security interests, this directive "imposed prior lifetime censorship, secrecy pledges, and lie-detector tests on *any* government employee with access to classified information."[3] Due to widespread controversy and congressional reaction, the president suspended, but did not withdraw, requirements for lifetime prior censorship and the use of lie-detector tests.[4] Nonetheless, in November 1985 Reagan issued an order authorizing lie-detector tests for thousands of government employees dealing with sensitive materials. The order appeared to include White House cabinet officers, leading Secretary of State George P. Shultz to threaten to resign if forced to take a lie-detector test. "The minute in this government I am told that I'm not trusted is the day I leave."[5] Also, over 120,000 government employees—outside the Central Intelligence Agency and the National Security Agency—already had signed lifetime censorship agreements under a 1981 nondisclosure requirement (Form 4193).[6]

Reagan's Executive Order 12333 authorized domestic surveillance by the CIA.[7] Early in Reagan's term, the CIA ended the longstanding practice of providing background information briefings on intelligence matters to reporters.[8] A Reagan executive order in December 1981 provided an executive definition of "special activities," which enhanced the CIA's role in pursuing covert operations and made congressional oversight more difficult.[9]

The president promoted and signed into law in October 1984 legislation permitting the CIA director to close "operational files" from public scrutiny under the Freedom of Information Act. In so doing, the president created a new exemption from the FOIA.[10]

One of the most controversial information control efforts by Reagan involved an attempt to stop leaks of classified information. On 12 January 1982 Reagan spokesman David Gergen held a briefing for reporters in which he delivered the following presidential statement:

> Unauthorized disclosure of classified information under the jurisdiction of the National Security Council and of classified intelligence reports is a problem of major proportions within the U.S. Government. The Constitution of the United States provides for the protection of individual rights and liberties, including freedom of speech and freedom of the press, but it also requires that Government functions be discharged efficiently and effectively, especially where the national security is involved. As President of the United States, I am responsible for honoring both constitutional requirements, and I intend to do so in a balanced and careful manner. I do not believe, however, that the Constitution entitles Government employees, entrusted with confidential information critical to the functioning and effectiveness of the Government, to disclose such information with impunity. Yet this is precisely the situation we have. It must not be allowed to continue.[11]

As Stephen Hess reports, the presidential statement then specified new policies. For example, " 'all contacts' with reporters in which classified information was to be discussed would require the 'advance approval of a senior official' and must be followed by a memorandum outlining 'all information provided to the media representatives.' Fewer officials would have access to intelligence documents." The administration would investigate unauthorized disclosures to determine the sources of national security leaks.[12]

Because of a severely negative press reaction, National Security Adviser William Clark issued new procedures on 2 February 1982, superseding the 12 January 1982 presidential order.[13] In effect, the more controversial elements of the order—controls on interviews and investigating leaks by "all legal methods"—were deleted. Nonetheless, the incident further revealed the extent to which the Reagan administration wanted to control access to information.

Other secrecy measures included the Intelligence Identities Protection Act of 1982, which prohibited intentional disclosure of the identities of covert agents and specified punishments for offenders.[14] The administration imposed costs on Freedom of Information Act requests, in part to discourage such requests. The fees could only be waived if the request clearly met a "public interest" standard based on several qualifying criteria.[15] The administration sought to exempt certain materials from FOIA requests by maintaining that the Privacy Act of 1974 precluded release of those materials.[16]

The administration's invasion of Grenada resulted in widespread criticism of excessive secrecy. During the early stages of the invasion, journalists could only move as close as Barbados, 160 miles northeast of Grenada. Two days passed before the military escorted a group of journalists to Grenada. Reporters fumed that they had been "left in the dark" and denied due access to the military action.[17] The administration argued that it did not want to endanger the military operation or the lives of journalists by escorting reporters to the attack. Critics of the policy maintained that the administration actually intended to cover up embarrassing information about the operation.

To accept the views of leading journalists, the Reagan administration went to unprecedented lengths to maintain and promote secrecy about its actions. *Newsday* managing editor Anthony Marro wrote that Reagan's administration went "well beyond other recent administrations in its attempts to bottle up information, to prevent public access to government officials and records, to threaten and intimidate the bureaucracy in order to dry up sources of information, and to prevent the press and public from learning how the government is functioning."[18] *Los Angeles Times* Washington bureau chief Jack Nelson complained that Reagan had "set a policy and tone for secrecy in government that exceeds anything since Watergate. In fact, not even during the Nixon years were so many steps taken to establish secrecy as government policy."[19]

Despite a penchant for secrecy, the administration never made a strong case for executive privilege. In an administration that showed no reluctance to control information, the lack of a strong stand on, or defense of, executive privilege is telling. Four cases of executive privilege in the Reagan administration demonstrate that this constitutional doctrine fared poorly even during the Reagan years.

Four Cases of Executive Privilege

The Department of the Interior and the
Mineral Lands Leasing Act, 1981–1982[20]

The first significant executive privilege controversy during the Reagan years occurred in the president's first year in office and put Department of the Interior Secretary James G. Watt in the national spotlight. In 1981 the Subcommittee on Oversight and Investigations of the House Committee on Energy and Commerce had been investigating the Mineral Lands Leasing Act (30 U.S.C. Sec. 181) because of a significant number of takeovers of American companies by foreign interests. The cabinet secretary responsible for implementation of the act had control over documents sought by the congressional investigating committee.

Secretary Watt determined that thirty-one requested documents contained sensitive information and he refused to supply them to Congress. The subcommittee responded with a subpoena on 28 September 1981, raising the stakes of the conflict.

The president requested the opinion of Attorney General William French Smith regarding the executive's right to withhold the contested documents. A 13 October 1981 letter from the attorney general to the president cited the necessity of an assertion of executive privilege over the documents. The attorney general offered a standard defense of executive privilege based on the needs to protect White House confidentiality and national interests. The letter stated the following: "All of the documents at issue are either necessary and fundamental to the deliberative process presently ongoing in the Executive Branch or relate to sensitive foreign policy considerations."[21]

Smith emphasized that internal staff discussions about unsettled issues would be compromised by public release of the documents. Furthermore, the documents contained the views of Canadian government officials expressed in confidence. Smith cited the landmark *U.S. v. Nixon* case as supportive of a claim of executive privilege in this instance. He concluded that "release of these documents would seriously impair the deliberative process and the conduct of foreign policy. There is, therefore, a strong public interest in withholding the documents from congressional scrutiny at this time."[22]

Smith's opinion went beyond a defense of executive privilege on mere confidentiality and national interest concerns. He maintained that by demanding confidential documents, members of Congress were trying to become participants in executive branch decision-making processes. Perhaps more provocatively, Smith alleged that Congress lacked a strong interest in executive branch information when requested merely for investigatory purposes:

> The interest of Congress in obtaining information for oversight purposes is, I believe, considerably weaker than its interest when specific legislative proposals are in question. . . . [T]he congressional oversight interest will support a demand for predecisional, deliberative documents in the possession of the Executive Branch only in the most unusual circumstances.[23]

The next day, 14 October 1981, Watt appeared before the subcommittee and submitted a memorandum from the president asserting executive privilege over the thirty-one contested documents. Watt also furnished the subcommittee with a copy of the attorney general's opinion. Watt further refused to answer subcommittee members' questions about matters pertaining to the documents. The president refused a subsequent request to release the documents.

The subcommittee did not accept the claim of executive privilege as valid. It solicited and received an opinion of the general counsel to the clerk of the House refuting the attorney general's legal opinion on executive privilege.[24] On 9 February 1982 the subcommittee voted to hold Watt in contempt and referred the conflict to the full committee. On 25 February 1982 the Committee on Energy and Commerce passed a resolution recommending that Watt be cited by the full House for contempt of Congress.

At this stage, the administration had the option to weigh the importance of protecting these documents against the likelihood of a House citation for contempt and further executive-legislative feuding over the matter. The administration decided to resolve the issue in Congress's favor and on 18 March 1982 made the contested documents available to the subcommittee for review. On 15 September 1982 the Committee on Energy and Commerce unanimously voted not to bring the contempt citation to the full House.

Having made a strong initial case for executive privilege, the administration backed down when pushed by Congress. Despite its claim that confidentiality and national interests were at stake, the administration decided instead to accommodate the legislature. The Justice Department did not take part in the negotiations resulting in the settlement. Assistant Attorney General Theodore Olson, who had written to the full committee chair expressing the administration's position and had appeared with Secretary Watt before the subcommittee on 14 October 1981, opposed the settlement terms.[25] The Reagan administration had decided in favor of a short-term political accommodation over defending a constitutional prerogative of the executive.

The EPA and Superfund, 1982–1983[26]

The most contentious debate over executive privilege in the Reagan administration concerned the refusal of the Environmental Protection Agency (EPA) to release to Congress certain documents pertaining to agency enforcement of hazardous waste laws (particularly "Superfund" cleanup regulations). Once again, the Oversight and Investigations Subcommittee of the House Committee on Energy and Commerce played a central role in the controversy. In 1982 that subcommittee had been investigating the agency's implementation of hazardous waste laws and had become frustrated by delays and nonresponses when requesting data on EPA efforts.

The Subcommittee on Investigations and Oversight of the House Public Works and Transportation Committee experienced similar difficulties in its own examination of EPA enforcement of hazardous waste laws. A pattern developed in which the EPA released some requested documents and the Justice Department forbade the release of others. The Justice Department assessed that it had the duty to protect the administration from undesired disclosure of sensitive materials by individual agencies. In this case, the Justice Department maintained that law enforcement efforts could be undermined by public disclosure of "enforcement sensitive" documents. The department did not want the EPA alone to determine which documents met the criterion of "enforcement sensitive."

On 21 October 1982 the chair of the House Committee on Energy and

Commerce, Rep. John Dingell (D-Mich.), issued a subpoena to EPA administrator Anne Gorsuch[27] directing her to appear before the committee with certain documents. The second investigating subcommittee, chaired by Rep. Elliot Levitas (D-Ga.), subpoenaed Gorsuch on 22 November 1982 to obtain withheld documents.

Despite Gorsuch's protests, the Justice Department urged the president to assert executive privilege over the documents. The White House counsel, Fred Fielding, assured Gorsuch that, unlike the Watt controversy, the administration would stand solidly behind this claim of executive privilege.

On 30 November 1982 President Reagan sent to the EPA a memorandum with an attached copy of a letter to Dingell from the attorney general "setting forth the historic position of the Executive Branch, with which I concur, that sensitive documents found in open law enforcement files should not be made available to Congress or the public except in extraordinary circumstances." The president instructed Gorsuch and her colleagues "not to furnish copies of this category of documents to the Subcommittees in response to their subpoenas."[28]

That same day, the attorney general issued a response to the two subcommittee chairs defending the administration's assertion of executive privilege. In this case, the attorney general did not cite traditional national security or foreign policy concerns as justification for executive privilege. Instead, he emphasized the sensitive nature of "internal deliberations" and the need to keep secret "prosecutorial strategy."[29] The letter also specified the president's official policy toward executive privilege, which had been issued on 4 November 1982.[30]

On 2 December 1982 Gorsuch appeared before the Levitas subcommittee and conveyed the president's insistence on asserting executive privilege. The subcommittee responded by voting Gorsuch in contempt. On 10 December 1982 the House Public Works Committee voted as well to hold her in contempt. The House of Representatives voted 259–105 on 16 December 1982 to find her in contempt of Congress. Within a few moments of that vote, the Justice Department filed suit against the House of Representatives.[31] The U.S. district attorney would not, as specified in the contempt statute, "bring the matter before the grand jury for their action" while the suit against the House was pending.[32]

On 3 February 1983 the district court of the District of Columbia granted the defendants' motion to dismiss the suit. In so doing, the court encouraged the two branches "to settle their differences without further judicial involvement."[33] The court did not address the claim of executive privilege but explained that "[i]f these two co-equal branches maintain their present adversarial positions, the Judicial Branch will be required to resolve the dispute by determining the validity of the Administrator's claim of executive privilege."[34]

Two weeks after the court dismissal of the suit, the administration struck a bargain with the Levitas subcommittee, agreeing to allow limited disclosure of certain documents. Gorsuch advocated full disclosure, but the White House disagreed. Dingell did not consider the Levitas agreement acceptable and continued to press for full disclosure of the disputed documents. On 1 March 1982 Dingell wrote a strongly worded letter to the president requesting full disclosure and emphasizing that the investigation would continue until the White House released the disputed documents.

As with the Watt case, in an effort to put the controversy to rest, the White House accepted an agreement to release the disputed documents. On 9 March 1983 Gorsuch resigned her position as EPA administrator and the White House agreed to release its documents to the Dingell committee in much less limited form than anticipated by the agreement with the Levitas subcommittee. The U.S. attorney presented the Gorsuch contempt citation to a grand jury, which unanimously decided not to indict her.

Although the administration initially had taken a strong stand on executive privilege, it backed down in the face of mounting political pressure. The decision to compromise did not settle the executive privilege controversy. The House Committee on the Judiciary further investigated the Justice Department's role in the controversy and concluded that the department had misused executive privilege by advocating the withholding of documents that had not been thoroughly reviewed.[35] The committee also alleged that the department withheld documents to cover up wrongdoing at EPA.[36] The administration's compromise served as a temporary political expedient that eventually allowed Congress to examine previously withheld documents and draw broader conclusions about the

exercise of executive privilege. Reagan may have won a temporary re-
prieve from political pressures, but he had lost ground in his effort to establish the viability of the doctrine of executive privilege.

The Rehnquist Memoranda, 1986[37]

On 17 June 1986 President Reagan nominated Associate Justice of the
Supreme Court William H. Rehnquist for the position of chief justice. The
president selected Rehnquist to replace retiring Chief Justice Warren
Burger. Reagan nominated federal appeals court judge Antonin Scalia to
fill the associate justice position opened up by Rehnquist's move to chief
justice.

Although eventually confirmed by the Senate, Rehnquist's nomination
was not without controversy. Members of the Senate Judiciary Committee requested Justice Department documents that Rehnquist had written
as the head of the Nixon administration Office of Legal Counsel. Rehnquist had no objection to his earlier memos being made available to the
committee. Nonetheless, the Reagan Justice Department refused to turn
over the memos and President Reagan invoked executive privilege to protect the documents that contained confidential legal advice.

With a Republican-controlled Senate, the administration may have felt
safe in invoking executive privilege in this case. Unfortunately for Reagan, a majority of the Judiciary Committee—eight Democrats and two
Republicans—said that they wanted to review the contested documents.
It became apparent that the committee had the votes to subpoena the
documents and even to delay the Rehnquist and Scalia confirmation proceedings. Members of the Reagan Justice Department disagreed on the
course of action to follow. Some advocated battling the Judiciary Committee all the way to the judicial branch. Others urged accommodation.

After several days of negotiations, the president waived his claim of executive privilege over the documents. The Justice Department and Judiciary Committee agreed upon an arrangement in which certain documents would be reviewed by selected senators and staff members.
Although the president had again backed away from an executive privilege claim, in this case he was able to ensure that a fairly narrow range of
documents would be made available rather than a comprehensive set of

documents from Rehnquist's tenure at the Nixon Justice Department. Judiciary Committee Democrats boasted that they had secured access to the most critical documents. The Justice Department spokesman also claimed victory for having limited the senators' access to only certain documents.

The controversy ended when senators expressed satisfaction that the Rehnquist memos contained no damaging information that would undermine his confirmation. Reagan may have weakened somewhat his claim to executive privilege by turning over specific documents, but he understood the implications of not giving in somewhat to the senators opposing his claim: a potentially serious threat to the Rehnquist and Scalia confirmations as well as another congressional subpoena of executive branch documents.

The President's Diaries, 1987[38]

Although some critics of the Reagan presidency went so far as to compare the Iran-contra controversy to the Watergate scandal, a major difference between presidential handling of these crises deserves to be acknowledged: whereas President Nixon conspired in a cover-up of executive branch wrongdoing, President Reagan cooperated with the congressional investigation. In all, the Reagan administration furnished over three hundred thousand White House, State Department, Defense Department, CIA, and Justice Department documents to Congress. The investigating committees deposed numerous executive branch officials. The president waived executive privilege for executive branch officials who testified before Congress.[39] The president had vowed to cooperate fully with the investigations: "I recognize fully the interest of Congress in this matter and the fact that in performing its important oversight and legislative role, Congress will want to inquire into what occurred. We will cooperate with these inquiries."[40]

The issue of executive privilege surfaced nonetheless when Chief of Staff Donald Regan revealed before the Senate Select Committee on Intelligence that the president kept a personal diary primarily for the purpose of aiding the future writing of his memoirs. Committee members raised the issue of access to the diaries, which contained some recollections of the Iran-contra affair. Regan protested that the president's diaries were purely personal, not subject to disclosure. The White House initially took the position as well that a president's diaries were personal and that disclosure of them "would infringe on the privacy of the president and others."[41]

A battle over executive privilege appeared imminent. Senator George Mitchell (D-Maine) declared the privacy issue irrelevant. "The decision ought not to be whether they are personal or not, but . . . whether they are relevant to our investigation, whether they shed light on answers to questions the committee wants."[42]

Assistant Attorney General William Bradford Reynolds offered a strong defense of executive privilege, arguing that acquiescence to congressional demands for information is tantamount to "near abdication" of the executive's constitutional powers.[43] That Reynolds' comments were made during the controversy over Reagan's diaries led to speculation about how the administration would resolve the controversy. Clearly, many members of the Reagan administration had urged the president to take an affirmative stand on executive privilege over his personal diaries.

On 2 February 1987 White House spokesman Marlin Fitzwater said that Reagan's notes were "very personal in nature," leading the White House to favor nondisclosure.[44] "There is a concern for invasion of the president's privacy and the privacy of others," Fitzwater explained. He added that the White House counsel and special counselor had determined that Reagan's notes were not relevant to the congressional inquiries. Soon after making these comments Fitzwater learned that the president decided not to assert executive privilege over his diaries. In his second statement Fitzwater emphasized the White House position of full cooperation with the investigation and added that "the president wants to get to the bottom of the matter and fix what went wrong."[45]

Perhaps no action by Reagan did more to harm the constitutional doctrine of executive privilege than to establish the precedent of turning over his personal diaries. If such materials are not entitled to protection, it is hard to imagine executive privilege being accepted for anything but the most compelling national security information. Even if Congress had subpoenaed the diaries, it is most likely the courts would have favored the president's claim of privilege. Although the *U.S. v. Nixon* case made clear that in a criminal investigation a president must supply subpoenaed evidence, the law makes no such absolute claim for congressional sub-poenas. In this case, as well as the earlier ones, Reagan chose not to defend his prerogatives and instead sought the most expedient solution to his immediate political problems.

Executive Privilege in the Reagan Administration

Although President Reagan invoked executive privilege on several occasions, he never fully exercised that power. When confronted by congressional demands for information, Reagan generally followed a pattern of initial resistance followed by accommodation of Congress's request. Reagan never made a concerted effort to defend his prerogative in this area. As a result, he further weakened a constitutional presidential power that already had lost stature because of Watergate. Because of Nixon's use of executive privilege to cover up White House wrongdoing, subsequent efforts to invoke that doctrine have been characterized as Nixonian attempts to conceal and deceive. Consequently, even an administration that went to great lengths to establish secrecy measures was reluctant to make a strong case for executive privilege.

The Reagan experiences also show that any effort to adopt a statutory definition or limitation on executive privilege would be frivolous. Limitations on the exercise of that power are provided for by the traditional separation of powers doctrine in which each branch employs whatever powers it has to resist encroachments by another branch. Congress has available many means by which to resist the exercise of executive privilege. For example, it can issue subpoenas, delay confirmation hearings, withhold support for administration programs, issue contempt citations, or even try to impeach the president. As the Reagan examples show, when Congress feels strongly about disclosure of executive branch information, it can force the president into a very difficult situation.

The president, of course, has the option of further resisting Congress's demands. He can even allow the dispute to rise to the level of a constitutional crisis to be decided at the judicial level. Reagan did not do that. He sought accommodations with Congress that would resolve his short-term political problems. A more vigorous defense of the constitutional doctrine of executive privilege will have to await another presidency.

GEORGE BUSH, 1989–1993

George Bush's presidency provides an important contrast to that of Ronald Reagan's. Despite his experience as the two-term vice president to Reagan, Bush brought a different leadership style to the White House. Whereas Reagan articulated effectively a philosophy of governance that provided some degree of coherence to his various programs, Bush expressed discomfort with what he called the "vision thing" and never clearly defined his administration's policy goals. Whereas Reagan was content to leave the details of governance to others, Bush practiced a more "hands-on" approach to presidential leadership. Furthermore, whereas Reagan came to the Oval Office as an outsider committed to change, Bush was the consummate Washington insider who sought to work within the system.

These differences in leadership style had important implications for how each administration tried to manage controversy over executive privilege. Reagan presented a formal memorandum outlining his administration's policy on executive privilege. When controversy over executive privilege arose, his administration responded by articulating constitutional principles regarding the prerogatives of the presidency. In the face of opposition from Congress as well as media criticism, Reagan backed down from his principled stands.

By contrast, Bush never issued a formal policy on executive privilege and he did not make any concerted effort to articulate constitutional principles as the bases for his actions. Bush's response to executive privilege controversies was never dogmatic; it tended to be bureaucratic: find some way to work around the problem without raising the level of conflict. Bush consequently had more success at withholding information than did his predecessor.

Bush's Policy on Executive Privilege

The Bush administration never adopted its own formal policy on the use of executive privilege. Instead, the 4 November 1982 Reagan memorandum on executive privilege remained in effect as the official Bush administration procedures on exercising that constitutional authority.

The Bush approach to executive privilege differed substantially from

Reagan's. Whereas the Reagan administration on several occasions boldly proclaimed its constitutional prerogative to assert executive privilege, and then had to back down in the face of congressional and popular opposition, the Bush administration adopted a much more politically feasible strategy toward that doctrine. Bush maintained in theory the Reagan policy of requiring the president personally to approve the use of executive privilege. His administration withheld information from Congress on many occasions without invoking executive privilege—in effect, without calling attention to the controversial doctrine. In brief, Bush's strategy was to further the cause of withholding information by invoking executive privilege only if absolutely necessary.

Perhaps there is no stronger indication of how far the doctrine of executive privilege has fallen into political disrepute than how the Bush administration sought to secure all of the benefits of governmental secrecy without making a case for this presidential power. Bush understood that to draw too much attention to the controversial doctrine only would have the effect that his predecessor experienced: public confrontations with Congress, congressional contempt citations, and critical media coverage of executive branch secrecy.

On many occasions, rather than invoke executive privilege, the Bush administration used other names for justifying withholding information or cited some other source of authority for doing the same. Among the phrases and justifications often used to defend withholding of information were "deliberative process privilege," "attorney-client privilege," "attorney work product," "internal departmental deliberations," "deliberations of another agency," "secret opinions policy," "sensitive law enforcement materials," and "ongoing criminal investigations."

These phrases and justifications are not all original to the Bush administration. Numerous administrations have, for example, withheld documents pertaining to "ongoing criminal investigations" in the Department of Justice without specifically citing executive privilege. What is telling, though, is the extent to which the Bush administration went to cloak the use of executive privilege under different names. As the chief investigator to the House Committee on the Judiciary, Jim Lewin, explained, "Bush was more clever than Reagan when it came to executive privilege. You have to remember that Bush really was our first bureaucrat president. He knew how to work the system. He avoided formally claiming executive privilege and instead called it other things. In reality, executive privilege was in full force and effect during the Bush years, probably more so than under Reagan."[46]

The Bush administration further downplayed, and hence weakened, the doctrine of executive privilege by failing to articulate or defend any constitutional arguments for its exercise. Bush was content to effectively concede the constitutional issues over executive privilege to the opponents to satisfy his short-term political need to avoid constitutional conflict while at the same time blocking congressional committees and the public from attaining certain information.

None of this is to suggest that Bush either did not believe in or never personally invoked executive privilege. On a few occasions Bush resorted to executive privilege when no other option was available to achieve the purpose of withholding information.

Bush's Exercise of Executive Privilege

Although President Bush never established his own formal procedures for using executive privilege, a number of controversies during his presidency bring to light how his administration exercised that power in a crafty, even hidden-hand, fashion.

The "Kmiec Memo," 1989

The first executive privilege statement by the Bush administration never involved the president and did not result in any substantive policy decision. On 24 March 1989 the assistant attorney general in the Department of Justice office of legal counsel, Douglas M. Kmiec, issued a memorandum proclaiming that under the doctrine of executive privilege, inspectors general are not obligated to provide to Congress "confidential information about an open criminal investigation."[47] Oddly enough, Kmiec did not issue the opinion memorandum in reaction to any specific controversy between the Bush administration and Congress. Nobody from the Bush administration requested the opinion. In fact, Kmiec offered the opinion as a response to a 3 June 1987 Reagan administration inquiry into how inspectors general should respond to congressional demands for information.[48] It is unclear why Kmiec—who held his Department of Justice position in both the Reagan and Bush administrations —waited almost two years to respond to the inquiry, after a change in administrations.

The Kmiec memo provided a brief historical justification for the doctrine of executive privilege. Furthermore, it stated that "Congress has a limited interest in the conduct of an ongoing criminal investigation and the executive branch has a strong interest in preserving the confidentiality of such investigations. Accordingly, in light of established executive branch policy and practice, and absent extraordinary circumstances, an IG should not provide Congress with confidential information concerning an open criminal investigation."[49]

In terms of influencing Bush administration use of executive privilege, the Kmiec memo amounted to nothing. General Counsel to the Clerk of the House Steven R. Ross and Deputy General Counsel Charles Tiefer responded that congressional committees did indeed have the "authority to obtain information on agency waste, fraud, and wrongdoing, from Inspectors General as from other agency officers. The Kmiec memo represents a gratuitous and unjustified break with a clear historic tradition and attempts to put aside explicit statutory language. It should [be] regarded as simply an error."[50] As Tiefer later explained, the Kmiec memo represented nothing more than an "abstract statement" that had no bearing on official policy or administration action. Indeed, during the Bush years, Congress met no resistance from inspectors general in its various requests for information.[51]

The Reagan Diaries, 1990[52]

The Bush administration reluctantly asserted executive privilege over the personal diaries of Ronald Reagan when the former national security adviser, John M. Poindexter, sought access to portions of those materials. Poindexter needed the Reagan diaries for the purpose of substantiating the claim that Reagan had authorized certain activities in the Iran-contra affair.

On 30 January 1990 a federal district court judge, Harold H. Greene, ordered Reagan to turn over to Poindexter excerpts from the diaries. Reagan's attorneys had been attempting since November 1989 to persuade Greene to cancel a subpoena for the diaries sought by the Poindexter defense. Greene instead ordered that the diary excerpts be released and gave Reagan's attorneys until 5 February 1990 to challenge that decision with an assertion of executive privilege. Greene had privately reviewed the Reagan diary excerpts and determined "that some but not all the diary entries produced in response to various subpoena categories are relevant to defendant's claim."[53]

On 2 February 1990 the Bush administration Department of Justice moved in federal court to delay the order that Reagan's diary excerpts be produced for Poindexter's Iran-contra trial. The department did so to keep Reagan's attorneys from having to assert executive privilege. The department maintained that the court order could become a "significant intrusion into what are probably a president's most personal records," possibly resulting in a "serious constitutional confrontation."[54]

The tactic failed and on 5 February 1990 Reagan asserted executive privilege over the diaries. In the attorney's brief for Reagan, the former president's lawyer, Theodore B. Olson, wrote that "these materials are the private reflections of the former president prepared for his personal deliberations and touch the core of the presidency."[55] The former president's spokesman maintained that Reagan had decided to invoke executive privilege to protect the privacy of future presidents.[56] In his formal motion to invoke executive privilege, Reagan maintained that he had no other choice because Judge Greene refused to disclose Poindexter's written statements of why the diary excerpts were important to the case, unless the former president claimed executive privilege.[57] Greene maintained that such a claim of executive privilege would require him to reexamine his earlier decision to compel release of the diary excerpts. In other words, Greene would have to determine whether the need for the excerpts in the trial must override any claim of executive privilege. The Bush administration followed by issuing its own claim of executive privilege over Reagan's diaries.

To further complicate the controversy, Judge Greene separately ordered Reagan to provide videotaped testimony in the Poindexter trial, giving the former president until 9 February 1990 to assert executive privilege and refuse to testify.

On that date, Reagan agreed to provide the videotaped testimony. The Bush administration Department of Justice that same day waived its claim of executive privilege in order to enable Reagan to present his testimony. Nonetheless, Judge Greene agreed to allow Reagan's attorneys and Bush administration lawyers to accompany the former president during the testimony so that they could advise him about when to refuse to answer questions on the grounds of executive privilege. Reagan's attorneys stated that the former president would defer to President Bush, "with respect to issues of executive privilege concerning national security or foreign affairs that may arise during the taking of the videotaped testimony."[58]

Reagan provided eight hours of videotaped testimony on 16 and 17 February 1990. He could not recall key events, information, and even some names in the Iran-contra affair and consequently did not provide any significant new information about the controversy.

On 21 March 1990 Judge Greene ruled in favor of the Reagan and the Bush administration claims of executive privilege over the diary excerpts. Greene had again privately reviewed the disputed diary entries and determined that they offered "no new insights" into the Iran-contra affair and, consequently, that the claims of executive privilege outweighed Poindexter's claim to need access to the diary entries. Greene determined that "the claims of executive privilege filed on behalf of the former president and of the incumbent president are sufficient under the facts presented here to defeat the defendant's demand." Furthermore, Poindexter's "showing of need for the diary excerpts and their indispensibility for the achievement of justice in this case is meager." He explained that Poindexter's case may have been stronger if Reagan had earlier refused to provide videotaped testimony. Greene made clear that he had overturned his earlier decision to compel release of the diary entries because of the assertions of executive privilege. He determined that "courts must exercise both deference and restraint when asked to issue coercive orders against a president's person or papers."[59]

The doctrine of executive privilege prevailed in this controversy. Significantly, it was Judge Greene, not the Reagan attorneys or the Bush administration, who forced the issue of executive privilege in this case. Reagan's attorneys avoided the use of the phrase "executive privilege" in their formal response to Judge Greene's deadline for asserting such authority as the basis for withholding the diary entries. The Bush administration initially tried to get around the issue of executive privilege, but the tactic failed to produce that result. When compelled to do so, Reagan's attorneys and the Bush administration claimed executive privilege.

The Persian Gulf War, 1990–1991

The Persian Gulf war raised many access-to-information controversies. As with any military operation, certain restrictions had to be placed on information about troop movements, campaign strategy, and weapons capabilities. The most controversial techniques for restricting military information were the journalist "pool system" and the "security review" process.

In brief, the pool system established specific rules governing how many journalists could cover events on the front lines, where the journalists could travel, and whom they could interview. Specifically, the U.S. military allowed selected journalists to travel to the front lines in groups of six or more persons to cover the war. The journalists had to travel with military escorts who then supervised the reporters' conversations with the troops. When the pool returned from what some journalists likened to a guided tour, all news stories and footage had to be submitted for a security review.[60] The U.S. military established this latter requirement to ensure that news reports did not disclose secret or sensitive information that could damage the allied war effort. The approved pool reports then would be shared among the press corps members stationed in Saudi Arabia.

The Bush administration did not use executive privilege as a basis for restricting press access to military information. Instead, the administration justified its many restrictions on the basis of national security concerns.

An executive privilege dispute did arise concerning congressional access to information regarding U.S.-Persian Gulf policy. On 3 January 1991 Rep. Barbara Boxer (D-Calif.) introduced in Congress a privileged resolution of inquiry, H.Res. 19, seeking specific information on Operation Desert Shield: the likelihood of a wider regional conflict in the Middle East; assessments of Iraqi military capabilities; projections of consequences of conflict on international oil supplies; assessments of U.S. vulnerabilities to terrorist attacks; information about U.S. efforts to seek support for Operation Desert Shield from other governments; memoranda of meetings between U.S. officials and foreign leaders; analyses of budgetary options for the military operation; analyses of postwar options for Iraq. The resolution called for the administration to provide all of this information within ten days.[61]

On 23 January 1991 the counsel to the President, C. Boyden Gray, responded as follows:

> The resolution requests extremely sensitive information that, if disclosed, could cause grave damage to the national security at this time of crisis in the Persian Gulf region.
>
> [The requested information concerns] some of our nation's most sensitive national security secrets, including war plans. Even indirect knowledge of those secrets, especially our war plans, would be of obvious use to Iraq in countering steps that the president has ordered, and may yet order, in accordance with H. J.Res. 77. It would be unconscionable to expose U.S. and coalition military personnel in the Persian Gulf region to the risks associated with disclosure of this kind of information.
>
> Because of the extraordinary sensitivity of such information, the courts have long recognized that the Constitution permits the president to protect such information from disclosure under the national security component of the executive privilege doctrine. This component of executive privilege also insulates from disclosure information relating to diplomatic discussions with foreign governments.
>
> Moreover, insofar as documents requested by H.Res. 19 reflect predecisional discussions, advice, recommendations, and budgetary or other analyses, they are also protected from disclosure by the deliberative process component of executive privilege.
>
> In short, we believe that enactment of H.Res. 19 would be contrary to the national interest, and that it would be unconstitutional.[62]

On 7 February 1991 the chairman of the House Committee on Foreign Affairs, Rep. Dante B. Fascell (D-Fla.), and the chairman of the House Committee on Armed Services, Rep. Les Aspin (D-Wisc.), wrote to President Bush requesting "a more responsive answer than the initial reply by Mr. Gray." The letter further requested that the information be presented in "timely fashion" so that Congress could fulfill its oversight responsibilities.[63]

Congress received much of the requested information, but too late to be used to assess administration policies. The White House dropped the use of executive privilege and accommodated Congress's request. On 20 February 1991 National Security Adviser Brent Scowcroft responded to the Fascell–Aspin letter by providing summary information from the White House, Department of Defense, and Department of State. He also explained that Central Intelligence Agency information relevant to the areas of inquiry would be provided separately in classified form. The White House presented the information in less detailed form than requested, but nonetheless dropped the use of executive privilege in response to congressional protest. Congress received much of the desired information and did not dispute the administration's final response that some details could not be provided given time constraints.[64] Widespread public support for Bush's military action also made Congress's efforts to compel release of all of the detailed information about the allied war effort politically difficult, to say the least. Consequently, the Bush administration was able to protect the information that it did not want to release without formally exercising executive privilege, without encouraging a constitutional conflict. Furthermore, by delaying a response to Boxer's request and then raising executive privilege, the Bush administration succeeded in denying Congress timely information that legislators could have used as a part of their decision-making process.

Department of Education and College Accreditation Standards, 1991[65]

In 1991 the Bush administration Department of Education challenged the use of cultural diversity standards in college accreditation decisions. Specifically, on 11 April 1991 Secretary of Education Lamar Alexander challenged the Middle States Association of Colleges and Schools practice of considering the degree of faculty, staff, and student diversity in colleges in deciding whether to grant accreditation. The Subcommittee on Human Resources and Intergovernmental Relations of the House Committee on Government Operations soon began an investigation into Alexander's controversial action. On 17 April 1991 the subcommittee chaired by Rep. Ted Weiss (D-N.Y.) requested Department of Education documents pertaining to Alexander's action.

Although the department furnished many of the requested documents, it also refused to supply others. On 7 May 1991 the department's general counsel, Edward Stringer, wrote to Weiss that certain documents had to be withheld from Congress. Stringer claimed the "attorney-client privilege" and "deliberative process privilege" as reasons for withholding documents.[66]

The subcommittee rejected these claims of privilege. Staff members of the subcommittee and of the Department of Education met on 13 May 1991 to try to resolve the dispute. No agreement could be reached and Stringer wrote another letter to Weiss to inform the chairman that the Department of Justice's office of legal counsel had advised the Department of Education to claim executive privilege over the documents.[67]

The next day the subcommittee rejected this use of executive privilege and voted 6–3, along party lines, to issue a subpoena for the disputed documents. The Department of Education chose not to fight the subpoena, withdrew its claim of executive privilege, and turned over to Congress all of the disputed documents.

President Bush never personally got involved in this controversy. Despite administration policy—carried over from the Reagan administration—that executive privilege could only be invoked either by the president or with his personal approval, the Department of Justice's office of legal counsel advised the Department of Education in this case to claim executive privilege. As the general counsel and the deputy general counsel to the clerk of the House wrote to Rep. Weiss,

> What was novel about this claim of privilege was the frankness with which the Office of Legal Counsel admitted that it was claiming executive privilege. The Justice Department's willingness to apply the term "executive privilege" to the decisional documents of a department, and to documents for which attorney-client privilege was attempted to be asserted, contrasts with other occasions when, for tactical reasons, the Justice Department has [devised] attempts at the withholding of similar records without admitting that it is really invoking executive privilege.[68]

The Department of Education had tried initially to devise other bases than executive privilege for withholding the documents before eventually claiming the constitutional doctrine. The trouble was, without presidential approval, the department had no legitimate grounds on which to assert executive privilege. President Bush obviously did not believe that the disputed documents were so important to protect from scrutiny that he was willing to risk a constitutional conflict over executive privilege.

Congress proved its ability to compel production of disputed documents through vigorous use of its authority to investigate and to subpoena evidence.

McDonnell Douglas A-12 Navy Aircraft Program Investigation, August–September 1991[69]

On 1 August 1991 the Subcommittee on Legislation and National Security of the House Committee on Government Operations unanimously voted to subpoena Secretary of Defense Richard Cheney for a document regarding cost overruns on the McDonnell Douglas A-12 navy aircraft program terminated in January 1991. The subcommittee, chaired by Rep. John Conyers (D-Mich.), gave Cheney until 9 August 1991 either to turn over the requested information or to respond to the subpoena.

On 8 August 1991 President Bush signed a memorandum to Cheney instructing the secretary of defense to claim executive privilege and, therefore, not to comply with the subpoena. The president instructed Cheney as follows:

> It is my decision that you should not release this document. Compelled release to Congress of documents containing confidential communications among senior Department officials would inhibit the candor necessary to the effectiveness of the deliberative process by which the Department makes decisions and recommendations concerning national defense, including recommendations to me as Commander-in-Chief. In my judgment, the release of the memorandum would be contrary to the national interest because it would discourage the candor that is essential to the Department's decision-making process. Therefore, I am compelled to assert executive privilege with respect to this memorandum and to instruct you not to release it to the subcommittee.[70]

What is interesting about this particular case is that although governmental appropriations—not national security concerns—were at issue, the Conyers committee chose not to challenge Bush's claim of executive privilege. Bush prevailed for a number of reasons. First, the White House successfully lobbied the minority party members of the Conyers committee to back the president after the assertion of executive privilege. Second, Conyers determined that with a committee divided along partisan lines there would be little support on Capitol Hill for a contempt citation against Cheney. Third, there would likely have been very little sentiment on Capitol Hill in favor of a contempt citation against Cheney, who happened to be a former House member and remained very popular in Congress.

Congress could claim only one small achievement in this battle over executive branch information. As a consequence of the Conyers committee's action the president personally claimed executive privilege and further established a precedent for the view that executive privilege only can be claimed or approved by the president himself, and not by any other member of the executive branch of government.

The Quayle Council and the FDA, 1991–1992[71]

In September 1991 the Human Resources and Intergovernmental Relations Subcommittee of the House Committee on Government Operations began an investigation into Food and Drug Administration (FDA) dealings with the Quayle Council on Competitiveness. In brief, the council had recommended a series of reforms of the FDA's drug approval process. The FDA accepted the recommendations, some of which were controversial.

The investigating subcommittee ran into difficulty receiving documents pertaining to the council's work on behalf of the FDA procedures. The FDA refused to provide certain documents that concerned "deliberative communications within the Council or otherwise reveal its deliberations."[72] On 13 November 1991 the subcommittee voted to subpoena the withheld documents and informed the FDA commissioner, David Kessler, that only the president could claim executive privilege over those materials. The subcommittee informed Kessler that he would be voted in contempt of Congress on 22 November 1991 if he did not deliver the disputed documents.

After several days of negotiation by the subcommittee with the White House counsel and the FDA, the White House decided against asserting executive privilege and agreed to release all of the disputed documents. The Bush administration gave in to the pressure from the subcommittee just one day before Kessler was to be held in contempt of Congress.

Unlike the Rocky Flats controversy (discussed hereafter), in this case the Bush administration, after weighing the relative risks associated with full disclosure and with nondisclosure, chose not to assert executive privilege. Congress succeeded again in forcing the issue of executive privilege from the cabinet level to the White House.

Rocky Flats Nuclear Weapons Plant Investigation, 1992[73]

In September 1992 the Subcommittee on Investigations and Oversight of the House Committee on Science, Space and Technology began seeking testimony from individuals with knowledge of a five-year FBI investigation into environmental crimes committed by Rockwell International at its Rocky Flats nuclear weapons plant in Golden, Colorado. Although ten criminal violations of environmental law had been acknowledged in the Rockwell plea bargain with the government, no individual culpability had been assigned. The subcommittee, chaired by Rep. Howard Wolpe (D-Mich.), subsequently became interested in examining the plea bargain.

The Department of Justice instructed certain individuals who had been called to testify before the Wolpe committee not to divulge various kinds of information pertaining to the Rocky Flats government investigations. For example, the department gave an FBI agent who investigated Rocky Flats instructions on what information to withhold. A department lawyer accompanied the man during a congressional inquiry to be sure that privileged information would not be compromised. The department similarly instructed the U.S. district attorney for Colorado and consequently he refused to cooperate with the congressional inquiry.

Wolpe responded by sending a letter to President Bush requesting that the president either personally assert executive privilege or direct the witnesses to the events to testify.[74] The president never responded to the request and consequently there was no presidential approval of the use of executive privilege in this case. The White House counsel, C. Boyden Gray, wrote to Wolpe to make clear that the White House had no intention of claiming executive privilege and that the Department of Justice and the investigating committee should work out their differences.[75]

Without presidential support for a claim of executive privilege, the Department of Justice could not withstand further pressure from Congress for candid testimony. The Wolpe committee threatened to hold the U.S. district attorney for Colorado in contempt of Congress unless certain conditions were met—most importantly, rescinding the Department of Justice "gag rule" over witnesses.[76] The Department of Justice agreed to the Wolpe committee's demands and waived all privileged information claims.[77]

What is noteworthy about this case is that the Department of Justice made privilege claims on behalf of the administration—without White House approval—and then backed down when the president would not support those claims. Congress used its powers of inquiry and subpoena to full effect in this case in order to get the information that it needed to carry out its investigative functions. Unlike the A-12 navy aircraft case, the president did not become personally involved, making it easier for Congress to prevail.

The Overseas Arrests Controversy, 1989–1992[78]

One of the most innovative secrecy devices of the Bush administration was the Department of Justice's "secret opinions policy." Under that policy, the department could refuse to show Congress legal memorandum opinions from the Office of Legal Counsel (OLC). The secret opinions policy itself was very controversial because Congress traditionally has not been denied access to OLC decision memoranda. During the Bush years, one such memorandum was especially controversial.

In 1989 the OLC issued an opinion entitled "Authority of the FBI to Override Customary or Other International Law in the Course of Extraterritorial Law Enforcement Activities." In brief, the memorandum—which overruled a 1980 Carter administration Department of Justice opinion—determined that the FBI could apprehend fugitives abroad without the permission of the host country. News of the memorandum resulted in congressional questions regarding the possible lack of statutory authority for such a policy and conflicts with international law.

Again, the administration made no claim of executive privilege when it refused to divulge the memorandum to Congress. It relied instead on the newly created "secret opinions policy," a position that Congress refused to accept as legitimate. Nonetheless, the last action taken by Congress was a Judiciary Committee vote to subpoena the memorandum. The issue had become more sensitive because of the January 1990 arrest of former Panamanian leader Manuel Antonio Noriega and the Department of Justice claim that disclosure of the memorandum could harm the government's case against the former dictator. The department also maintained that the attorney-client privilege would be violated by release of the memorandum because federal agencies in the future would become hesitant to rely on the department for confidential legal advice.

In the end, both sides "won." A Supreme Court decision upheld the practice of apprehending fugitive criminals in foreign territories. Furthermore, the Department of Justice and the House Committee on the Judiciary agreed to an arrangement whereby committee members could review, but not copy, department documents pertaining to the memorandum as well as the memorandum itself. The committee declared itself victorious and the Bush administration, no longer able to keep the information from Congress, leaked the full memorandum to the *Washington Post*.

INSLAW Documents Controversy, 1991–1992[79]

One government secrecy controversy that remains unresolved concerns a congressional investigation into allegations that Reagan administration Department of Justice officials conspired to force the INSLAW computer company into bankruptcy and to then have INSLAW's leading software product bought by another company. When a subcommittee of the House Committee on the Judiciary sought documents regarding the INSLAW controversy, the Bush administration initially refused to release the documents, citing the "attorney-client privilege." The Bush White House never formally asserted executive privilege over these documents, although it did consider that option.[80] Instead, after a subcommittee subpoena of the disputed documents and a vote of the full committee to do the same, the Department of Justice chose to partially comply with congressional demands. The department turned over the vast majority of requested materials, yet refused to turn over every document relevant to the congressional inquiry.

The Bush Department of Justice adopted the position that, in ongoing proceedings in which members of the department itself are involved, certain materials must be protected by the traditional attorney-client relationship. Therefore, even though Congress has the power of inquiry, the prerogative of the attorney-client relationship during ongoing proceedings must override that power. Furthermore, Congress's power of inquiry is more compelling when a dispute involves legislation than when a dispute concerns the ongoing operations of another branch of government.

There has been no formal resolution to this interbranch dispute. The Bush administration never fully complied with the congressional subpoenas and furthermore declared numerous requested documents "missing." Consequently, the Bush administration partially succeeded in withholding information from Congress without any presidential assertion of executive privilege; Congress partially succeeded in gaining access to disputed executive branch documents. More recently, the Clinton administration Justice Department has been reviewing INSLAW documents in order to edit and remove materials pertaining to national security.

Executive Privilege in the Bush Administration

The Bush administration demonstrated that it may be easier to withhold information in the post-Watergate environment by not asserting executive privilege. Instead, avoid the controversial doctrine, to the extent possible, and claim other justifications for withholding materials.

Bush did not avoid the use of executive privilege altogether. He personally instructed the use of executive privilege in one information dispute with Congress (the A-12 navy aircraft controversy) and reluctantly claimed executive privilege to protect his predecessor's diaries from a court subpoena.

More often than not, Bush avoided the controversial doctrine. On a number of occasions, when lower-level officials claimed executive privilege, Bush chose not to personally approve the use of that doctrine and instead accommodated Congress's demands (e.g., the Persian Gulf war document request, the Quayle Council controversy, the Rocky Flats dispute, the overseas arrests memorandum controversy, the INSLAW investigation). Even though Congress claimed victory in some of these informational disputes, administration efforts to withhold information often succeeding in denying Congress timely access to materials.

In general, during the Bush years, Congress achieved at least a partial victory when it challenged administration exercise of secrecy policies. But Congress did not, and could not, challenge every such exercise. Although Congress achieved its goal of having the controversial overseas arrests memorandum made public, it was able to do so only after having learned unexpectedly of the existence of such a policy memorandum. The Bush administration Department of Justice "secret opinions policy" shielded vast amounts of information from congressional and public scrutiny. Consequently, the administration lost some information battles with Congress, but it won the information "war" by employing innovative and far-reaching secrecy devices, using executive privilege cautiously, and denying the timely release of information.

THE POST-WATERGATE PRESIDENCY

When it comes to the use of executive privilege, the post-Watergate presidents have had to operate in the shadow of Richard M. Nixon. The abuse of executive privilege in the Nixon White House made the exercise of that power very difficult for subsequent administrations. The examination of post-Watergate executive privilege controversies reveals the following:

- Because of the taint of Watergate, presidents have been reluctant to exercise certain constitutional prerogatives, such as executive privilege.

- No post-Watergate president, not even Jimmy Carter, has rejected outright the legitimacy of executive privilege. Every one has considered that power a legitimate presidential prerogative and has exercised that power at one time or another.

- Successive presidential administrations, Republican and Democrat alike, have tried to find ways to achieve all the benefits of executive privilege while avoiding, when possible, the use of the phrase "executive privilege."

- Because of Watergate, Congress has become especially vigilant in its attempts to constrain presidential exercise of prerogative powers. Consequently, Congress is less deferential to claims of executive privilege than it used to be.

- No post-Watergate administration has been willing to take an aggressive posture toward executive privilege to reestablish the political viability of that constitutional doctrine. Clearly, each administration has perceived the political costs to be too great.

The United States needs to return to a pre-Watergate understanding of the legitimacy of executive privilege in our constitutional order. This understanding is informed by the writings of the American founders and the historical exercise of executive privilege, and refined somewhat by the lessons of the post-Watergate era. In brief, it was far better when the legitimacy of executive privilege was widely accepted and a certain trust was placed in elected officials to exercise their constitutional responsibilities and powers judiciously. It is unhealthful to the political system to have executive branch officials developing duplicitous schemes to withhold information without using executive privilege. It is time to reestablish the unarguable constitutional legitimacy of executive privilege among members of Congress, the executive branch, the public, and the news media (the courts have not wavered in conferring the constitutional stamp of legitimacy), and, consequently, to return to an earlier understanding of how this particular executive prerogative can best be exercised and constrained.

CHAPTER 6

Resolving the Dilemma

★————————————————————————★

The dilemma of executive privilege is that of permitting governmental secrecy in a political system predicated on leadership accountability. On the surface, the dilemma is a complex one to resolve: How can democratically elected leaders be held accountable by the public when they are able to deliberate in secret or to make secretive decisions?

The evidence shows that presidential exercise of the doctrine of executive privilege fits comfortably within the embrace of our constitutional system. That constitutional doctrine has evolved over the course of our history and traditionally has been accepted by the coordinate branches of government as a legitimate executive branch power.

Nonetheless, in more recent years, the doctrine of executive privilege has fallen into disrepute because of the leadership abuses of one presidency. Members of Congress consequently show little or no deference to presidential exercise of executive privilege. Presidential administrations seek various means for withholding information, oftentimes by disguising executive privilege. The pattern of executive branch recriminations against legislators for meddling where they don't belong and legislative branch accusations that executive branch failure to divulge all information constitutes criminal activity has been unhealthful to our governing system. Currently there appears to be a lack of recognition by the political branches of each other's legitimate powers and interests in the area of governmental secrecy. To restore some sense of comity and cooperation between the political branches on issues of executive branch secrecy, the following points must be recognized.

First, executive privilege is a legitimate constitutional doctrine validated by the writings of the constitutional Framers, broad residual executive powers contained in Article II of the Constitution, historical exercise, congressional acceptance, and judicial opinion. The weight of the evidence clearly refutes the assertion that executive privilege is a "constitutional myth." Consequently, presidential administrations should not be devising schemes for achieving the ends of executive privilege while avoiding any mention of the constitutional doctrine. Furthermore, Congress must recognize that the executive branch—like the legislative and judicial branches—has a legitimate need to deliberate in secret and that not every assertion of executive privilege is automatically a devious attempt to conceal wrongdoing.

Second, executive privilege is not an unlimited, unfettered presidential power. Executive privilege should be exercised only rarely and for the most compelling reasons. Congress has the right—and often the duty—to challenge presidential assertions of executive privilege when such assertions clearly are not related to such legitimate needs as protecting national security or the candor of internal deliberations.

Third, there are no clear, precise constitutional boundaries that determine, a priori, whether any particular claim of executive privilege is legitimate. The resolution to the dilemma of executive privilege is found in the political ebb and flow of our separation of powers system. There is, in fact, no need for any precise definition of the constitutional boundaries surrounding executive privilege. Such a power cannot be subject to precise definition because it is impossible to determine in advance all of the circumstances under which presidents may have to exercise that power. A return to the traditional separation of powers theory provides the appropriate resolution to the dilemma of executive privilege and democratic accountability.

RESOLVING THE DILEMMA: THE SEPARATION OF POWERS

In response to such a constitutional dilemma as posed by presidential use of executive privilege, it is often tempting to try to devise a remedy that would eliminate any potential future conflict. The preeminent critic of executive privilege, Raoul Berger, believes that there is just one answer to the question of how to resolve this constitutional dilemma: eliminate the source of power from which the dilemma originates. In Berger's view, "secrecy in the operations of government is an abomination."[1] Berger concludes that the case of the Nixon presidency proves that point. Under the Nixon presidency, Berger writes, " 'confidentiality' was the vehicle for the cover-up of criminal acts and conspiracies by [Nixon's] aides, an instrument he repeatedly employed to the obstruction of justice."[2]

Berger's assessment of Nixon's exercise of executive privilege is unarguable. Yet many of the critiques of executive privilege—within both Congress and the academic community—focus on the incredible abuses of a single presidency. Generalizing from the abuses of power in the Nixon White House, many critics of executive privilege maintain that, therefore, there must be completely open deliberations within the executive branch of government (a position never adopted even by the "open" presidencies of Gerald R. Ford or Jimmy Carter). These critics, while having identified an undeniable problem, call for simplistic, blanket solutions. That is, if such a power as executive privilege can potentially be abused, then it must be eliminated in favor of completely open, public deliberations. They perceive such openness as the only means by which to assure accountability from the executive branch.[3]

Underlying this argument against executive privilege is the view that Congress must always be supreme in the lawmaking process given the need for democratic accountability and the specific powers conferred upon the legislative branch by Article I of the Constitution. Some scholars see no exceptions to that rule. Berger dismisses the existence of residual or prerogative powers for the president, even in foreign affairs and emergency situations. David Gray Adler argues that the Constitution makes Congress the supreme branch in the conduct of foreign policy and war. "The president is vested with only modest authority in this area and is clearly only of secondary importance."[4] Adler maintains that the end of the Cold War eliminates any rationale for executive preeminence in foreign policy.[5]

James W. Ceaser argues that the belief that Congress must always be supreme in the lawmaking process, even at the expense of tying the hands of the executive during times of emergency, "is based on a narrow and legalistic understanding of the Constitution and on a failure to recognize the real purpose for which the founders adopted the theory of separation of powers."[6] The failure to understand or to accept the founders' theory of the separation of powers has resulted in the quest for absolutes on the issue of executive privilege. Modern-day congressionalists seek ways to deny presidential powers because such powers can be abused. The congressionalists subsequently elevate the exception—the abuse of power—into the rule, leading to the call for broad, sweeping solutions.

Many of former president Nixon's defenders, on the other hand, elaborated the equally suspect argument that Congress and the public have no authority to limit and constrain the exercise of executive powers. The extreme statement of this view was Nixon's claim that any action undertaken by the president is legitimate. Nixon's attorneys submitted the argument that how the executive privilege is exercised "is a matter of presidential judgment alone."[7] In the case *U.S. v. Sirica* (1973) Judge George MacKinnon expressed best of all the notion of an unlimited executive privilege: "In my opinion an absolute privilege exists for presidential communications. . . . [S]trict confidentiality is so essential to the deliberative process that it should not be jeopardized by any possibility of disclosure."[8]

Neither the congressional supremacy view nor the imperial presidency view presents an accurate assessment of the separation of powers system. Neither provides a workable resolution to the dilemma of executive privilege. Yet only a proper understanding of the separation of powers doctrine can help resolve the inherent conflict between governmental secrecy and the "right to know."

The alternative proposed by the congressional supremacists—completely open executive branch deliberations—is worse than the danger that they seek to eliminate. Any power once created can be abused. And because secrecy is vital to the proper functioning of the presidency, periodic attempts to abuse this power may be an unavoidable price that must be accepted. To demand that presidents exercise their powers fully to move forward an activist policy agenda, that they strictly conform to the letter of every legal and constitutional provision in the exercise of their powers, and yet remain fully subordinate to the legislative authority in all areas, is to expect nothing less than an ideal world—one in which the trustworthiness of chief executives never is at issue; the legal and constitutional provisions pertaining to the presidency are unmistakably clear and consistent, and do not unduly constrain the exercise of presidential authority; and legislators are concerned only with high-minded matters of policy and the public good. As the founders understood so well, such a state of affairs never will exist given the undeniable flaws of human beings. There are better ways to check the potential abuse of power than total elimination of the source of power. The dilemma of executive privilege can be resolved by means other than eliminating that authority altogether or effectively trying to do so through the use of onerous legalistic constraints.

Furthermore, the pro-imperial presidency view—the one in which the chief executive exercises his authority unfettered by congressional constraints, Congress defers to executive fiat, and the only check on presidential power takes place on election day—also misunderstands the separation of powers doctrine. The resolution to the dilemma of executive privilege is not simply to allow the president to determine for himself the scope and limits of his own authority.

Only a proper understanding of the separation of powers doctrine can resolve the dilemma of executive privilege and the right to know. Such an understanding begins with the writings of the most influential thinkers of modern constitutionalism, Locke and Montesquieu. Locke articulated a system of separated powers to limit the potential for governmental tyranny. As Louis W. Koenig has written, "John Locke would have been flabbergasted" by the Nixon assertion that any action undertaken by the president is legal.[9] Yet limited governmental power can never bow to the "fundamental law of nature" that counsels self-preservation. Therefore, Locke advocated a strong executive, capable of acting with unity and "despatch," and given the "power to act with discretion, for the public good, without the prescription of the law, and sometimes against it."[10] Montesquieu similarly advocated a governmental system in which power checks power while still leaving the executive independent of direct popular will when necessary.

A proper understanding of the separation of powers also is rooted in the founding period and the early years of the Republic. The founders recognized an implied constitutional prerogative of presidential secrecy—a power that they believed was necessary and proper. The leading founders either exercised or acknowledged the right of executive branch secrecy in the early years of the Republic. In devising our constitutional system, they sought to limit governmental powers to reduce the threat of tyranny. But this perceived need to limit power never implied either weak government or a subordinate executive branch. As political scientist L. Peter Schultz has written, "The separation of powers constitutes an attempt to solve one of the major problems of government, that of providing for both reasonable government and forceful government without sacrificing either."[11]

The leading founders exercised considerable foresight in establishing a constitutional system capable of adapting to the needs of changing times. That foresight has been especially useful to the conduct of foreign policy—the area in which claims of executive privilege are especially compelling. When it came to writing the executive articles of the Constitution, the Framers exercised great care not to constrain executive power with constitutional exactitude.

Finally, a proper understanding of the separation of powers doctrine is founded on the notion that there are inherent limitations on the prerogative powers of the presidency. The eventual resolution of the Nixon administration scandals shows that Congress and the judiciary, when given good reason to believe that the claim of privilege is being abused, have institutional mechanisms that can be used to compel the president to divulge information. The separation of powers system provides the vital mechanisms by which the other branches of government can challenge executive claims of privilege.

The answer to the question of how executive privilege can properly be exercised and constrained is found in an examination of the roles of the other branches of government in ensuring that the executive branch does not abuse the right to withhold information.

The Role of Congress

One proposed solution to the dilemma of executive privilege is to establish a statutory definition of that power, specifying the circumstances under which executive privilege can be exercised.[12] Fortunately, no such legislative solution has been enacted. Any a priori "solution" is bound to fail given the impossibility of determining all of the circumstances under which executive privilege may be exercised in the future. As former attorney general Edward Levi has explained, "The lesson of history is that the reasonableness of an assertion of confidentiality cannot be determined in advance on the basis of neat categories."[13]

As the examination of post-Watergate executive privilege controversies has made clear, Congress already has the institutional capability to challenge claims of executive privilege by means other than eliminating the right to withhold information or attaching statutory restrictions on the exercise of that right. For example, if members of Congress are not satisfied with the response to their demands for information, they have the option of retaliating by withholding support for the president's agenda or for his executive branch nominees. Recall that the threat by a Senate committee not to confirm a prominent presidential nomination until a separate access to information dispute had been resolved resulted in President Nixon ceding to the senators' demands. If information can be withheld only for the most compelling reasons, it is not at all unreasonable for Congress to try to force the president's hand by making him weigh the importance of withholding the information against that of moving forward a nomination or piece of legislation. Presumably, information being withheld for purposes of vital national security or constitutional concerns would take precedence over pending legislation or a presidential appointment. If not, then there appears to be little justification in the first place for withholding the information.

Congress possesses numerous other means by which to compel presidential compliance with requests for information. One is the control Congress maintains over the governmental "purse-strings," a formidable power over the executive branch. Additionally, Congress often relies on the subpoena power and the contempt of Congress charge to compel release of withheld information. It is not merely the exercise of these powers that matters, but the threat that Congress may resort to such powers. During the Reagan–Bush years, Congress had a great deal of success at compelling executive branch disclosure of information through the subpoena and contempt of Congress powers.

In the extreme case, Congress also has the power of impeachment—the ultimate weapon with which to threaten the executive. Clearly this congressional power cannot routinely be exercised as a means of compelling disclosure of information and consequently is not going to constitute a real threat in commonplace information disputes. Nonetheless, in the case of a scandal of Watergate-like proportions, in which all other remedies have failed, Congress can threaten to exercise its ultimate power over the president.

In the vast majority of cases—as recent history verifies—it can be expected that the president will comply with requests for information rather than withstand increased belligerence from Congress.

If certain members of Congress believe that the executive privilege power is too formidable, the answer resides not in crippling presidential authority, but in exercising to full effect the vast array of powers already at Congress's disposal. Sotirios A. Barber contends that presidential pre-eminence in foreign policy-making "cannot be explained by comparing the executive and legislative powers enumerated in the Constitution." Barber correctly explains that Congress possesses formidable powers, but at times has failed to fully exercise them.[14] Three decades ago Sen. J. William Fulbright (D-Ark.) argued that Congress too often acquiesced to presidential authority in foreign affairs and charged his colleagues not to allow the chief executive to act unilaterally in foreign policy in a secretive fashion. "I conclude that when the president, for reasons with which we can all sympathize, does not invite us into his high-policy councils, it is our duty to infiltrate them as best we can."[15]

Louis Koenig nonetheless refutes the oft-stated belief that the presidency has become imperial while Congress's powers have atrophied. Koenig cites the example of the Nixon presidency as proof that Congress both possesses and has exercised formidable powers when it has so chosen.

> The imperial presidency thesis excessively downgrades Congress and misstates the historical experience of the presidency. Time and again, Congress prevailed over Nixon. Congress ended his once secret war in Cambodia by cutting off its funds. His claims of massive powers to impound funds or abolish programs were rejected both by Congress and the courts. His modest program proposals were rejected by Congress more frequently than any other contemporary president. Ultimately, Nixon's certain impeachment by the House of Representatives drove him from the presidency. . . . [The presidency] contains substantial weaknesses of power which the imperial thesis obscures.[16]

The resolution of executive-legislative disagreements over withheld information need not occur through such combative techniques. Rooted in the separation of powers doctrine is the notion that the potential stalemate that results from executive branch refusal to release secretive information can be overcome by mutual accommodation and compromise. Former attorney general William French Smith mistakenly believes that there are inherent problems with holding any members of Congress in confidence regarding sensitive information.[17] In fact, the divulging of sensitive information to a few trusted and highly respected members of Congress has succeeded in the past. For example, during the Second World War, President Roosevelt frequently confided sensitive national security information to trusted members of Congress, and they respected the sanctity of that information. In times of great uncertainty over the appropriateness of withholding information, the president can, in secret chambers, discuss the problem with a few highly trusted members of Congress.

The area of treaty negotiations is particularly complex because of the obvious need for confidential discussions combined with the Senate's constitutional authority of "advice and consent." In diplomatic negotiations, to publicly divulge negotiating positions before agreements have been arrived at is highly imprudent. The flexibility of negotiating positions is compromised by such revelations, making highly difficult, if not impossible, the achievement of an agreement between or among the parties. Supreme Court Chief Justice William Rehnquist has testified that the use of private discussions between the president and some members of Congress can satisfy both Congress's right to know and the needs of diplomatic negotiations.

> Frequently the problem of overly broad public dissemination of such negotiations can be solved by testimony in executive session, which informs the members of the committee of Congress without making the same information prematurely available throughout the world. The end is not secrecy as to the end product—the treaty—which of course should be exposed to the fullest public scrutiny, but only the confidentiality as to the negotiations which lead up to the treaty.[18]

A statutory resolution to the dilemma of executive privilege is not needed. Congress already possesses the constitutional means by which to challenge executive branch withholding of information. As the examination of the post-Watergate presidencies has shown, Congress has had a good deal of success using its existing powers to compel disclosure of withheld information. In fact, Congress appears to have gained the upper hand in its disputes with the executive branch over information policy. When it comes to the issue of executive privilege, there is no convincing evidence for the view that the president is imperial, capable of doing whatever he wants.

The Role of the Courts

In the realms of foreign affairs and national security policy-making, the courts generally have been deferential to the so-called political branches. The judiciary's role in the separation of powers scheme is not regarded as one of arbitrating conflicts between the political branches over how foreign policy should be conducted. On many occasions, the courts have recognized that the judicial branch may not be best suited to deciding complex matters of foreign affairs, national security, and intelligence policy.[19] Constitutional scholar Louis Fisher explains the usual judicial response to congressional attempts to pose constitutional challenges to the president's national security decisions:

> Congress must be prepared, and willing, to exercise the ample powers within its arsenal. When it acquiesces to executive initiatives, the record clearly shows that legislative inaction will not be cured by judicial remedies. Four times during the Reagan administration, members of Congress filed suit in federal court to have President Reagan's military actions in El Salvador, Nicaragua, Grenada, and the Persian Gulf held unconstitutional and illegal. Four times the federal courts gave Congress the same message: if you fail to challenge the president, don't come to us. Justice Lewis Powell put it well in the treaty termination case of *Goldwater v. Carter* (1979): "If the Congress chooses not to confront the president, it is not our task to do so." [444 U.S. 996, 998] Congress has the constitutional power. It needs also the institutional courage and constitutional understanding to share with the president the momentous decision to send U.S. forces into combat.[20]

But this recognition of the limitations on the role of the courts does not undermine the function of the judiciary in arbitrating constitutional, rather than policy, disputes. As the Supreme Court affirmed in *U.S. v. Nixon*, the separation of powers doctrine does not guarantee "an absolute, unqualified presidential privilege of immunity from judicial process under all circumstances. The president's need for complete candor and objectivity from advisers calls for great deference from the courts. However, when the privilege depends solely on the broad, undifferentiated claim of public interest in the confidentiality of such conversations, a confrontation with other values arises."[21] The Court made clear that when a claim of privilege is made to protect national security or foreign policy deliberations, such a claim is difficult for another branch to overcome in a balancing of constitutional powers.[22] But while upholding the "constitutionally based" nature of the privilege, the Court also made clear that the privilege may, at times, have to defer to the constitutionally based powers of a coordinate branch of government. Although the Court did not specify the exact balance of powers among the branches, it did affirm that the judicial branch has the authority to compel production of information claimed to be privileged when such information is needed as evidence in a criminal case.

> We conclude that when the ground for asserting privilege as to subpoenaed materials sought for use in a criminal trial is based only on the generalized interest in confidentiality, it cannot prevail over the fundamental demands of due process of law in the fair administration of criminal justice. The generalized assertion of privilege must yield to the demonstrated, specific need for evidence in a pending criminal trial.[23]

Other court cases affirm that it is appropriate to apply a balancing test of competing interests when disputes arise over executive branch information policies.[24] In the *U.S. v. Nixon* case, the Supreme Court exhibited the capacity of the judiciary to pose as a viable check on executive abuses of the privilege.

There also is considerable legal precedent for *in camera* review of sensitive information by the courts.[25] Rather than simply compelling disclosure of privileged information for open court review, it may be appropriate for the executive branch to satisfy the court in secret chambers of the necessity of nondisclosure. The courts have repeatedly affirmed their right to decide in particular cases whether the necessity of protecting sensitive information does indeed outweigh the need for evidence in criminal justice matters.[26] And little evidence exists to support the claim that the judiciary does not administer this duty carefully and prudently. As

Chief Justice John Marshall asserted in the *U.S. v. Burr* (1807) decision, the president has the right to protect privileged information, but this right does not override the authority of the judiciary to review protected documents:

> The president, although subject to the general rules which apply to others, may have sufficient motives for declining to produce a particular paper, and those motives may be such as to restrain the court from enforcing its production. . . . I can readily conceive that the president might receive a letter which it would be improper to exhibit in public. . . . The occasion for demanding it ought, in such a case, to be very strong, and to be fully shown to the court before its production could be insisted on. . . . Such a letter, though it be a private one, seems to partake of the character of an official paper, and to be such as ought not on light ground be forced into public view.[27]

The judiciary clearly plays a less active role than Congress in resolving executive privilege disputes. Institutional conflict between the political branches should most often resolve informational controversies. Constant judicial intervention in such controversies is neither practical nor desirable. Nonetheless, the courts must often get involved in those conflicts in which they are a party and in disputes that the political branches cannot resolve without judicial intervention.

SECRECY AND DEMOCRATIC ACCOUNTABILITY

The dilemma of executive privilege cannot be resolved with constitutional exactitude. To try to do so would be to attempt to impose a solution that is antithetical to our constitutional culture. The dilemma can best be resolved on a case-by-case basis, through the normal ebb and flow of politics as envisioned by the Framers of our governing system. Exactitude cannot be achieved in a government that must accommodate ever-changing circumstances. The genius of the American constitutional system is its enormous capacity to maintain its legitimacy and stability by adapting to changing circumstances without sacrificing underlying fundamental values.

The search for constitutional absolutes—executive privilege is a myth, or, executive privilege is an unfettered prerogative—is misguided. Our constitutional system cannot guarantee certitude with regard to how every information policy dispute in government will be resolved. Nor should it. Two executive privilege claims that, on the surface, appear equally valid may be treated very differently from one another given different circumstances (e.g., political composition of Congress, membership of a particular investigating committee, popularity of the president, etc.). In the Bush administration, one presidential claim of executive privilege that had little to do with national security concerns prevailed in part because of the popularity of a cabinet member who may otherwise have been held in contempt of Congress and in part because of the lack of followthrough by the chair of the committee in charge of the investigation. On numerous other occasions, Congress prevailed over the administration's claims of privilege either because of its vigorous challenges to those actions or due to the unwillingness of post-Watergate presidents to resist congressional demands.

It is implausible that a strict, legalistic definition of executive privilege could have determined in advance the appropriate resolution to each controversy. What is problematic in the post-Watergate years is the delegitimization of executive privilege due to Nixon's abuses of power. Congress does not accept presidential exercise of executive privilege as proper and constitutional. Presidents generally seek to attain all the benefits of executive privilege without invoking the constitutional doctrine, often by devious and deceptive means. Many advocates of the strong presidency now decry the so-called imperial Congress and the legislature's propensity to solve informational disputes through resort to narrow legalisms.[28] Rather than appropriately exercising the separation of powers mechanism to moderate presidential power, more and more often members of the political branches are adopting intransigent positions. This development represents a regrettable deviation from the constitutional Framers' notion of the separation of powers and from the traditional dynamic that occurred between the political branches over executive branch secrecy until the Nixon years. Through the normal political process of confrontation, compromise, and accommodation, the coordinate branches for years had satisfactorily resolved their differences over executive privilege matters. We cannot solve our modern dilemma by resorting to the solution that was rejected by the Framers—constitutional certitude.

Michael Foley makes the point that constitutional dogmatism could have the effect of dangerously exposing the unresolvable elements of the separation of powers doctrine and the inconsistencies of the constitutional system. He correctly explains that certain constitutional problems are not amenable to definitive solutions.[29] In fact, an advanced constitutional culture is one that tolerates and even cultivates the existence of what he calls "abeyances," defined as "those constitutional gaps which remain vacuous for positive and constructive purposes."[30] Foley's thesis is most germane to the analysis of how to resolve the dilemma of executive privilege:

> There is simply more to be gained by cultivating and protecting abeyances and in preventing political issues and institutional differences from inciting intransigent divisions and entrenched constitutional dogmatism. In not extending claims to their logical but provocative conclusions; in not seeking to maximize advantages irrespective of their repercussions; and in promoting "comity" by which positions are acknowledged and honoured in the cause of achieving a means of cooperation within a context brooding with adversity, political participants can transform immobilism into productive interplay. The unremitting dissonance of a separated powers system, therefore, can condition those who work within it to the need to strive continuously against a background of conflict and dispute, in order to achieve any sense of common purpose.[31]

Critics of executive privilege nonetheless make the case that such a prerogative power is potentially dangerous, thereby requiring either elimination of that power or the imposition of severe legal constraints on its exercise. Such resolutions to the dilemma of executive privilege are antithetical to the nature of a constitutional system that tolerates and cultivates abeyances. Those resolutions demonstrate a lack of understanding of a separation of powers system in which the exercise of prerogative powers is recognized as a necessity in unusual circumstances. James W. Ceaser makes the point that the exercise of prerogative powers is appropriate for unusual circumstances and that "the exception or extreme case need not define the rule."[32] Ceaser disputes the assumption of some congressionalists that the nation's legislature "performs its proper duty in a separation of powers system only when it ties the executive's hands and attempts to force the nation to run its foreign policy through the instrument of law."[33] In creating the separation of powers system, the Framers did not envision the resort to strict legalisms as the means to resolve customary interbranch disputes. Ceaser's explanation of the Framers' theory of the separation of powers is germane to this analysis:

> The executive power, although it cannot always be subject to precise limitations, can still be watched, checked, and supervised by other institutions possessing an equal or greater regard among the people. Following this theory, the founders placed the greater part of the law-making power in Congress, thereby reducing the prospect that the prerogative power would ever be carried over into normal governance. Moreover, the very presence of institutions as powerful as the Congress and the Supreme Court could serve to check the executive power. Finally, there is a sense in which the founders made the legislative power supreme not so much by giving it the law-making power as by giving it the power to impeach and convict the president. By this means the legislature can dismiss the person exercising the executive power, even though it cannot exercise that power itself.[34]

Many critics of executive privilege too readily assume that any invocation of that power is, by definition, suspect—that no one wants to refuse to disclose information unless he or she has "something to hide." To avoid future Watergate-like scandals, to resolve the dilemma of executive privilege, they offer solutions that are more troublesome than the problems they wish to eliminate. The resolution to this dilemma is, in a sense, right before our eyes. The founders' theory of separation of powers offers the necessary mechanisms by which prerogative powers can be exercised, challenged, and constrained.

Although there is no need for any statutory definition of, or limitations on, executive privilege, the post-Watergate years demonstrate that it is prudent for each presidential administration to adopt a set of procedures on how it will exercise executive privilege. The failure of the Ford and Carter administrations to do so—although perhaps necessitated by the political environment of the mid- to late 1970s—resulted in a great deal of confusion both within each administration and between the political branches. There is no small irony to the fact that these two presidencies—predicated on promises to be "open" and in every way possible unlike the Nixon administration—in failing to adopt their own executive privilege guidelines operated officially under the guidelines established in the Nixon memorandum. Reagan adopted new executive privilege guidelines in 1982, which remained in effect throughout the Reagan–

Bush years. The Bush administration did not routinely abide by those guidelines.

To avoid confusion regarding the exercise of executive privilege, it would be eminently sensible for each new administration to promulgate guidelines on the use of that power. These guidelines need not diverge substantially, or even at all, from one administration to the next. But a presidential directive should be issued by each administration to make unmistakably clear how members of the executive branch are to handle executive privilege matters. The proposed guidelines should not be posed in the form of legalisms, but rather, should merely outline the formal procedures of the administration for handling and resolving executive privilege issues. The guidelines, too, should identify only broad categories of areas in which issues of executive privilege may arise. The traditional categories are national security, confidential deliberations, enforcement of criminal justice, and privacy of executive branch officials. Specific cases of executive privilege should be dealt with as they arise, as all such cases cannot be anticipated in advance.

Regardless of how the guidelines are set up—whether, for example, the president must personally assert executive privilege, or the use of that power can be approved by the attorney general—ultimately, responsibility for the exercise of that prerogative resides with the president. Consequently, accountability really is not compromised by the exercise of executive privilege because the result of the use of that power will have to be justified to the electorate at some point or to one or both of the coordinate branches of government. To accept the legitimacy of a properly constrained executive privilege power in our system of separated powers is to place an important trust in our president that he will exercise this power prudently and in the public interest, and to know that we can hold him accountable for the manner in which he discharges such constitutional authority.

Notes

PREFACE AND ACKNOWLEDGMENTS

1. Raoul Berger, *Executive Privilege: A Constitutional Myth* (Cambridge: Harvard University Press, 1974).

2. Raoul Berger, "The Incarnation of Executive Privilege," *UCLA Law Review* 22 (October 1974): 29.

3. Berger, *Executive Privilege*, viii.

4. See, for example, L. Gordon Crovitz and Jeremy A. Rabkin, eds., *The Fettered Presidency: Legal Constraints on the Executive Branch* (Washington, D.C.: American Enterprise Institute, 1989); Eric Felten, *The Ruling Class: Inside the Imperial Congress* (Washington, D.C.: Heritage Foundation, 1993); Gordon S. Jones and John A. Marini, eds., *The Imperial Congress* (New York: Pharos Books, 1988).

5. Jones and Marini, *Imperial Congress*.

INTRODUCTION: THE DILEMMA OF SECRECY AND
DEMOCRATIC ACCOUNTABILITY

1. Woodrow Wilson, *Congressional Government* (Gloucester, Mass.: Peter Smith, 1973), 198.

2. David Wise, *The Politics of Lying: Government Deception, Secrecy, and Power* (New York: Random House, 1973), 64.

3. Ibid., 140. Wise later qualifies his argument by suggesting that it is acceptable for government in some cases to keep secrets; once the information gets out, however, all restraints are lifted (150).

4. Ibid., 140.

5. Morton H. Halperin and Daniel N. Hoffman, *Top Secret: National Security and the Right to Know* (Washington, D.C.: New Republic Books, 1977), 31.

6. James Wiggins, *Freedom or Secrecy* (New York: Oxford University Press, 1956), x.

7. Quoted in U.S. Congress, *Availability of Information to Congress*, Hearings before a Subcommittee of the Committee on Government Operations, House of Representatives, 93d Cong., 1st Sess., 3, 4, 19 April 1973, 81.

8. Michael A. Ledeen, "Secrets," in Simon Serfaty, ed., *The Media and Foreign Policy* (New York: St. Martin's Press, 1991), 121.

9. Ibid., 122–23.

10. Harold Evans, "The Norman Conquest: Freedom of the Press in Britain and America," in Serfaty, *Media and Foreign Policy*, 189.

11. Ibid., 192.

12. Stansfield Turner, *Secrecy and Democracy: The CIA in Transition* (Boston: Houghton Mifflin, 1985), 4.

13. Daniel P. Franklin, *Extraordinary Measures: The Exercise of Prerogative Powers in the United States* (Pittsburgh: University of Pittsburgh Press, 1991), 13.

14. *Board of Education v. Pico*, 457 U.S. 853, 867 (1982); *First National Bank v. Bellotti*, 435 U.S. 765, 783 (1978); *Stanley v. Georgia*, 394 U.S. 557, 564 (1969). See the analysis of A. Stephen Boyan, Jr., "Presidents and National Security Powers: A Judicial Perspective," paper presented at the annual meeting of the American Political Science Association, Washington, D.C., 1–4 September 1988.

15. Louis Henkin, *Constitutionalism, Democracy, and Foreign Affairs* (New York: Columbia University Press, 1990), 20.

CHAPTER 1: THE ARGUMENTS AGAINST EXECUTIVE PRIVILEGE

1. See speech of Rep. George Meader (R-Mich.) to the House, 10 March 1958: "It is amazing to me that a nonexistent, imaginary, so-called 'Executive privilege,' nowhere recognized in the Constitution, in statutes, or in court decisions, can seriously be advanced to destroy the expressly vested legislative power, as well as the investigative power which inheres in it." Quoted in "'Privilege' Is Scored," *New York Times*, 11 March 1958, 19.

2. Raoul Berger, *Executive Privilege: A Constitutional Myth* (Cambridge: Harvard University Press, 1974).

3. Theodore Roosevelt, *The Autobiography of Theodore Roosevelt*, ed. Wayne Andrews (New York: Scribner's, 1958), 197–200.

4. William Howard Taft, *Our Chief Magistrate and His Powers* (New York: Columbia University Press, 1916), 138.

5. David Gray Adler, "Presidential Prerogative and the National Security State: The Corruption of the Constitution," paper presented at the annual meeting of the American Political Science Association, San Francisco, Calif., 30 August 1990, 1.

6. Ibid., 6.

7. Harold Hongju Koh, *The National Security Constitution: Sharing Power after the Iran-Contra Affair* (New Haven, Conn.: Yale University Press, 1990), 4.

8. Louis Henkin, *Constitutionalism, Democracy, and Foreign Affairs* (New York: Columbia University Press, 1990), 36.

9. Quoted in Berger, *Executive Privilege*, 41.

10. Alan Swan, "Statement before the Subcommittee on Separation of Powers of the Committee on the Judiciary," *Executive Privilege*, U.S. Senate, 92d Cong., 1st Sess., 1971, 245. Berger notes that "in the Constitution the Framers provide for limited secrecy by Congress alone, thereby excluding executive secrecy from the public" (cited from "The Incarnation of Executive Privilege," *UCLA Law Review* 22 [October 1974]: 15–16).

11. Morton Halperin and Daniel N. Hoffman, *Top Secret: National Security and the Right to Know* (Washington, D.C.: New Republic Books, 1977), 88.

12. Berger, "Incarnation of Executive Privilege," 17.

13. George C. Calhoun, "Confidentiality and Executive Privilege," in Thomas M. Franck, ed., *The Tethered Presidency: Congressional Restraints on Executive Power* (New York: New York University Press, 1981), 173.

14. Raoul Berger, "Executive Privilege vs. Congressional Inquiry," *UCLA Law Review* 12 (1965): 1058–60.

15. Berger, "Statement," 1971, 278. Article I, Section 6 (1) of the Constitution provides that "for any speech or debate in either House [members] shall not be questioned in any other place." Berger points out that there is no comparable guarantee in Article II against anyone else examining the executive.

16. Berger, *Executive Privilege*, 41.

17. Quoted in Berger, "Statement," 1971, 278.

18. Ibid. According to Berger, "The Founders did not view the President with awe but with apprehension." See "Incarnation of Executive Privilege," 20.

19. David Gray Adler, "The Supreme Court and Presidential Power in Foreign Affairs: *Curtiss-Wright* and Judicial Deference," paper presented at the annual meeting of the Western Political Science Association, Newport Beach, Calif., 22–24 March 1990, 14.

20. Adler, "Presidential Prerogative," 6.

21. Berger, *Executive Privilege*, 131.

22. Adler, "Supreme Court and Presidential Power," 18.

23. Berger, *Executive Privilege*, 127.

24. Berger, "Statement," 1971, 283.

25. J. William Fulbright, "Statement before the Subcommittee on Separation of Powers of the Committee on the Judiciary," 1971, 31.

26. *Inland Waterways Corp. v. Young*, 309 U.S. 518, 534 (1940).

27. *Powell v. McCormack*, 395 U.S. 486, 546 (1969). See also *United States v. Morton Salt Co.*, 338 U.S. 632, 647 (1950): once powers are "granted, they are not lost by being allowed to lie dormant, any more than nonexistent powers can be prescribed by an unchallenged exercise."

28. Sam Ervin, "Statement before the Subcommittee on Separation of Powers of the Committee on the Judiciary," 1971, 4.

29. Stuart Symington, "Statement before the Subcommittee on Separation of Powers of the Committee on the Judiciary," 1971, 221.

30. *McGrain v. Daugherty*, 273 U.S. 135, 161 (1927).

31. *Exxon Corp. v. FTC*, 589 F. 2d 582, 589 (D.C. Cir. 1978), *cert. denied*, 441 U.S. 943 (1979); *FTC v. Owens-Corning Fiberglass Corp.*, 626 F. 2d 966, 970 (D.C. Cir. 1980).

32. U.S. Congress, *Executive-Legislative Consultation on Foreign Policy: Strengthening Executive Branch Procedures*, Congress and Foreign Policy Series, No. 2, U.S. House of Representatives (Washington, D.C.: U.S. Government Printing Office, May 1981), 35–36.

33. Ibid., 30.

34. Irving Janis, *Groupthink* (Boston: Houghton Mifflin, 1982).

35. James MacGregor Burns, *Leadership* (New York: Harper and Row, 1978), 410.

36. U.S. Congress, *Executive-Legislative Consultation on Foreign Policy*, 40.

37. Ervin, "Statement," 1971, 3–4.

38. Bruce Miroff, "Secrecy and Spectacle: Reflections on the Dangers of the Presidency," in Paul Brace, Christine B. Harrington, and Gary King, eds., *The Presidency in American Politics* (New York: New York University Press, 1989), 157.

39. Ibid., 152–53.

40. Quoted in David Wise, *The Politics of Lying: Government Deception, Secrecy, and Power* (New York: Random House, 1973), 339.

41. 5 U.S.C. § 552 (1966).

42. Hanson W. Baldwin, "Managed News: Our Peacetime Censorship," *Atlantic Monthly*, April 1963, 53.

43. Wise, *Politics of Lying*, 149–50.

44. Ibid., 149.

45. Quoted in Miles Beardsley Johnson, *The Government Secrecy Controversy* (New York: Vantage Press, 1967), 39.

46. U.S. Congress, *Freedom of Information; Executive Privilege; Secrecy in Government*, Hearings before the Subcommittee on Administrative Practice and Procedure and Separation of Powers of the Committee on the Judiciary, United States Senate and the Subcommittee on Intergovernmental Relations of the Committee on Government Operations, 93d Cong., 1st Sess., 10, 11, 12 April; 8, 9, 10, 16 May; 7, 8, 11, 26 June 1973 (3 vols.), 2:209.

47. Thomas I. Emerson, "The Danger of State Secrecy," in Ronald Pynn, ed., *Watergate and the American Political Process* (New York: Praeger, 1975), 60.

48. Wise, *Politics of Lying*, 64.

49. Ibid., 343.

50. Ibid., 344. See also A. Stephen Boyan, Jr., "Presidents and National Security Powers: A Judicial Perspective," paper presented at the annual meeting of

the American Political Science Association, Washington, D.C., 1–4 September 1988, 3: "It does not take an Iran-Contra affair or a Watergate to remind us that an appeal to national security offers a handy reason to avoid public scrutiny of unwise or mistaken policies or of abuses of constitutional rights."

51. Berger, "Incarnation of Executive Privilege," 11, 21, 26–27, 29; Norman Dorsen and John Shattuck, "Executive Privilege: The President Won't Tell," in Norman Dorsen and Stephen Gillers, eds., *None of Your Business: Government Secrecy in America* (New York: Penguin Books, 1975), 27–60; Note, "Military and State Secrets Privilege," *Yale Law Journal* (1982): 579.

52. Halperin and Hoffman, *Top Secret*, 2.

53. Symington, "Statement," 1971, 222.

54. Berger, "Incarnation of Executive Privilege," 26–27.

55. Quoted in Itzhak Galnoor, ed., *Government Secrecy in Democracies* (New York: New York University Press, 1977), vii.

CHAPTER 2: THE ARGUMENTS IN FAVOR OF EXECUTIVE PRIVILEGE

1. Archibald Cox, "Executive Privilege," *U. Pa. Law Review* 122 (1974): 1388.

2. Harold Laski, *The American Presidency* (New York: Harper and Row, 1940), 155.

3. Raoul Berger, "Executive Privilege vs. Congressional Inquiry," *UCLA Law Review* 12 (1965): 1060.

4. Niccolò Machiavelli, *The Prince* (New York: Modern Library, 1950).

5. Niccolò Machiavelli, *The Discourses* (New York: Modern Library, 1950), Book I, chapters 3, 9.

6. Ibid., Book I, chapter 2; Book III, chapter 1.

7. Thomas Hobbes, *Leviathan* (Cambridge: Cambridge University Press, 1991).

8. John Locke, *Second Treatise of Government* (Indianapolis: Bobbs-Merrill, 1952), chapter 12, sections 143–48.

9. Ibid., sections 146–48.

10. Ibid., chapter 14, section 166.

11. On this point, see James W. Ceaser, "In Defense of Separation of Powers," in Robert A. Goldwin and Art Kaufman, eds., *Separation of Powers: Does It Still Work?* (Washington, D.C.: American Enterprise Institute, 1986), 168–93.

12. Baron de Montesquieu, *The Spirit of the Laws* (New York: Hafner, 1966), Book II.

13. Ibid.

14. Paul Peterson, "The Constitution and the Separation of Powers," in Gary McDowell, ed., *Taking the Constitution Seriously: Essays on the Constitution and Constitutional Law* (Dubuque: Kendall/Hunt, 1981), 195.

15. Edward S. Corwin, *The President: Office and Powers, 1787–1948*, 3d ed. (New York: New York University Press, 1948), 10.

16. Ibid., 15–16.

17. Quoted in Daniel Hoffman, *Governmental Secrecy and the Founding Fathers* (Westport, Conn.: Greenwood Press, 1981), 21. Even George Mason referred to the secrecy of the Constitutional Convention as "a proper precaution" because it averted "mistakes and misrepresentations until the business shall have been completed, when the whole may have a very different complexion from that in which the several parts might in their first shape appear if submitted to the public eye." Quoted in Max Farrand, ed., *The Records of the Federal Convention of 1787* (New Haven: Yale University Press, 1967), 3:28, 32.

18. Warren Burger, "'A Republic, If You Can Keep It': A Bicentennial Commentary," *Presidential Studies Quarterly* 18 (Summer 1988): 468.

19. *U.S. v. Nixon*, 418 U.S. 683, 705 (1974).

20. Michael Foley, *The Silence of Constitutions* (London: Routledge, 1989).

21. J. W. Peltason, *Corwin and Peltason's Understanding the Constitution*, 11th ed. (New York: Holt, Rinehart, and Winston, 1988), 84.

22. Quoted in Robert Green McCloskey, ed., *The Works of James Wilson* (Cambridge: Harvard University Press, 1967), 1:294, 296.

23. *Marbury v. Madison*, 1 Cranch 137, 166 (1803).

24. Quoted in Daniel L. Feldman, *The Logic of American Government: Applying the Constitution to the Contemporary World* (New York: William Morrow, 1990), 82.

25. Quoted in George B. Galloway, *History of the House of Representatives* (New York: Thomas Y. Crowell, 1961), 236–37.

26. Quoted in Raoul Berger, "Statement before the Subcommittee on Separation of Powers of the Committee on the Judiciary," *Executive Privilege*, U.S. Senate, 92d Cong., 1st Sess., 1971, 278.

27. Peterson, "Constitution," 205.

28. Berger, "Executive Privilege vs. Congressional Inquiry," 1060, 1117.

29. Ibid., 1117.

30. Raoul Berger, *Executive Privilege: A Constitutional Myth* (Cambridge: Harvard University Press, 1974), 10–11.

31. Ceaser, "Separation of Powers," 171.

32. Gary Schmitt, "Executive Privilege," in Joseph Bessette and Jeffrey Tulis, eds., *The Presidency in the Constitutional Order* (Baton Rouge: Louisiana State University Press, 1981), 157–58.

33. *Watkins v. U.S.*, 354 U.S. 178 (1957); *Wilkinson v. U.S.*, 365 U.S. 399 (1961).

34. *U.S. v. Nixon*, 418 U.S. 683 (1974).

35. Schmitt, "Executive Privilege," 159.

36. Ibid., 160.

37. Berger, "Executive Privilege vs. Congressional Inquiry," 1078.

38. Quoted in Glenn A. Phelps, "George Washington and the Founding of the Presidency," *Presidential Studies Quarterly* 17 (Spring 1987): 345.

39. Ibid., 350, 354.

40. *3 Annals of Congress* (1792), 493.

41. Paul Ford, *The Writings of Thomas Jefferson* (New York: Putnam, 1892), 1:189–90.

42. Adam Breckenridge, *The Executive Privilege* (Lincoln: University of Nebraska Press, 1974), 31.

43. Abraham Sofaer, "Executive Privilege: An Historical Note," *Columbia Law Review* 75 (1975): 1319.

44. Ibid., 1321; Abraham Sofaer, "Executive Power and Control over Information: The Practice under the Framers," *Duke Law Journal* 1977 (March 1977): 8.

45. James Richardson, *A Compilation of the Messages and Papers of the Presidents* (New York: Bureau of National Literature, 1897), 1:186–87.

46. *5 Annals of Congress* (1796), 771, 782–83.

47. Ibid., 773.

48. Quoted in Schmitt, "Executive Privilege," 188n.

49. Ibid., 187n.

50. William Nisbet Chambers, *Political Parties in a New Nation: The American Experience, 1776–1809* (London: Oxford University Press, 1963), 134–35; Sofaer, "Executive Power and Control over Information," 13–14.

51. Sofaer, "Executive Power and Control over Information," 16–17.

52. Thomas P. Abernathy, *The Burr Conspiracy* (New York: Oxford University Press, 1954).

53. *16 Annals of Congress* (1806–7), 336.

54. Richardson, *Compilation*, 1:400.

55. Ford, *Writings of Thomas Jefferson*, 55.

56. Quoted in Dumas Malone, *Jefferson the President: First Term, 1801–1805* (Boston: Little, Brown, 1970), 320.

57. Quoted in Louis Henkin, *Foreign Affairs and the Constitution* (Mineola, N. Y.: Foundation Press, 1972), 297–98.

58. Sofaer, "Executive Power and Control over Information," 19–24.

59. Ibid., 28–45.

60. Quoted in Schmitt, "Executive Privilege," 169.

61. *House Journal*, 18th Cong., 2d Sess. (1825), 102.

62. Richardson, *Compilation*, 2: 847.

63. Ibid., 3:1172.

64. Ibid., 3:1200. Jackson later refused a House request for information on the settlement of the northeastern boundary, calling such disclosure "incompatible with the public interest." See ibid., 3:1346.

65. Ibid., 7:3065. See also Charles Warren, *The Making of the Constitution* (Boston: Harvard University Press, 1947), 177.

66. Richardson, *Compilation*, 7:3234.

67. Ibid., 11:5123. In 1886 Cleveland supported the opinion of his attorney general that documents pertaining to the dismissal of U.S. District Attorney

George M. Duskin should not be divulged to the Senate. See Edward S. Corwin, *The President: Office and Powers, 1787–1957*, 4th ed. (New York: New York University Press, 1957), 429.

68. Richardson, *Compilation*, 12:5673–74.

69. Corwin, *President*, 429.

70. Ibid., 429–30.

71. Quoted in Berger, *Executive Privilege*, 229.

In December 1906 a Senate resolution called on the president to furnish information on the dismissal of the three military companies, "if not incompatible with the public interest." Sen. John Spooner (R-Wisc.) responded that Congress could not compel disclosure of information "which, if made public, would result in very great harm to our foreign relations." Spooner noted that there are circumstances "where the president would be at liberty obviously to decline to transmit information to Congress or to either House of Congress" (quoted in Corwin, *President*, 428).

Although William Howard Taft disagreed with Roosevelt's "stewardship theory" of the presidency, he defended the right of the chief executive to withhold information. With regard to the constitutional provision that the president inform Congress through the State of the Union address, Taft wrote that Congress did not thereby have the power "to elicit from him [the president] confidential information which he has acquired for the purposes of enabling him to discharge his constitutional duties if he does not deem the disclosure of such information prudent or in the public interest" (William Howard Taft, *Our Chief Magistrate and His Powers* [New York: Columbia University Press, 1916], 129–32).

72. *65 Cong. Rec.* (1924), 6087.

73. "Hoover Refuses Pact Data and 2 Senators Join Foes," *New York Times*, 12 July 1930, 1; "Treaty Foes Seek Debate Limitation to Get Vote in Week," *New York Times*, 17 July 1930, 1.

74. Summarized from U.S. Congress, *Contempt of Congress*, Report of the Committee on Public Works and Transportation, House of Representatives, 97th Cong., 2d Sess., 15 December 1982, 107–8.

75. Cited in William Rehnquist, "Statement before the Subcommittee on Separation of Powers of the Committee on the Judiciary," 1971, 432.

76. Francis Rourke, *Secrecy and Publicity* (Baltimore: Johns Hopkins University Press, 1961), 71.

77. *The Public Papers of the Presidents: Harry S Truman, 1948*, 228.

78. U.S. Congress, *Investigation of the GSA Strike*, Hearings before a Special Subcommittee of the Committee on Education and Labor, House of Representatives, 80th Cong., 2d Sess., 1948, pt. 2, 8.

79. Ibid., pt. 1, 12.

80. *The Public Papers of the Presidents: Harry S Truman, 1950*, 240.

81. S. Rep. No. 2108, 81st Cong., 2d Sess. (1950), 9.

82. *The Public Papers of the Presidents: Harry S Truman, 1951*, 289.

83. U.S. Congress, *Military Situation in the Far East*, Hearings before the Committee on Armed Services and the Committee on Foreign Relations, U.S. Senate, 82d Cong., 1st Sess., 1951.

84. *The Public Papers of the Presidents: Harry S Truman, 1952–1953*, 199.

85. Ibid.

86. Ibid., 235–36.

87. *The Public Papers of the Presidents: Dwight D. Eisenhower, 1954*, 483–84.

88. Quoted in Fred I. Greenstein, *The Hidden-Hand Presidency* (New York: Basic Books, 1982), 204.

89. Ibid., 205.

90. Ibid., 205, 207.

91. *Washington Post*, 18 May 1954, 14.

92. Quoted in John P. Roche and Leonard W. Levy, eds., *The Presidency* (New York: Harcourt, Brace and World, 1964), 36.

93. Quoted in Harold Chase and Allen Lerman, eds., *Kennedy and the Press* (New York: Thomas Y. Crowell, 1965), 8.

94. Quoted in Thomas M. Franck and Edward Weisband, eds., *Secrecy and Foreign Policy* (New York: Oxford University Press, 1974), 5.

95. U.S. Congress, *Military Cold War Education and Speech Review Policies*, Hearings before the Special Preparedness Subcommittee of the Committee on Armed Services, U.S. Senate, 87th Cong., 2d Sess., 1962, 508–9.

96. Ibid., 513–14. The president subsequently wrote a letter to his secretary of state issuing the same directive as given to the secretary of defense.

97. Clark R. Mollenhoff, *Washington Cover-Up* (Garden City, N.Y.: Doubleday, 1962), 239.

98. Richard M. Pious, *The American Presidency* (New York: Basic Books, 1979), 352.

99. *Executive Privilege*, U.S. Senate, 1971, 35.

100. Ibid., 39.

101. U.S. Congress, *Nominations of Abe Fortas and Homer Thornberry*, Hearings before the Committee on the Judiciary, U.S. Senate, 90th Cong., 2d Sess., 1968, pt. 2, 1347.

102. Ibid., 1363.

103. Ibid., 1348.

104. Rehnquist, "Statement before the Subcommittee on Separation of Powers of the Committee on the Judiciary," 1971, 435.

105. Peterson, "Constitution," 194.

106. *First National Bank v. Banco Nacional de Cuba*, 406 U.S. 759 (1972); *Haig v. Agee*, 453 U.S. 291 (1981); *Oetjen v. Central Leather Co.*, 246 U.S. 297 (1918); *U.S. v. Curtiss-Wright Corp.*, 299 U.S. 304 (1936); *U.S. v. Truong Dinh Hung*, 629 F. 2d 908 (1980).

107. A. Stephen Boyan, Jr., "Presidents and National Security Powers: A Judicial Perspective," paper presented at the annual meeting of the American Polit-

ical Science Association, Washington, D.C., 1–4 September 1988, 2. See *U.S. v. Macintosh*, 283 U.S. 605 (1931), in which Justice George Sutherland wrote for the majority that normally constitutionally protected liberties could effectively be suspended during wartime. Sutherland was careful to note that the exception to the rule had to be construed narrowly—only under truly extraordinary circumstances could the government adopt extraordinary actions.

108. 299 U.S. 304 (1936). The Court has relied on *Curtiss-Wright* in support of broad delegations of legislative authority to the chief executive. See *Ex parte Endo*, 323 U.S. 283, 298 (1944); *Zemel v. Rusk*, 381 U.S. 1, 17 (1965); *Goldwater v. Carter*, 444 U.S. 996, 1000 (1979).

109. 299 U.S. 304, 305 (1936). Writing for the majority in *Carter v. Carter Coal Co.*, 298 U.S. 238, 295 (1936), Sutherland declared that unenumerated "inherent" federal powers do not exist in domestic affairs. External affairs, he wrote, are "a wholly different matter which it is not necessary now to consider."

110. 299 U.S. 304, 307–8 (1936).

111. Ibid., 319–20.

112. *Zemel v. Rusk*, 381 U.S. 1, 17 (1965).

113. *Department of Navy v. Egan*, 484 U.S. 518, 527 (1988).

114. *U.S. v. Truong Dinh Hung*, 629 F. 2d 908, 913 (1980). The court held that "attempts to counter foreign threats to the national security require the utmost *stealth, speed*, and *secrecy*. . . . The executive branch not only has superior expertise in the area of foreign intelligence, it is also constitutionally designated as the preeminent authority in foreign affairs" (913, 914).

115. *INS v. Chadha*, 462 U.S. 919 (1983); *Bowsher v. Synar*, 478 U.S. 714 (1986).

116. *Chicago and Southern Airlines v. Waterman Steamship Corporation*, 333 U.S. 103, 111 (1948).

117. *U.S. v. Reynolds*, 345 U.S. 1, 10 (1952).

118. Ibid., 8.

119. Joseph W. Bishop, "The Executive's Right to Privacy," *Yale Law Journal* 66 (February 1957): 487.

120. Brit Hume, "Mighty Mouth," *The New Republic*, 1 September 1986, 20.

121. Bill Gertz and Peter LaBarbera, "Congressmen Have Right to Reveal Secrets, Wright Says," *Washington Times*, 27 September 1988, A1. See also Bill Gertz and Peter LaBarbera, "Wright Draws Fire for Spilling Secrets," *Washington Times*, 21 September 1988, A1, A11.

122. Daniel Schorr, "Cloak and Dagger Relics," *Washington Post*, 14 November 1985, A23.

123. *Contempt of Congress*, House of Representatives, 86n.

124. Robert L. Borosage, "Para-Legal Authority and Its Perils," *Law and Contemporary Problems* 40 (1976): 187.

125. George C. Calhoun, "Confidentiality and Executive Privilege," in Thomas M. Franck, ed., *The Tethered Presidency: Congressional Restraints on Executive Power* (New York: New York University Press, 1981), 179.

126. Ibid., 178. Former consultant to the National Security Council, Michael A. Ledeen, provides an insider's perspective on the policy effects of exposing secrets:

Some years ago, I heard Bobby Inman—then deputy director of Central Intelligence—argue against a proposed covert action on the grounds that "this sort of thing always leaks from the oversight committees." The proposal was scrapped, just as others were when Senator Joseph Biden threatened to "leak" them if, against his recommendations, they were put into effect. So, by bringing Congress into the act, some secret actions are blocked, and others are sabotaged by leaks from hostile legislators. (Michael A. Ledeen, "Secrets," in Simon Serfaty, ed., *The Media and Foreign Policy* [New York: St. Martin's Press, 1991], 126)

127. Ledeen, "Secrets," 123.

128. Averell Harriman, "Statement before the Subcommittee on Separation of Powers of the Committee on the Judiciary," 1971, 353.

129. William P. Bundy, "Statement before the Subcommittee on Separation of Powers of the Committee on the Judiciary," 1971, 320–21.

130. Leonard G. Ratner, "Executive Privilege, Self Incrimination, and the Separation of Powers Illusion," *UCLA Law Review* 22 (October 1974): 94.

131. Theodore H. White, *Breach of Faith: The Fall of Richard Nixon* (New York: Atheneum, 1975), 203. Arthur S. Miller similarly writes that "executive privilege is akin to the 'state secrets' privilege; as such, it may be invoked for the benefit of the nation, not the individual. It is not something behind which a president's peccadilloes or other derelictions can be hidden" (Arthur S. Miller, "Executive Privilege: A Political Theory Masquerading as Law," in Harold C. Relyea, ed., *The Presidency and Information Policy* [New York: Center for the Study of the Presidency, 1981], 54).

132. *U.S. v. Nixon*, 483 U.S. 683, 705–6, 708 (1974).

133. *Federal Open Market Committee of the Federal Reserve System v. Merrill*, 413 F. Supp. 494 (D. D. C. 1979).

134. *Watkins v. U.S.*, 354 U.S. 178 (1957); *Wilkinson v. U.S.*, 365 U.S. 399 (1961).

135. *McGrain v. Daugherty*, 273 U.S. 135 (1927); *Sinclair v. United States*, 279 U.S. 263 (1929).

136. *Senate Select Committee v. Nixon*, 498 F. 2d 725, 731 (1974): "The sufficiency of the Committee's showing must depend solely on whether the subpoenaed evidence is demonstrably critical to the responsible fulfillment of the Committee's functions."

137. Robert G. Dixon, Jr., "Congress, Shared Administration, and Executive Privilege," in Harvey C. Mansfield, Sr., ed., *Congress against the President* (New York: Praeger, 1975), 134.

138. *U.S. v. Marchetti*, 466 F. 2d 1309 (1972).

139. *Weissman v. CIA*, 565 F. 2d 692 (D.C. Cir. 1977); *Phillippi v. CIA*, 655 F. 2d 1325 (D.C. Cir. 1981).

140. Ledeen, "Secrets," 124–25.

141. Benjamin R. Civiletti, "Intelligence Gathering and the Law: Conflict or Compatibility," *Fordham Law Review* 48 (1980): 887–88.

142. Quoted in *Contempt of Congress*, 83n. A classic study of secrecy and legislative inquiry is Irving Younger, "Congressional Investigations and Executive Secrecy: A Study in the Separation of Powers," *University of Pittsburgh Law Review* 20 (1959): 755–84.

143. Rehnquist, "Statement before the Subcommittee on Separation of Powers of the Committee on the Judiciary," 1971, 434.

144. *U.S. v. Pink*, 315 U.S. 203 (1942).

145. Richard Pious, *The American Presidency* (New York: Basic Books, 1979), 55.

146. Ibid.

147. *New York Times v. United States*, 403 U.S. 713, 728 (1971). Stewart also wrote the following:

> I think there can be but one answer. . . . The responsibility must be where the power is. If the Constitution gives the Executive a large degree of *unshared power* in the conduct of foreign affairs and the maintenance of our national defense, then under the Constitution the Executive must have the largely *unshared duty* to determine and preserve the degree of internal security necessary to exercise that power successfully. . . . It is clear to me that it is the *constitutional duty of the executive*—as a matter of *sovereign prerogative* and not as a matter of law as the courts know law—through the promulgation and enforcement of executive regulations to *protect the confidentiality necessary* to carry out its responsibilities in the fields of international relations and national defense. (728–30)

148. *Gravel v. United States*, 408 U.S. 606 (1972).

149. David M. O'Brien, *Storm Center: The Supreme Court in American Politics*, 2d ed. (New York: W. W. Norton, 1990), 150–51.

150. *Souicie v. David*, 448 F. 2d 1067, 1080 (D. C. Cir. 1971).

151. Calhoun, "Confidentiality," 174.

152. Raoul Berger, "The Incarnation of Executive Privilege," *UCLA Law Review* 22 (October 1974): 29.

153. Ibid.

CHAPTER 3: UNDERMINING A CONSTITUTIONAL DOCTRINE— RICHARD NIXON AND THE ABUSE OF EXECUTIVE PRIVILEGE

1. Quoted in Norman Dorsen and John H. F. Shattuck, "Executive Privilege, the Congress, and the Courts." Reprinted in U.S. Congress, *Executive Privilege; Se-*

crecy in Government; Freedom of Information, Hearings before the Subcommittee on Intergovernmental Relations of the Committee on Government Operations and the Subcommittees on Separation of Powers and Administrative Practice and Procedure of the Committee on the Judiciary, U.S. Senate, 93d Cong., 1st Sess., 10–12 April; 8–10, 16 May; and 7, 8, 11, 16 June 1973 (3 vols.), 3:155.

2. Letter from Rep. John E. Moss to President Richard M. Nixon, 28 January 1969, Folder: "Executive Privilege (2)," Box 13, Edward Schmults Files, Gerald R. Ford Library, Ann Arbor, Mich.

3. Letter from President Richard M. Nixon to Rep. John E. Moss, 7 April 1969, Folder: "Executive Privilege (2)," Box 13, Edward Schmults Files, Gerald R. Ford Library, Ann Arbor, Mich.

4. Memorandum from President Richard M. Nixon to Executive Department Heads, 24 March 1969, Folder: "Executive Privilege [1973]," White House Staff Files, Ronald Ziegler Alphabetical Subject File, Nixon Presidential Materials Project, Alexandria, Va.

5. Ibid.

6. *The Public Papers of the Presidents: Richard M. Nixon, 1973,* 253. In his 31 January 1973 press conference, Nixon said that he would be "as liberal as possible" about allowing White House aides to testify before Congress. He further added that "we are not going to use executive privilege as a shield for conversations that might just be embarrassing to us, but that really don't deserve executive privilege" (60–61).

7. Ibid., 254.

8. Raoul Berger, *Executive Privilege: A Constitutional Myth* (Cambridge: Harvard University Press, 1974), 254–55.

9. *The Public Papers of the Presidents: Richard M. Nixon, 1973,* 253.

10. U.S. Congress, *Availability of Information to Congress,* Hearings before a Subcommittee of the Committee on Government Operations, House of Representatives, 93d Cong., 1st Sess., 3, 4, 19 April 1973, 1.

11. Adam C. Breckenridge, *The Executive Privilege: Presidential Control over Information* (Lincoln: University of Nebraska Press, 1974), 119–20.

12. Louis Fisher, "Congress and the Removal Power," *Congress and the Presidency* 10 (Spring 1983): 75.

13. Letter, Sen. Sam Ervin, Jr., to Rep. L. H. Fountain, 2 April 1974; U.S. Congress, *Survey on Executive Privilege,* Subcommittee on Separation of Powers of the Committee on the Judiciary, U.S. Senate, 93d Cong., 1st Sess., 5 March 1973. Oddly enough, even though the scientists had been excluded from participation on the advisory boards due to their alleged Communist Party, U.S.A. affiliations, many of them had received substantial HEW grants.

14. Breckenridge, *Executive Privilege,* 7–8.

15. Ibid., 93–94; Berger, *Executive Privilege,* 259.

16. *Environmental Protection Agency v. Mink,* 410 U.S. 73 (1973).

17. See Breckenridge, *Executive Privilege*, 19–20, 94–96.

18. See *The White House Transcripts* (New York: *New York Times*/Bantam, 1974), 163–64.

19. Memorandum from President Richard M. Nixon to Leonard Garment, 2 May 1973, White House Staff Files, H. R. Haldeman, Folder: "Action Completed—Outbox Material," Box 281, Larry Higby Files, Nixon Presidential Materials Project.

20. *U.S. v. Nixon*, 418 U.S. 683 (1974).

21. Stephen E. Ambrose, *Nixon: Ruin and Recovery, 1973–1990* (New York: Simon and Schuster, 1991), 384.

22. 418 U.S. 683, 712 (1974).

23. Ibid., 708.

24. Ibid., 712.

25. *Nixon v. Administrator of General Services*, 433 U.S. 425 (1977).

26. Brief of Richard M. Nixon in Opposition to Plaintiffs' Motion for Summary Judgment, *Senate Select Committee on Presidential Campaign Activities v. Nixon*, 366 F. Supp. 51 (D. D. C. 1973), 16.

27. Brief of Richard M. Nixon in Opposition, *In re Grand Jury Subpoena Duces Tecum to Nixon*, 360 F. Supp. 1 (D.D.C. 1973), 12–13 (hereinafter Brief II).

28. "Nixon: A President May Violate the Law," *U.S. News and World Report*, 30 May 1977, 65.

29. Ibid.

30. House of Representatives, *Availability of Information to Congress*, 308.

31. Brief II, 4.

32. Letter from President Richard M. Nixon to Judge John Sirica, 25 July 1973, White House Central Files, FE4–1 (1 May 1973 to 30 September 1973), Nixon Presidential Materials Project.

33. Quoted in the U.S. Congress, *Executive Privilege—Secrecy in Government*, Hearings before the Subcommittee on Intergovernmental Relations of the Committee on Government Operations, U.S. Senate, 94th Cong., 1st Sess., 29 September and 23 October 1975, 598.

34. U.S. Congress, *Freedom of Information; Executive Privilege; Secrecy in Government*, Hearings before the Subcommittee on Administrative Practice and Procedure and Separation of Powers of the Committee on the Judiciary, and the Subcommittee on Intergovernmental Relations of the Committee on Government Operations, U.S. Senate, 93d Cong., 1st Sess. 10, 11, 12 April; 8, 9, 10, 16 May; 7, 8, 11, 26 June 1973 (3 vols.), 1:35.

35. Ibid., 39.

36. "Nixon: A President May Violate the Law," 65.

37. Quoted in *Availability of Information to Congress*, 308.

38. Dorsen and Shattuck, "Executive Privilege," 158–59.

39. Quoted in U.S. Congress, *Freedom of Information*, 39.

40. Quoted in Ambrose, *Nixon*, 76.

41. Ibid.

42. Quoted in Congressional Quarterly, *Watergate: Chronology of a Crisis* (Washington, D.C.: Congressional Quarterly Press, 1974), 2:6.

43. Brief II, 23.

44. Ibid., 2–3.

45. Letter from President Richard M. Nixon to Sen. Sam J. Ervin, 6 July 1973, White House Central Files, FE4–1 (1 May 1973 to 30 September 1973), Nixon Presidential Materials Project.

46. Letter from President Richard M. Nixon to Sen. Sam J. Ervin, 4 January 1974, White House Central Files, FE4–1 (1 May 1973 to 30 September 1973), Nixon Presidential Materials Project.

47. *The Public Papers of the Presidents: Richard M. Nixon, 1973,* 253.

48. Brief II, 18.

49. Quoted in William S. Moorhead, "Operation and Reform of the Classification System in the United States," in Thomas M. Franck and Edward Weisband, eds., *Secrecy and Foreign Policy* (New York: Oxford University Press, 1974), 99–100.

50. *The White House Transcripts,* 163–64.

51. "Nixon: A President May Violate the Law," 65.

52. Ambrose, *Nixon,* 114. In a memorandum to John Ehrlichman, the president advocated that the White House counter press criticism of administration use of executive privilege and of the FBI for domestic surveillance by conveying that the previous Democrat administrations had engaged in similar activities. See letter from President Richard M. Nixon to John Ehrlichman, 4 March 1973, President's Personal File: "Memoranda: 1969–1974," Nixon Presidential Materials Project.

CHAPTER 4: THE POST-WATERGATE YEARS—THE "OPEN" PRESIDENCIES OF GERALD R. FORD AND JIMMY CARTER

1. Letter from John E. Moss to President Gerald R. Ford, 15 August 1974, Folder: "Executive Privilege (2)," Box 13, Philip W. Buchen Files, Gerald R. Ford Library, Ann Arbor, Mich. (hereinafter, GRFL).

2. Letter from Max L. Friedersdorf to John E. Moss, 16 August 1974, Folder: "Executive Privilege (2)," Box 13, Philip W. Buchen Files, GRFL.

3. Letter from Reps. John N. Erlenborn and William S. Moorhead to President Gerald R. Ford, 13 August 1974; letter from Sens. Sam Ervin, Edmund S. Muskie, and William V. Roth to President Gerald R. Ford, 22 August 1974; letter from Max Friedersdorf to Rep. John N. Erlenborn, 16 August 1974; letters from William E. Timmons to Sens. Sam Ervin, Edmund S. Muskie, and William V. Roth, 28 August 1974, Folder: "Executive Privilege—General (2)," Box 13, Edward Schmults Files, GRFL.

4. Memorandum from Stanley Ebner to Philip W. Buchen, 19 September 1974, Folder: "Executive Privilege (2)," Box 13, Philip W. Buchen Files, GRFL.

5. Memorandum from William E. Timmons to Philip W. Buchen, 23 September 1974, Folder: "Executive Privilege (2)," Box 13, Philip W. Buchen Files, GRFL.

6. White House Schedule Proposal, 23 September 1974, Folder: "Executive Privilege (2)," Box 13, Philip W. Buchen Files, GRFL.

7. Agenda: Meeting with Moorhead and Erlenborn, 9 October 1974, Folder: "Executive Privilege (2)," Box 13, Philip W. Buchen Files, GRFL.

8. Memorandum from Doug Metz to Philip W. Buchen, 24 September 1974, Folder: "Executive Privilege—General (2)," Box 13, Edward Schmults Files, GRFL.

9. Memorandum from Dudley Chapman to Philip W. Buchen, 25 September 1974, Folder: "Executive Privilege—General (2)," Box 13, Edward Schmults Files, GRFL.

10. Memorandum from Dudley Chapman to Philip W. Buchen, et al., 5 November 1974, Folder: "Executive Privilege—General (1)," Box 13, Edward Schmults Files, GRFL.

11. Participants in the discussion included Solicitor General Robert Bork; Assistant Attorney General for the Office of Legal Counsel Antonin Scalia; former adviser to presidents Kennedy and Johnson, Martin Richman; Department of Justice Officer Robert L. Keuch; and two members of Ford's White House staff, Rod Hills and James Wilderotter. Note from Robert L. Keuch to Rod Hills, 7 April 1975, Folder: "Executive Privilege (4)," Box 13, Philip W. Buchen Files, GRFL.

12. Memorandum from Philip W. Buchen to Members of the Cabinet and Senior White House Staff, 21 November 1975, Folder: "Executive Privilege (5)," Box 13, Philip W. Buchen Files, GRFL.

13. Memorandum from the Office of the Attorney General—Privilege of the Executive Branch to Withhold Information from Congressional Committees, November 1975, Folder: "Executive Privilege (3)," Box 13, Philip W. Buchen Files, GRFL.

14. Gerald R. Ford, *A Time to Heal* (Norwalk, Conn.: Easton Press, 1987), 134.

15. Clifton Daniel, "Ford's Speech: Same Priorities," *New York Times*, 13 August 1974, 21.

16. Author interview with John W. Hushen, Washington, D.C., 14 May 1990.

17. Stanley I. Kutler, *The Wars of Watergate: The Last Crisis of Richard Nixon* (New York: Alfred A. Knopf, 1990), 570.

18. Quoted in Memorandum from Philip W. Buchen to Members of the Cabinet and Senior White House Staff, 21 November 1975, Folder: "Executive Privilege (5)," Box 13, Philip W. Buchen Files, GRFL.

19. Dom Bonafede, Daniel Rapoport, and Joel Havemann, "The President versus Congress: The Score since Watergate," *National Journal*, 29 May 1976, 738; Robert G. Dixon, "Congress, Shared Administration, and Executive Privilege," in Harvey C. Mansfield, Sr., ed., *Congress against the President* (New York: Praeger, 1975), 129.

20. See Memorandum from Dudley Chapman to Philip W. Buchen, et al., 5

November 1974, Folder: "Executive Privilege (1)," Box 13, Edward Schmults Files, GRFL. See also Memorandum from Philip W. Buchen to Members of the Cabinet and Senior White House Staff, 21 November 1975.

21. Memorandum from Philip W. Buchen to Members of the Cabinet and Senior White House Staff, 21 November 1975.

22. This section is summarized from the following sources: Memorandum from Philip W. Buchen to Members of the Cabinet and Senior White House Staff, 21 November 1975; Richard Ehlke, "Congressional Access to Information from the Executive: A Legal Analysis," *CRS Report to Congress* (Washington, D.C.: Congressional Research Service, 10 March 1986), 41–43; Peter M. Shane, "Negotiating for Knowledge: Administrative Responses to Congressional Demands for Information," *Administrative Law Review* 44 (Spring 1992): 202–3.

23. 50 U.S.C. App. 2406(c) (1969).

24. U.S. Congress, *Contempt Proceedings against Secretary of Commerce, Rogers C. B. Morton*, Hearings before the Subcommittee on Oversight and Investigations of the Committee on Interstate and Foreign Commerce, House of Representatives, 94th Cong., 1st Sess. (1975), 11.

25. This section is summarized from the following sources: Richard Ehlke, "Congressional Access to Information: Selected Problems and Issues," *CRS Report to Congress* (Washington, D.C.: Congressional Research Service, 16 October 1979), 19–21; idem, "Congressional Access to Information from the Executive: A Legal Analysis," 20n; Memorandum from Philip W. Buchen to Members of the Cabinet and Senior White House Staff, 21 November 1975.

26. House Report No. 94–693, 94th Cong., 1st Sess. (1975). Quoted in Ehlke (1979), 19–20.

27. Letter from President Ford to Rep. Otis Pike, 19 November 1975. Quoted in Ehlke (1979), 20n.

28. Memorandum from Philip W. Buchen to Members of the Cabinet and Senior White House Staff, 21 November 1975.

29. This section is summarized from the following sources: A. Stephen Boyan, ed., *Constitutional Aspects of Watergate* (Dobbs Ferry, N. Y.: Oceana, 1979), 5:183–88; Ehlke (1986), 9–14.

30. Boyan, *Constitutional Aspects of Watergate*, 5:184.

31. *United States v. AT&T*, 419 F. Supp. 454 (D. D. C. 1976).

32. *United States v. AT&T*, 551 F. 2d 384 (D. C. Cir. 1976).

33. *United States v. AT&T*, 567 F. 2d 121 (D. C. Cir. 1977).

34. 567 F. 2d 121, 131–33.

35. Letter from Reps. Richardson Preyer and Paul N. McCloskey, Jr., to President Jimmy Carter, 13 June 1977, File: "Executive Privilege, 3–6/77," Box 130, Margaret McKenna Files, Jimmy Carter Library, Atlanta, Ga. (hereinafter, JCL).

36. Letter from Rep. Richardson Preyer to Robert J. Lipshutz, 1 June 1978, File: "Executive Privilege, 1/78–7/79," Box 130, Margaret McKenna Files, JCL.

37. Letter from Reps. Richardson Preyer and Paul N. McCloskey, Jr., to Presi-

dent Jimmy Carter, 27 September 1978, File: "Executive Privilege, 1/78–7/79," Box 130, Margaret McKenna Files, JCL.

38. Letters from Frank Moore to Reps. Richardson Preyer and Paul N. McCloskey, Jr., 10 October 1978, Box FE 2–1, White House Central File (WHCF)—Subject File, JCL.

39. In July 1979 Rep. John Erlenborn (R-Ill.) also requested from the White House that there be some response to the Preyer–McCloskey letters. At this late date in Carter's term, the general counsel to the Office of Management and Budget wrote a memorandum to Lipshutz asking if there had been any response to various executive privilege inquiries as well as how to respond to members of Congress seeking information about the administration's policy (Memorandum from Robert P. Bedell to Robert J. Lipshutz, 12 July 1979, File: "Executive Privilege, 1/78–7/79," Box 130, Margaret McKenna Files, JCL).

40. There are numerous memoranda on these White House discussions in File: "Executive Privilege, 7–12/77," Box 130, Margaret McKenna Files, JCL. In particular, see Memorandum from Edward C. Newton to Margaret McKenna, 12 May 1977; Memorandum from Patricia M. Wald to Heads of Offices, Bureaus, and Divisions, 29 June 1977; Memorandum from Bob Lipshutz to Margaret McKenna, 6 July 1977; Memorandum from James W. Moorman to Patricia M. Wald, 8 July 1977; Memorandum from Thomas J. Madden to Patricia M. Wald, 11 July 1977; Memorandum from Myron C. Baum to Patricia M. Wald, 13 July 1977; Memorandum from Kevin D. Rooney to Patricia M. Wald, 14 July 1977; Memorandum from John M. Harmon to Patricia M. Wald, 19 July 1977; Memorandum from Patricia M. Wald to Heads of Offices, Boards, and Divisions, 20 July 1977; Memorandum from Gilbert G. Pompa to Patricia M. Wald, 20 July 1977.

41. See the following memoranda in File: "Executive Privilege, 7–12/77," Box 130, Margaret McKenna Files, JCL: Memorandum from Margaret McKenna to Patricia M. Wald and John Harmon, 18 July 1977; Memorandum from Eric L. Richard to Margaret McKenna, 25 July 1977; Memorandum from Margaret McKenna to Doug Huron, 10 August 1977; Memorandum from Doug Huron to William Nichols, 15 August 1977; Route Slip from Ron Kienlen to Doug Huron, 14 October 1977 (this correspondence contains copies of all departmental responses to the proposed executive order); Memorandum from Eric L. Richard to Working Group on Disclosure of Information to Congress, 25 October 1977; Memorandum from Eric L. Richard Working Group on Disclosure of Information, 3 November 1977.

42. See "Congressional Requests for Information from the Executive Branch" and other memoranda on executive privilege in Box FE-1, WHCF-Subject File, JCL.

43. Memorandum, "Congressional Requests for Information from the Executive Branch," 1977 [no specific date provided], Box FE-1, WHCF-Subject File, JCL.

44. Letter from Rep. John E. Moss to President Jimmy Carter, 11 October

1977, Box FE 2–1, WHCF-Subject File, JCL. Frank Moore wrote to Moss acknowledging that Carter received the letter and would keep the congressman's "comments under consideration." Letter from Frank Moore to Rep. John E. Moss, 20 October 1977, Box FE 2–1, WHCF-Subject File, JCL.

45. Memorandum from Robert Lipshutz to White House Staff, 8 February 1979, Box FE-2, WHCF-Subject File, JCL.

46. Memorandum from Doug Huron and Barbara Bergman to Lloyd Cutler, 6 March 1980, File: "Executive Privilege, 6/77–11/80," Box 74, Lloyd Cutler Files, JCL.

47. Memorandum from Lloyd Cutler to Reubin O'D. Askew, 22 October 1980, File: "Executive Privilege, 6/77–11/80," Box 74, Lloyd Cutler Files, JCL.

48. Memorandum from Lloyd N. Cutler to Heads of All Units Within the Executive Office of the President and the Senior White House Staff, 31 October 1980, File: "Executive Privilege, 6/77–11/80," Box 74, Lloyd Cutler Files, JCL.

49. Memorandum from Lloyd N. Cutler to the Attorney General, 31 October 1980, File: "Executive Privilege, 6/77–11/80," Box 74, Lloyd Cutler Files, JCL.

50. Memorandum from Zoe E. Baird to Lloyd N. Cutler, 10 November 1980, File: "Executive Privilege, 6/77–11/80," Box 74, Lloyd Cutler Files, JCL.

51. Memorandum from Robert Lipshutz and Margaret McKenna to President Jimmy Carter, 30 April 1977, Box FE-1, WHCF-Subject File, JCL.

52. Memorandum from Margaret McKenna and Robert Lipshutz to President Jimmy Carter, 11 May 1977, File: "Executive Privilege, 1977," Box 15, Robert Lipshutz Files, JCL.

53. Memorandum from Juanita M. Kreps to President Jimmy Carter, 21 November 1977, File: "Executive Privilege, 1977," Box 15, Robert Lipshutz Files, JCL.

54. Letter from Juanita M. Kreps to Rep. Benjamin S. Rosenthal, 21 November 1977, File: "Executive Privilege, 1977," Box 15, Robert Lipshutz Files, JCL.

55. Memorandum from Robert Lipshutz to President Jimmy Carter, 29 November 1977, File: "Executive Privilege, 1977," Box 15, Robert Lipshutz Files, JCL.

56. Memorandum from Robert Lipshutz to Stuart Eizenstat, 23 November 1977, File: "Executive Privilege, 1977," Box 15, Robert Lipshutz Files, JCL.

57. Memorandum from Robert Lipshutz to President Jimmy Carter, 30 November 1977, File: "Executive Privilege, 1977," Box 15, Robert Lipshutz Files, JCL.

58. Letter from Rep. Benjamin S. Rosenthal to James Griffin, 12 July 1978, File: "Executive Privilege, 1978," Box 15, Robert Lipshutz Files, JCL.

59. Memorandum of Conversation, 25 July 1978, File: "Executive Privilege, 1978," Box 15, Robert Lipshutz Files, JCL.

60. Letter from C. Fred Bergsten to Rep. Benjamin S. Rosenthal, 25 July 1978, File: "Executive Privilege, 1978," Box 15, Robert Lipshutz Files, JCL.

61. Memorandum from Robert H. Mundheim to Robert Lipshutz, 13 Septem-

ber 1978, File: "Executive Privilege, 1978," Box 15, Robert Lipshutz Files, JCL. Lipshutz agreed with Mundheim's recommendation. See Memorandum from Robert J. Lipshutz to Robert H. Mundheim, 18 September 1978, File: "Executive Privilege, 1978," Box 15, Robert Lipshutz Files, JCL.

62. U.S. Congress, *Contempt Proceedings against Secretary of Health, Education and Welfare, Joseph A. Califano, Jr.*, Hearings before the Subcommittee on Oversight and Investigations of the Committee on Interstate and Foreign Commerce, House of Representatives, 95th Cong., 2d Sess., 16 August 1978.

63. Letter from Sarah Weddington to Sen. Harrison A. Williams, 31 January 1979, File: "Executive Privilege, 1979," Box 15, Robert Lipshutz Files, JCL.

64. Transcript of 31 January 1979 news conference, File: "Executive Privilege, 1979," Box 15, Robert Lipshutz Files, JCL.

65. Memorandum from Robert Lipshutz to Margaret McKenna and Doug Huron, 2 February 1979, File: "Executive Privilege, 1979," Box 15, Robert Lipshutz Files, JCL.

66. Memorandum from Robert Lipshutz to White House Staff, 8 February 1979, File: "Executive Privilege, 1979," Box 15, Robert Lipshutz Files, JCL.

67. Memorandum from Robert Lipshutz and Margaret McKenna to President Jimmy Carter, 23 May 1977, File: "Executive Privilege, 1977," Box 15, Robert Lipshutz Files, JCL.

68. Letter from Lloyd Cutler to Rep. Samuel S. Stratton, 30 September 1980, File: "Executive Privilege, 6/77–11/80," Box 74, Lloyd Cutler Files, JCL. Cutler noted that the president had previously taken the exceptional position of waiving the privilege against compulsory testimony by White House aides when the president's brother had been implicated in a scheme to represent Libyan interests in the United States for a substantial fee.

69. Proclamation No. 4744, 45 Fed. Reg. 22,864 (3 April 1980).

70. U.S. Congress, *The Petroleum Import Fee: Department of Energy Oversight*, Hearings before a Subcommittee of the Committee on Government Operations, House of Representatives, 96th Cong., 2d Sess., 8, 24, 29 April 1980, 1–8.

71. Ibid., 142. *Independent Gasoline Marketers Council v. Duncan*, 492 F. Supp. 614 (D.D.C. 1980).

CHAPTER 5: THE POST-WATERGATE YEARS—RONALD REAGAN,
GEORGE BUSH, AND THE ERA OF DIVIDED GOVERNMENT

1. Memorandum from President Reagan to Heads of Executive Departments and Agencies, "Procedures Governing Responses to Congressional Requests for Information," 4 November 1982.

2. Diana M. T. K. Austin, "The Reagan Administration and the Freedom of Information Act," in Richard O. Curry, ed., *Freedom at Risk: Secrecy, Censorship, and Repression in the 1980s* (Philadelphia: Temple University Press, 1988), 71–72; Da-

vid Sadofsky, *Political and Legal Control of Information* (New York: Praeger, 1990), 84.

3. Austin, "Reagan Administration," 72.

4. Ibid.

5. Quoted in David S. Broder, *Behind the Front Page: A Candid Look at How the News Is Made* (New York: Simon and Schuster, 1987), 187.

6. Austin, "Reagan Administration," 72.

7. Ibid., 73–74; Donna A. Demac, *Keeping America Uninformed: Government Secrecy in the 1980s* (New York: Pilgrim Press, 1984), 96.

8. Demac, *Keeping America Uninformed*, 92.

9. John D. Lees, "Environmental Deregulation and Intelligence Gathering under Reagan—Contrasting Experiences of Policy Change," in John D. Lees and Michael Turner, eds., *Reagan's First Four Years: A New Beginning?* (New York: Manchester University Press, 1988), 221.

10. Ibid., 219–20; Austin, "Reagan Administration," 73.

11. "Protection of Classified National Security Council and Intelligence Information," *Weekly Compilation of Presidential Documents* 18 (January 1982), 24–25.

12. Stephen Hess, *The Government/Press Connection: Press Officers and Their Offices* (Washington, D.C.: Brookings Institution, 1984), 90.

13. Ibid., 91–92.

14. Lees, "Environmental Deregulation," 219.

15. Demac, *Keeping America Uninformed*, 96.

16. Ibid., 97.

17. *Time*, 7 November 1983, 66.

18. Quoted in Broder, *Behind the Front Page*, 186.

19. Quoted in Mark Hertsgaard, *On Bended Knee: The Press and the Reagan Presidency* (New York: Farrar Straus Giroux, 1988), 222.

20. The following sequence of events is summarized from two congressional reports: (1) U.S. Congress, *Executive Privilege: Legal Opinions Regarding Claim of President Ronald Reagan in Response to a Subpoena Issued to James G. Watt, Secretary of the Interior*, Subcommittee on Oversight and Investigations, Committee of Energy and Commerce, House of Representatives, 97th Cong., 1st Sess. (Washington, D.C.: U.S. Government Printing Office, 1981); (2) U.S. Congress, *Contempt of Congress*, Committee on Energy and Commerce, House of Representatives, 97th Cong., 2d Sess. (Washington, D.C.: U.S. Government Printing Office, 1982).

21. *Executive Privilege*, 2.

22. Ibid., 2–3.

23. Ibid., 3–4.

24. *Contempt of Congress*, Committee on Energy and Commerce, 42–45.

25. U.S. Congress, *Investigation of the Role of the Department of Justice in the Withholding of Environmental Protection Agency Documents from Congress in 1982–1983,*

House of Representatives, Committee on the Judiciary, 99th Cong., 1st Sess. (Washington, D.C.: U.S. Government Printing Office, 1985), 28.

26. The following sequence of events is summarized from the following sources: *Investigation of the Role*; U.S. Congress, *Contempt of Congress*, Committee on Public Works and Transportation, House of Representatives, 97th Cong., 2d Sess. (Washington, D.C.: U.S. Government Printing Office, 1982); Jonathan Lash, Katherine Gillman, and David Sheridan, *A Season of Spoils: The Reagan Administration's Attack on the Environment* (New York: Pantheon Books, 1984).

27. In the midst of this controversy Gorsuch married Robert Burford and changed her surname. For purposes of clarity, I shall refer to her throughout this chapter as Anne Gorsuch.

28. *Contempt of Congress*, Committee on Public Works and Transportation, 42–43.

29. Ibid., 36.

30. Ibid., 37.

31. *United States of America v. The House of Representatives*, 556 F. Supp. 150 (D. D. C. 1983). Some members of Congress objected to the administration being referred to in the suit as the "United States of America." No doubt, they had a point given the fact that the case involved a conflict between co-equal branches of the U.S. government. See Lash, Gillman, and Sheridan, *Season of Spoils*, 76.

32. Lash, Gillman, and Sheridan, *Season of Spoils*, 76–77.

33. 556 F. Supp. 150, 153 (D. D. C. 1983).

34. Ibid., 152.

35. *Investigation of the Role*, 11.

36. Ibid., 17.

37. The sequence of events surrounding the Rehnquist memos is derived from reports in *Congressional Quarterly Weekly Report* and the *Washington Post*. See Nadine Cohodas, "Rehnquist Rebuts Criticism, Confirmation Seems Likely," *Congressional Quarterly Weekly Report*, 2 August 1986, 1764–65; idem, "Rehnquist, Scalia Headed for Confirmation," *Congressional Quarterly Weekly Report*, 9 August 1986, 1844–46; Al Kamen and Howard Kurtz, "Rehnquist Told in 1974 of Restriction in Deed," *Washington Post*, 6 August 1986, A1, 6; David Broder, "Those Memos Will Tell," *Washington Post*, 6 August 1986, A15; Howard Kurtz and Al Kamen, "Rehnquist Not in Danger over Papers," *Washington Post*, 7 August 1986, A1, 14; Howard Kurtz, "Rehnquist Memos Described," *Washington Post*, 7 August 1986, p. A15.

38. The sequence of events surrounding the controversy over Reagan's diaries is summarized from several *Washington Post* news reports: Bob Woodward and David Hoffman, "President's Memoir File Includes Iran Notes," *Washington Post*, 1 February 1987, A1, 16; Al Kamen, "'Executive Privilege' Hailed," *Washington Post*, 1 February 1987, A16; W. Dale Nelson, "Reagan Iran Notes Report Confirmed," *Washington Post*, 2 February 1987, A16; David Hoffman, "President Offers to Share Iran Sales Notes with Hill," *Washington Post*, 3 February 1987, A1, 8.

39. Louis Fisher, "Congress as Macromanager of the Executive Branch," in James P. Pfiffner, ed., *The Managerial Presidency* (Pacific Grove, Calif.: Brooks/Cole, 1991), 232.

40. Woodward and Hoffman, "President's Memoir," A16. Despite these actions and the president's pledge, Independent Counsel Lawrence E. Walsh's controversial Iran-contra report maintained that "Reagan administration officials deliberately deceived the Congress and the public about the level and extent of official knowledge of and support for these operations." Quoted in George Lardner, Jr., and Walter Pincus, "Iran-Contra Report Castigates Reagan," *Washington Post*, 19 January 1994, A1.

41. Nelson, "Reagan Iran Notes," A16.

42. Ibid.

43. Kamen, " 'Executive Privilege' Hailed," A16.

44. Hoffman, "President Offers," A1.

45. Ibid., A8.

46. Author interview with Jim Lewin, by telephone, 19 November 1992.

47. Memorandum from Douglas M. Kmiec to Oliver B. Revell, "Congressional Requests for Information from Inspectors General Concerning Open Criminal Investigations," 24 March 1989, 1. Reprinted in U.S. Congress, *Department of Justice Authorization for Appropriations for Fiscal Year 1990*, House of Representatives, Committee on the Judiciary, 101st Cong., 1st Sess. (Washington, D.C.: U.S. Government Printing Office, 1989) (hereinafter, Kmiec memo).

48. Memorandum from Steven R. Ross and Charles Tiefer, "Justice Department Memorandum Directing the Withholding from Congress of Inspector General Information," 2 May 1989, 2. Reprinted in ibid., 78.

49. Kmiec memo, 7–8. Reprinted in ibid., 71–72.

50. Memorandum from Steven R. Ross and Charles Tiefer, "Justice Department," 12. Reprinted in ibid., 88.

51. Author interview with Charles Tiefer, by telephone, 23 November 1992.

52. This section is summarized from various news reports in the *New York Times*, *Washington Post*, and *Wall Street Journal*.

53. David Johnston, "Reagan Is Ordered to Provide Diaries in Poindexter Case," *New York Times*, 31 January 1990, A20.

54. Tracy Thompson, "Justice Department Asks Delay on Reagan Diary Ruling," *Washington Post*, 3 February 1990, A3.

55. David Johnston, "Reagan Rejects Poindexter Plea to Yield Diaries," *New York Times*, 6 February 1990, A1.

56. Ibid.

57. Paul M. Barrett and Amy Dockser Marcus, "Reagan's Videotaped Testimony Ordered," *Wall Street Journal*, 6 February 1990, B10. Reagan's attorney had met the 5 February 1990 deadline for formally refusing to release the diary entries but never used the phrase "executive privilege" in so refusing. That led to some confusion over whether Reagan had met Judge Greene's condition of having to

assert executive privilege by that date as the basis for the refusal. Reagan's attorney, Theodore B. Olson, made it clear on 7 February 1990 that Reagan indeed had relied upon executive privilege as the basis for withholding the diaries:

> No court has declared that the protection afforded the privilege for confidential presidential communications may be invoked only by reciting the phrase executive privilege. However, if this court intended . . . that the privilege may only be invoked in that fashion, the former president reaffirms that was, indeed [his] intention. (Joe Pichirallo, "Reagan Attorneys Assert Executive Privilege," *Washington Post*, 8 February 1990, A4.)

58. David Johnston, "Reagan to Give Tape Testimony on Iran-Contra," *New York Times*, 10 February 1990, 28.

59. David Johnston, "Poindexter Loses Fight for Reagan Notes," *New York Times*, 22 March 1990, A20. The issue of executive privilege also arose in connection with the Iran-contra trial of Lt. Col. Oliver North. In this case, North sought to subpoena Reagan's diaries and the testimonies of President Reagan and President-Elect Bush. The three subpoenas were quashed. Because earlier conspiracy charges against North had been dropped, Judge Gerhard A. Gesell determined that the defendant's needs in this case did not overcome the "presumptive privilege" accorded to the president and the president-elect. See Comment, "Legitimacy: The Sacrificial Lamb at the Altar of Executive Privilege," *Kentucky Law Journal* 78 (1990): 822–25; Joe Pichirallo and Ruth Marcus, "Reagan, Bush Subpoenaed by North; White House to Fight Testimony Demand," *Washington Post*, 31 December 1988, A1, 12; Ruth Marcus, "Subpoenaing the President," *Washington Post*, 1 January 1989, A7; Michael Wines, "Key North Counts Dismissed by Court," *New York Times*, 14 January 1989, 1, 7; George Lardner, Jr., "North Asks Court to Overturn Convictions," *Washington Post*, 7 February 1990, A3.

60. Peter Schmeiser, "Shooting Pool," *The New Republic*, 18 March 1991, 21; Sydney H. Schanberg, "A Muzzle for the Press," in Micah L. Sifry and Christopher Cerf, eds., *The Gulf War Reader: History, Documents, Opinions* (New York: Random House, 1991), 370.

61. H.Res. 19, 102d Cong., 1st Sess., 3 January 1991.

62. Letter from C. Boyden Gray to Rep. Dante B. Fascell, 23 January 1991.

63. Letter from Reps. Dante B. Fascell and Les Aspin to President George Bush, 7 February 1991.

64. Letter from Brent Scowcroft to Rep. Dante B. Fascell, 20 February 1991.

65. The following sequence of events is summarized from the following sources: Letter from Rep. Ted Weiss to Rep. John Conyers, Jr., 21 May 1991; Memorandum from Steven R. Ross and Charles Tiefer to Rep. Ted Weiss, 20 June 1991; Kenneth J. Cooper, "Executive Privilege at Education Department," *Washington Post*, 17 May 1991, A23.

66. Letter from Edward Stringer to Rep. Ted Weiss, 7 May 1991.

67. Letter from Edward Stringer to Rep. Ted Weiss, 13 May 1991.

68. Memorandum from Steven R. Ross and Charles Tiefer to Rep. Ted Weiss, 20 June 1991.

69. This section is based on the following sources: Patricia A. Gilmartin, "Congress Increases C-17 Scrutiny in Wake of Reported Cost Overruns," *Aviation Week & Space Technology*, 2 September 1991, 25–26; personal interviews with Charles Tiefer, deputy general counsel to the clerk of the House of Representatives, 23 November 1992; Eric Thorson, staff member, House Committee on Government Operations, 20 November 1992; Morton Rosenberg, specialist in American public law, American Law Division, Congressional Research Service, 21 November 1992; U.S. Congress, *Oversight Hearing on the A-12 Navy Aircraft*, Hearings before the Legislation and National Security Subcommittee of the Committee on Government Operations, House of Representatives, 102d Cong., 1st Sess., 11 April and 24 July 1991; U.S. Congress, *A-12 Navy Aircraft: System Review and Recommendations*, Twenty-First Report by the Committee on Government Operations, House of Representatives, 102d Cong., 2d Sess., 27 August 1992.

70. Memorandum from President George Bush to Secretary of Defense Richard Cheney, "Congressional Subpoena for an Executive Branch Document," 8 August 1991.

71. This section is based on the following sources: U.S. Congress, *The Quayle Council's Plans for Changing FDA's Drug Approval Process: A Prescription for Harm*, Twenty-Sixth Report by the Committee on Government Operations, House of Representatives, 102d Cong., 2d Sess., 9 October 1992; Dana Priest, "Competitiveness Council under Scrutiny," *Washington Post*, 26 November 1991, A19.

72. Letter from Kay Holcombe, acting associate commissioner for legislative affairs, FDA, to Rep. Ted Weiss, 16 October 1991. Quoted in, *Quayle Council's Plans*, 6.

73. This section is based on the following sources: author interviews with Charles Tiefer, Morton Rosenberg, and Monica Wrobelewski; various congressional documents provided by Ms. Wrobelewski, including: Statements of Rep. Howard Wolpe before the Subcommittee on Investigations and Oversight of the House Committee on Science, Space and Technology, 23 September, 2 and 5 October 1992.

74. Letter from Rep. Howard Wolpe to President Bush, 24 September 1992.

75. Letter from C. Boyden Gray to Rep. Howard Wolpe, 1 October 1992.

76. Letter from Rep. Howard Wolpe to Attorney General William P. Barr III, 5 October 1992.

77. Letter from Assistant Attorney General W. Lee Rawls to Rep. Howard Wolpe, 5 October 1992.

78. This section is based on the following sources: Joan Biskupic, "Panel Challenges Thornburgh over Right to Documents," *Congressional Quarterly Weekly Report*, 27 July 1991, 2080; David Johnston, "Administration to Fight House Panel's Subpoena," *New York Times*, 30 July 1991, A12; U.S. Congress, *Department of Justice Authorization for Appropriations, Fiscal Year 1992*, Hearings before the Commit-

tee on the Judiciary, House of Representatives, 102d Cong., 1st Sess., 11 and 18 July 1991; interviews with Morton Rosenberg, 21 November 1992, and Charles Tiefer, 23 November 1992.

79. This section is based on the following sources: Joan Biskupic, "Panel Challenges Thornburgh over Right to Documents," *Congressional Quarterly Weekly Report*, 27 July 1991, 2080; U.S. Congress, *The Attorney General's Refusal to Provide Congressional Access to "Privileged" INSLAW Documents*, Hearings before the Subcommittee on Economic and Commercial Law of the Committee on the Judiciary, House of Representatives, 101st Cong., 2d Sess., 5 December 1990; U.S. Congress, *Department of Justice Authorization for Appropriations, Fiscal Year 1992*, Hearings before the Committee on the Judiciary, House of Representatives, 102d Cong., 1st Sess., 11 and 18 July 1991; "The INSLAW Investigation," *Washington Post*, 29 May 1993, A30.

80. David Johnston, "Administration to Fight House Panel's Subpoena," *New York Times*, 30 July 1991, A12.

CHAPTER 6: RESOLVING THE DILEMMA

1. Raoul Berger, "The Incarnation of Executive Privilege," *UCLA Law Review* 22 (October 1974): 29.

2. Ibid.

3. See the commentary of Sen. J. William Fulbright in U.S. Congress, *Executive Privilege*, Hearings before the Subcommittee on Separation of Powers of the Committee on the Judiciary, U.S. Senate, 92d Cong., 1st Sess., 1971, 18–47.

4. David Gray Adler, "Presidential Prerogatives and the National Security State: The Corruption of the Constitution," paper presented at the annual meeting of the American Political Science Association, San Francisco, Calif., 30 August–2 September 1990, 2.

5. Ibid., 32.

6. James W. Ceaser, "In Defense of Separation of Powers," in Robert A. Goldwin and Art Kaufman, eds., *Separation of Powers—Does It Still Work?* (Washington, D.C.: American Enterprise Institute, 1986), 190.

7. Brief of Richard M. Nixon in Opposition to Plaintiffs' Motion for Summary Judgment, *Senate Select Committee on Presidential Campaign Activities v. Nixon*, 366 F. Supp. 51 (D. D. C. 1973), 16.

8. *U.S. v. Sirica*, 487 F. 2d 700, 742 (D. C. Cir. 1973).

9. Louis W. Koenig, *The Chief Executive* (New York: Harcourt, Brace, Jovanovich, 1986), 11.

10. John Locke, *The Second Treatise of Government* (Indianapolis: Bobbs-Merrill, 1952), chapter 14, section 160.

11. L. Peter Schultz, "The Separation of Powers and Foreign Affairs," in Goldwin and Kaufman, eds., 119.

12. See, for example, James Hamilton and John C. Grabow, "A Legislative Pro-

posal for Resolving Executive Privilege Disputes Precipitated by Congressional Subpoenas," *Harvard Journal of Legislation* 22 (Winter 1984): 145–72.

13. Letter from Edward Levi to Vice President Nelson Rockefeller, 13 June 1975.

14. Sotirios A. Barber, "The Supreme Court and Congress's Responsibilities in Foreign Affairs," in Gary L. McDowell, ed., *Taking the Constitution Seriously: Essays on the Constitution and Constitutional Law* (Dubuque, Iowa: Kendall/Hunt, 1981), 231.

15. J. William Fulbright, *The Arrogance of Power* (New York: Vintage Books, 1966), 46.

16. Koenig, *Chief Executive*, 11–12.

17. Letter from William French Smith to Rep. John D. Dingell, 30 November 1982. Cited in U.S. Congress, *Contempt of Congress*, Report of the Committee on Public Works and Transportation, House of Representatives, 97th Cong., 2d Sess., 15 December 1982, 79.

18. William Rehnquist, "Statement before the Subcommittee on Separation of Powers of the Committee on the Judiciary," 434.

19. *Atlee v. Laird*, 347 F. Supp. 689 (E.D. Pa. 1972); *affirmed without opinion*, 411 U.S. 911 (1973); *Chicago & Southern Airlines v. Waterman Steamship Co.*, 333 U.S. 111 (1948); *Coleman v. Miller*, 307 U.S. 433 (1939); *Crockett v. Reagan*, 558 F. Supp. 893 (1982); *Holtzman v. Schlesinger*, 484 F. 2d 1307 (2d Cir. 1973), *cert. denied*, 416 U.S. 936 (1974); *New York Times Co. v. United States*, 403 U.S. 713 (1971; Justice Stewart concurring); *Oetjen v. Central Leather Corp.*, 246 U.S. 297 (1918); *U.S. v. Belmont*, 301 U.S. 324 (1937); *U.S. v. Curtiss-Wright Corp.*, 299 U.S. 304 (1936); *U.S. Presbyterian Church in U.S.A. v. Reagan*, 557 F. Supp. 61 (1982).

20. Louis Fisher, "War Powers: The Need for Collective Judgment," in James A. Thurber, ed., *Divided Democracy: Cooperation and Conflict between the President and Congress* (Washington, D.C.: Congressional Quarterly Press, 1991), 215.

21. *U.S. v. Nixon*, 418 U.S. 683, 706 (1974).

22. Ibid., 706, 710.

23. Ibid., 713.

24. See *Senate Select Committee on Presidential Campaign Activities v. Nixon*, 498 F. 2d 725 (D.C. Cir. 1974); *United States v. AT&T*, 521 F. 2d 384 (D.C. Cir. 1976) and 567 F. 2d 121 (D.C. Cir. 1977).

25. *Farnsworth Cannon v. Grimes*, 635 F. 2d 268 (4th Cir. 1980); *Nixon v. Sirica*, 487 F. 2d 700 (D.C. Cir. 1973); *U.S. v. Boyce*, 594 F. 2d 1246 (9th Cir. 1979), *cert. denied*, 444 U.S. 855 (1979); *U.S. v. Jolliff*, 548 F. Supp. 229 (1981); *U.S. v. Lyon*, 567 F. 2d 777 (8th Cir. 1977), *cert. denied*, 435 U.S. 918 (1978).

26. *Committee for Nuclear Responsibility, Inc. v. Seaborg*, 463 F. 2d 788 (D.C. Cir. 1971); *Kaiser Aluminum & Chemical Corp. v. U.S.*, 157 F. Supp. 939 (1958).

27. *U.S. v. Burr*, 25 Fed. Cas. 187, 190, 191–92 (No. 14,694) (C.C.D. Va.1807).

28. See Gordon S. Jones and John A. Marini, eds., *The Imperial Congress* (New York: Pharos Books, 1988); L. Gordon Crovitz and Jeremy A. Rabkin, eds., *The*

Fettered Presidency: Legal Constraints on the Executive Branch (Washington, D.C.: American Enterprise Institute, 1989); Terry Eastland, *Energy in the Executive: The Case for an Active Presidency* (New York: Free Press, 1992).

29. Michael Foley, *The Silence of Constitutions* (London: Routledge, 1989), 77.
30. Ibid., xi.
31. Ibid., 76.
32. Ceaser, "In Defense of Separation of Powers," 176.
33. Ibid., 190.
34. Ibid., 176.

Index

accountability, xii, 1–3, 5, 10, 11, 14, 15, 17–18, 20, 142, 144, 153–57
Adams, John, 36
Adams, John (Deputy General Counsel), 44, 45
Adler, David Gray, 9–10, 12, 13, 144
Alexander, Lamar: challenge to college accreditation standards, 132–33
American Telephone and Telegraph Company (AT&T): role in electronic surveillance, 94–96
Articles of Confederation, 26
Askew, Reuben, 101
Aspin, Rep. Les: request for information on Operation Desert Shield, 131
Atlee v. Laird, 347 F. Supp. 689 (E.D. Pa. 1972), *affirmed without opinion*, 411 U.S. 911 (1973), 185n. 19
Audubon Society: suit against Carter administration, 102

Baldwin, Hanson W., 18
Barber, Sotirios A., 149

Barr, Joseph W., 47
Bay of Pigs, 19, 20, 47
Berger, Raoul: on executive branch secrecy, xi, xii, 1, 8–9, 10, 20, 27, 30–31, 82, 114; on foreign policy powers, 13; on the Framers, 25, 31–32; on impeachment, 11, 30; on legislative power of inquiry, 11–12, 15, 22, 30–31, 55; on legislative secrecy, 10, 27; on Nixon's use of executive privilege, 60, 144; on the state of the union power, 11–12, 31–32; on treaty-making powers, 13–14, 28
Bergman, Barbara: memorandum on executive privilege, 100–101
Bergsten, C. Fred: on need for confidential deliberations, 104
Biden, Sen. Joseph, 52
Bill of Rights, 2, 5
Bishop, Joseph W., 52
Board of Education v. Pico, 457 U.S. 853 (1982), 160n. 14
Bowsher v. Synar, 478 U.S. 714 (1986), 168n. 115

proceedings, 26; on withholding information, 36, 38

Marbury v. Madison, 1 Cranch 137 (1803), 30, 164n. 23

Marro, Anthony, 114

Marshall, John: executive discretionary powers, 30; opinion in *Marbury v. Madison* (1803), 30; opinion in *U.S. v. Burr* (1807), 152–53

Mason, George: on secrecy of Constitutional Convention, 164n. 17

Mathews, F. David: challenge of congressional request for information, 91–92

McCarthy, Sen. Joseph, 44–45, 61

McCloskey, Rep. Paul N.: letters to Carter, 98–99

McDonnell Douglas A-12 Navy Aircraft Program investigation, 134–35, 137, 139

McGrain v. Daugherty, 273 U.S. 135 (1927), 15, 162n. 30, 169n. 135

McKenna, Margaret: on executive privilege in Carter administration, 102, 105

McKinley, William: on executive branch secrecy, 42

Meader, Rep. George: on executive privilege, 160n. 1

Metz, Doug: executive privilege memorandum, 87

Miller, Arthur S., 169n. 131

Miroff, Bruce, 17

Mitchell, Sen. George: on Reagan's diaries, 122

Mitchell, John: withholding confidential FBI reports, 68

Mollenhoff, Clark, 3

Monroe, James: Steward incident, 38

Montesquieu, Baron de: modern constitutionalism, 22, 25; separation of powers, 22, 24, 146

Moore, Frank, 99

Moorhead, Rep. William S.: letter to Ford on executive privilege, 85–86

Morris, Governeur: Article II, 29; Constitutional Convention, 29

Morton, Rogers C. B.: congressional testimony of, 92–93; response to Moss inquiry, 92

Moss, Rep. John E.: appeal of AT&T case, 95–96; on executive privilege, 18; letter to Ford, 85; letter to Johnson, 47; letter to Kennedy, 47; letter to Nixon, 63–64; request for information from Office of Export Administration, 92–93; request for survey of hospitals, 91–92; response to Carter on proposed executive order, 100

Mundheim, Robert H.: on "governmental privilege," 104

Muskie, Sen. Edmund S.: letter to Ford on executive privilege, 86

National Security Act of 1947: "sources and methods proviso," 56

National Security Administration (NSA), 112

National security concerns, 2, 6, 18, 20, 21, 49–53, 70, 79–80

National Security Council (NSC), 3, 53, 81, 93–94

National Security Directive 84 (1983), 112

Nelson, Jack, 114

New York Times Co. v. United States, 403 U.S. 713 (1971), 58–59, 170n. 147, 185n. 19

Nixon, Richard M.: 4, 17, 94, 120–21; abuse of executive privilege, 6–7, 19–20, 54, 60–63, 70–82, 121, 123, 140, 144, 147, 154, 173n. 52; correspondence with Nguyen Van Thieu, 91; defense of executive privilege claims, 72–80, 145, 146; on

U.S. v. Nixon, 418 U.S. 683 (1974), 27, 54–55, 71, 74–75, 80–82, 94, 115, 122–23, 151–52, 164n. 19, 169n. 132, 172n. 20, 185n. 21
U.S. v. Pink, 315 U.S. 203 (1942), 170n. 144
U.S. Presbyterian Church in U.S.A. v. Reagan, 557 F. Supp. 61 (1982), 185n. 19
U.S. v. Reynolds, 345 U.S. 1 (1952), 51, 168n. 117
U.S. v. Sirica, 487 F. 2d 700 (D.C. Cir. 1973), 184n. 8
U.S. v. Truong Dinh Hung, 629 F. 2d 908 (1980), 167n. 106, 168n. 114

Van Devanter, Willis: opinion in *McGrain v. Daugherty*, 15
Vietnam War, 19, 81, 91

Walsh, Lawrence E.: Iran-contra report of, 181n. 40
war powers, 9, 13
Warren, Earl: on presidential privilege, 14
Washington, George: 32; precedents for executive privilege, 33–36
Watergate, 3, 6–7, 19, 60, 70–84, 86, 87, 89, 96, 97, 102, 109, 121, 123, 139, 140–41, 148–49, 154

Watkins v. U.S., 354 U.S. 178 (1957), 164n. 33, 169n. 134
Watt, James G.: withholding information from Congress, 115–19
Weddington, Sarah: congressional testimony prohibited, 104–5
Weiss, Rep. Ted: challenges secrecy in Bush administration, 132–33
Weissman v. CIA, 565 F. 2d 692 (D.C. Cir. 1977), 170n. 139
White, Theodore H., 54
Wiggins, James, 3
Wilkinson v. U.S., 365 U.S. 399 (1961), 164n. 33
Williams, Sen. Harrison A.: on congressional testimony, 104–5
Wilson, Charles, 45
Wilson, James: on executive power and secrecy, 29–30
Wilson, Woodrow: on representative government, 1
Wise, David, 1–2
Wolpe, Rep. Howard: role in Rocky Flats investigation, 136–37
World War II, 57–58, 150
Wright, Rep. Jim: on government secrecy, 52

Zemel v. Rusk, 381 U.S. 1 (1965), 51, 168n. 108

LIBRARY OF CONGRESS CATALOGING-IN-PUBLICATION DATA

Rozell, Mark J.

    Executive privilege : the dilemma of secrecy and democratic accountability /
Mark J. Rozell.

        p.   cm. — (Interpreting American politics)
    Includes bibliographical references and index.
    ISBN 0-8018-4899-7 (alk. paper). — ISBN 0-8018-4900-4 (pbk. : alk.
paper)
    1. Executive privilege (Government information)—United States.
2. Executive privilege (Government information)—United States—
History.   I. Title.   II. Series.
JK468.S4R67   1994
353.03'28—dc20   94-6801